Study Guide

for use with

The Macro Economy Today

Ninth Edition

Bradley R. Schiller
American University

Prepared by
Linda Wilson
University of Texas – Arlington

Kevin Klein
Illinois College

Boston   Burr Ridge, IL   Dubuque, IA   Madison, WI   New York   San Francisco   St. Louis
Bangkok   Bogotá   Caracas   Kuala Lumpur   Lisbon   London   Madrid   Mexico City
Milan   Montreal   New Delhi   Santiago   Seoul   Singapore   Sydney   Taipei   Toronto

Study Guide for use with
THE MACRO ECONOMY TODAY
Bradley R. Schiller

Published by McGraw-Hill/Irwin, an imprint of The McGraw-Hill Companies, Inc., 1221 Avenue of the Americas, New York, NY 10020. Copyright © 2003, 2000, 1997 by The McGraw-Hill Companies, Inc.
All rights reserved.

2 3 4 5 6 7 8 9 0 QPD/QPD 0 9 8 7 6 5 4 3 2

ISBN 0-07-247192-1

www.mhhe.com

Table of Contents

STUDY GUIDE

Preface

This study guide is written to accompany *The Macro Economy Today*, 9th edition, by Bradley R. Schiller. The overall focus of the Study Guide is to reinforce the economic principles and concepts presented in the textbook. Each section of each chapter has a particular objective.

The *Quick Review* and *Learning Objectives* sections provide brief summaries of the basic contents of the corresponding text chapters.

The *Using Key Terms* section allows students to practice using the words defined in each chapter in a crossword puzzle format.

The *True or False* and *Multiple Choice* sections help students apply economic principles in a familiar problem-solving setting. This will help greatly in the preparation for exams.

The *Problems and Applications* section lets students discover economic principles for themselves. Students not only learn the techniques that economists use, but they also discover the basis for the economic concepts they have learned.

Semester after semester, students have difficulty with the same concepts and make the same mistakes. The section called *Common Errors* addresses some of these problems, and provides an explanation using appropriate economic principles.

Online Learning Center

The Online Learning Center is an exciting feature of the *The Macro Economy Today*'s 9th edition. The Student Center provides a number of ways to supplement your study efforts including Chapter Summaries, Key Terms, Multiple Choice Quizzes, Web-Based Projects, News Flashes, *New York Times* articles, DiscoverEcon, and PowerPoint slides.

A summary of each feature is provided below along with instructions on how to use it.

Chapter Summary – This is a simple summary of the material covered in the text for each chapter. To access this feature, choose the chapter number you want to work on and then click on the *Chapter Summary* link in the left-hand column.

Key Terms – This section lists the chapter's key terms, and provides a definition for each term. To access this feature, choose the chapter number you want to work on and then click on the *Key Terms* link.

Multiple Choice Quiz – This is a 15 question multiple choice quiz that tests how well you learned the concepts covered in the chapter. After answering the questions, you can submit the quiz for grading and send the results of the quiz to your professor by e-mail. To access this feature, choose the chapter number you want to work on and then click on the *Multiple Choice Quiz* link in the left-hand column. After answering the quiz questions, click the "Submit Answers" button to have the quiz automatically graded.

Web-based Activities – There are two interactive activities provided for each chapter. These activities allow you to explore each chapter's content through a series of questions that are tied to specific World Wide Web links. To access this feature, choose the chapter number you want to work on and then click on the *Web-based Activities* link.

Web-based Projects – These projects are designed to help you use the World Wide Web to explore economic questions. In these projects, you are asked a series of questions relevant to the content you are exploring in class. To find the answers, you must explore specific content located on the World Wide Web by following the links provided. These projects also have a collaborative feature that may be assigned by your professor. With this feature you collaborate with other students in your class to develop answers to specific questions together. To access this feature, simply click on the *Web-based projects* link and choose the topic relevant to the material being covered in class or the material assigned by your professor.

NewsFlashes – As up-to-date as *The Economy Today* is, it can't foretell the future. As the future becomes the present, however, Brad Schiller writes 2 page *News Flashes* describing major economic events in the news and relating them to specific text references. To access this feature, simply click on the *NewsFlashes* link and choose the topic relevant to the material being covered in class or the *NewsFlash* assigned by your professor.

New York Times **news articles** – This section contains news articles from the New York Times that are relevant to the course. To access this feature, simply click on the *New York Times News* link and choose the chapter number you want to work on.

DiscoverEcon – Software specifically designed to supplement Brad Schiller's *The Economy Today*, 9e was developed by Gerald Nelson at the University of Illinois, Urbana-Champaign. This software is designed to be an interactive textbook that parallels the paper textbook. DiscoverEcon is available with the textbook either on the web or on CD-ROM. When you purchased your new textbook, you should have found either an online code card or a CD folder inside the package.   If you received a code card, follow the instructions on the back of the code card to access the online version of DiscoverEcon and enter your unique code. If you received a CD folder, follow the instructions for installation in the User's Manual inside the folder.

PowerPoints – Developed using Microsoft PowerPoint software, these slides are a great step-by-step review of the key points and graphs in each of the book's 36 chapters. To access this feature, choose the chapter number you want to work on and then click on the *PowerPoints* link in the left-hand column. Click on the chapter file that appears on the screen. It will take a few seconds for your computer to launch PowerPoint, but once you see the first slide, you can begin using the arrow keys to move from slide to slide within the chapter.

If you need additional help, you can click on Help Center to scroll through a list of help topics, or send your question to the webmaster via e-mail by selecting the Feedback option.

PART 1   Basic Concepts

CHAPTER 1

Economics: The Core Issues

Quick Review

- Resources (land, labor, capital, and entrepreneurship) are considered scarce, even when they seem abundant, because there are not enough resources to satisfy all of society's wants.

- Because resources are limited, society must make choices about what to produce. Choosing to produce one thing means giving up the opportunity to produce something else. Economists refer to the best forgone alternative as opportunity cost.

- Economists illustrate these choices by drawing a production-possibilities curve. This curve shows the combinations of goods and services a society could produce if it were operating efficiently and all of its resources were fully employed.

- The production-possibilities curve appears bowed out from the origin because of the law of increasing opportunity costs, which occurs because resources are not equally well suited to the production of all goods.

- If society uses its resources inefficiently, it will produce inside the production-possibilities curve. Additional resources and technological advances result in an outward shift of the production-possibilities curve. This is known as economic growth.

- Every society confronts the problem of scarcity and must somehow answer these basic questions: WHAT is to be produced?
  HOW should it be produced?
  FOR WHOM should the output be produced?

- In the United States, our choices are largely accomplished through the market mechanism. The "invisible hand" of the market mechanism coordinates the production and consumption decisions of millions of individuals and directly affects the allocation of the economy's resources. In some economies the market mechanism has not been allowed to work. Planned (or command) economies, like that of the old Soviet Union, are good examples of this.

- When the market mechanism fails to provide goods and services efficiently and equitably – a situation called "market failure" – the public sector must provide assistance. However, it is possible that government intervention will make the situation even worse, which is referred to as "government failure."

1

- It is useful to break economics into two categories: microeconomics and macroeconomics. Microeconomics focuses on a specific individual, firm, industry, or government agency; macroeconomics focuses on the entire economy.

Learning Objectives

After reading Chapter 1 and doing the following exercises, you should:

1. Understand the debate concerning market allocation vs. government allocation of resources.
2. Understand that economics is the study of how to allocate society's scarce resources – land, labor, capital, and entrepreneurship.
3. Know that scarcity occurs because resources are not sufficient to satisfy all of society's wants.
4. Be able to define and illustrate opportunity costs using a production-possibilities curve.
5. Understand the law of increasing opportunity costs.
6. Be able to demonstrate efficiency, growth, unemployment, and underemployment using a production-possibilities curve.
7. Know why every economy must answer the same basic questions – WHAT, HOW, FOR WHOM.
8. Be able to distinguish macroeconomic issues from microeconomic issues.
9. Be able to describe how the market mechanism seeks to allocate society's resources to their most valued use.
10. Be aware that there is serious debate and controversy over how the economy works.
11. Be able to discuss the tradeoffs inherent in the "peace dividend."
12. Be able to describe the mixed economy and distinguish market failure from government failure.

Using Key Terms

Fill in the puzzle on the opposite page with the appropriate terms from the list of Key Terms at the end of the chapter in the text.

Across

1. The reason there is no such thing as a "free lunch."
3. Occurs when government intervention fails to improve economic outcomes.
6. Represented by land, labor, capital, and entrepreneurship.
7. Economic study concerned with the behavior of individuals, firms, and government agencies.
11. The study of how best to allocate society's scarce resources.
14. Referred to as the "invisible hand" by Adam Smith.
16. Latin term meaning "other things remaining equal."
17. Economic policy supported by Adam Smith.

Down

2. The curve represented in Figure 1.1 in the text.
4. The assembling of resources to produce new or better products.
5. The study of the economy as a whole.
8. The use of both market signals and government directives to select the mix of output.
9. Illustrated in Figure 1.5 in the text by the outward shift of the production-possibilities curve.
10. Occurs when the market mechanism results in the wrong mix of output.
12. Final goods used to produce other goods.
13. The idea that there are not enough resources available to satisfy all desires.
15. Every point on the production-possibilities curve represents a situation of _____.

Puzzle 1.1

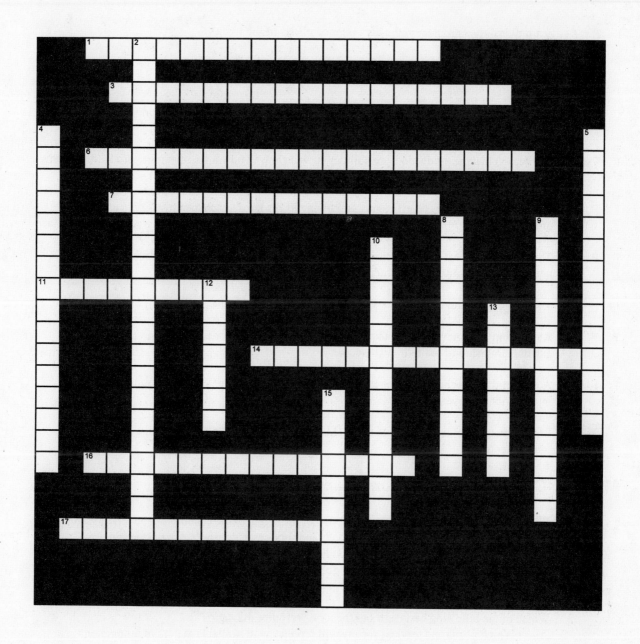

True or False: *Circle your choice and explain why any false statements are incorrect.*

T F 1. Scarcity is only a problem in the very poor countries of the world.

T F 2. Students do not pay tuition in public school, so from society's point of view, there is no opportunity cost involved in their education.

T F 3. A production-possibilities curve can be drawn only if a scarce resource prevents unlimited production of a product.

T F 4. One reason that the production-possibilities curve is bowed outward is that more production means the economy is less efficient in producing output.

T F 5. If the economy is fully and efficiently employing its resources, then the only way to acquire more of one good, *ceteris paribus*, is to accept less of something else.

T F 6. The opportunity cost of a good increases as more of the good is produced because resources are not equally well-suited to the production of all goods.

T F 7. The economy achieves the greatest efficiency when it is inside the production-possibilities curve.

T F 8. An economy will never be able to produce a combination of goods and services outside of its existing production-possibilities curve.

T F 9. A market-driven economy is not capable of solving the problems created by pollution without intervention by government.

T F 10. Price signals direct the answers to the WHAT, HOW, and FOR WHOM decisions in a laissez-faire economy.

Multiple Choice: *Select the correct answer.*

_____ 1. Which of the following is the best description of the origin of the economic problem of scarcity?
   (a) Humans have limited wants for goods and services and resources are also limited.
   (b) Humans have limited wants for goods and services and resources are unlimited.
   (c) Humans have unlimited wants for goods and services but resources are limited.
   (d) Humans have unlimited wants for goods and services and resources are also unlimited.

_____ 2. Which of the following best describes the term "resource allocation"?
   (a) Which goods and services society will produce with available factors of production.
   (b) How society spends the income of individuals based on resource availability.
   (c) How society purchases resources, given its macroeconomic goals.
   (d) How individual market participants decide what to produce given fixed resource constraints.

_____ 3. A consequence of the economic problem of scarcity is that:
   (a) Choices have to be made about how resources are used.
   (b) There is never too much of any good or service produced.
   (c) The production of goods and services has to be controlled by the government.
   (d) The production-possibilities curve is bowed outward.

_____ 4. Which of the following is *not* a factor of production?
   (a)   A college professor.
   (b)   A chalkboard used in an economics classroom.
   (c)   The $10 million donated to the college by wealthy alumni.
   (d)   The land on which a college is located.

_____ 5. Centrally planned economies are most likely to underestimate the value of:
   (a)   Land.
   (b)   Labor.
   (c)   Capital.
   (d)   Entrepreneurship.

_____ 6. Which of the following describes how resources are typically allocated in the U.S. economy?
   (a)   By tradition.
   (b)   By democratic vote.
   (c)   By markets.
   (d)   By government.

_____ 7. I plan on going to a $5 movie this evening instead of studying for an exam. The total opportunity cost of the movie:
   (a)   Depends on how I score on the exam.
   (b)   Is $5.
   (c)   Is what I could have purchased with the $5 plus the study time I forgo.
   (d)   Is the forgone studying I could have done in the same time.

_____ 8. The opportunity cost of installing a traffic light at a dangerous intersection is:
   (a)   Negative, since it will reduce accidents.
   (b)   The best possible alternative bundle of other goods or services that must be forgone in order to build and install the traffic light.
   (c)   The time lost by drivers who approach the intersection when the light is red.
   (d)   The cost of the stoplight plus the cost savings from a reduction in the number of accidents.

_____ 9. Which of the following events would cause the production-possibilities curve to shift inward?
   (a)   Immigration into a country increases.
   (b)   New factories are built.
   (c)   A technological breakthrough occurs.
   (d)   A terrorist attack destroys roads, bridges, and factories.

_____ 10. Which of the following events would cause the production-possibilities curve to shift outward?
   (a)   The economy's capital stock increases.
   (b)   A new, strong plastic is developed for use in building houses.
   (c)   More women enter the labor force.
   (d)   All of the above.

_____ 11. The slope of the production-possibilities curve provides information about:
   (a)   The growth of the economy.
   (b)   Technological change in the economy.
   (c)   Opportunity costs in the economy.
   (d)   All of the above.

_____ 12. The law of increasing opportunity cost explains:
   (a)   How everything becomes more expensive as the economy grows.
   (b)   The shape of the production-possibilities curve.
   (c)   Inflation.
   (d)   All of the above.

_____ 13. When an economy is producing efficiently it is:
    (a) Producing a combination of goods and services outside the production-possibilities curve.
    (b) Getting the most goods and services from the available resources.
    (c) Experiencing decreasing opportunity costs.
    (d) All of the above are correct.

_____ 14. In a market economy, the answer to the WHAT to produce question is determined by:
    (a) Direct negotiations between consumers and producers.
    (b) Producer profits and sales.
    (c) Government directives.
    (d) A democratic vote of all producers.

_____ 15. In a market economy, the answer to the HOW to produce question is determined by:
    (a) Government planners.
    (b) The production possibilities curve.
    (c) The least-cost method of production.
    (d) The method of production that uses the least amount of labor.

_____ 16. The trend toward greater reliance on the market mechanism by former communist societies is evidence of:
    (a) Government failure.
    (b) Market failure.
    (c) The failure of a mixed economy.
    (d) _Ceteris paribus._

_____ 17. Which of the following are major macroeconomic goals of the economy?
    (a) Full employment.
    (b) Control of inflation.
    (c) Economic growth.
    (d) All of the above.

_____ 18. Microeconomics focuses on the performance of:
    (a) Individual consumers, firms and government agencies.
    (b) Firms only.
    (c) Government agencies only.
    (d) The economy as a whole.

_____ 19. Reread the _In the News_ article "Bush Seeking Defense Increase." The article illustrates that increased military spending causes:
    (a) The production-possibilities curve to shift outward, _ceteris paribus._
    (b) The production-possibilities curve to shift inward, _ceteris paribus._
    (c) The production-possibilities curve to bow outward from the origin, _ceteris paribus._
    (d) Society to give up the production of civilian goods, _ceteris paribus._

_____ 20. Reread the _World View_ article "North Korea Says It Is Running Out of Food." Implicitly, the article is suggesting that the maintenance of an army results in:
    (a) An opportunity cost in terms of consumer goods.
    (b) An opportunity cost in terms of investment goods only.
    (c) No opportunity cost because the army keeps the country safe.
    (d) No opportunity cost because the soldiers are being paid.

_____ 21. The slope of a curve at any point is given by the formula:
    (a) The change in y coordinates between two points divided by the change in their x coordinates.
    (b) The change in x coordinates between two points divided by the change in their y coordinates.
    (c) The percentage change in y coordinates between two points divided by the percentage change in their x coordinates.
    (d) The percentage change in x coordinates between two points divided by the percentage change in their y coordinates.

_____ 22. When the relationship between two variables changes:
    (a) There is movement from one point on a linear curve to another point on the same curve.
    (b) The entire curve shifts.
    (c) The labels on the axes must be changed.
    (d) The curve becomes linear.

_____ 23. A linear curve can be distinguished by:
    (a) The continuous change in its slope.
    (b) The same slope throughout the curve.
    (c) The changing relationship between the two variables.
    (d) A shift in the curve.

Problems and Applications

Exercise 1

Suppose you have only 20 hours per week to allocate to study or leisure. The following table indicates the tradeoff between leisure time (not studying) and the grade-point average achieved as a result of studying.

Table 1.1

	(a)	(b)	(c)	(d)	(e)
Leisure time (hours / week)	20	18	14.5	10	0
Grade-point average	0	1.0	2.0	3.0	4.0

1. In Figure 1.1, draw the production-possibilities curve that represents the possible combinations from Table 1.1.

Figure 1.1

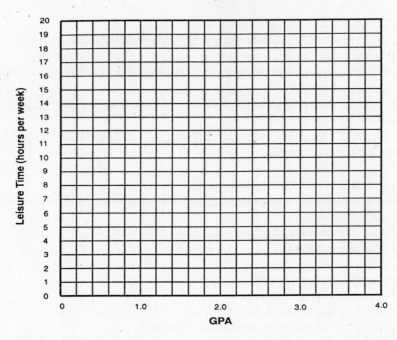

2. Using the information above, what is the opportunity cost of raising your grade-point average from 2.0 to 3.0? _____

3. What is the opportunity cost of raising your grade-point average from 3.0 to 4.0?

   _____

4. Why does the opportunity cost of improving your grade-point average increase?

   _____

Exercise 2

This exercise is similar to the problem at the end of Chapter 1 in the text. It provides practice in drawing and interpreting a production-possibilities curve and demonstrating shifts of such a curve.

1. A production-possibilities schedule showing the production alternatives between corn and lumber is presented in Table 1.2. Plot combination *A* in Figure 1.2 and label it. Do the same for combination *B*. In going from combination *A* to combination *B*, the economy has sacrificed _____ billion board feet of lumber production per year and has transferred the land to production of _____ billion bushels of corn per year. The opportunity cost of corn in terms of lumber is _____ board feet per bushel.

Table 1.2

Combination	Quantity of corn (billions of bushels per year)	Quantity of lumber (billions of board feet per year)
A	0	50
B	1	48
C	2	44
D	3	38
E	4	30
F	5	20
G	6	0

2. In answering Question 1 you determined the opportunity cost of corn when the economy is initially producing only lumber (combination *A*). Using the information in Table 1.2, plot the rest of the production-possibilities combinations in Figure 1.2 and label each of the points with the appropriate letter. Connect the points to form the production-possibilities curve.

Figure 1.2

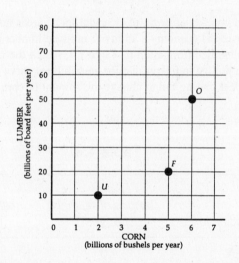

3. When Table 1.3 is completed, it should show the opportunity cost of corn at each possible combination of lumber and corn production in the economy. Opposite "1st billion bushels" insert the number of board feet per year of lumber sacrificed when the economy shifts from combination *A* to combination *B*. Complete the table for each of the remaining combinations.

Table 1.3

Corn production (billions of bushels per year)	Opportunity cost of corn in terms of lumber (billions of board feet per year)
1st billion bushels	_____
2nd billion bushels	_____
3rd billion bushels	_____
4th billion bushels	_____
5th billion bushels	_____
6th billion bushels	_____

4. In Table 1.3, as more corn is produced (as the economy moves from combination *A* toward combination *G*), the opportunity cost of corn (falls, rises, remains the same), which illustrates the law of _____.

5. Suppose that lumber companies begin to clear-cut forest areas instead of cutting them selectively. Clear-cutting improves the economy's ability to produce lumber but not corn. Table 1.4 describes such a situation. Using the information in Table 1.4, sketch the new production-possibilities curve in Figure 1.2 as you did the initial production-possibilities curve based on Table 1.3. For which combination does clear-cutting fail to change the amount of corn and lumber produced?

_____

Table 1.4

Combination	Corn (billions of bushels per year)	Lumber (billions of board feet per year)
A'	0	75
B'	1	72
C'	2	66
D'	3	57
E'	4	45
F'	5	30
G'	6	0

6. After the introduction of clear-cutting most of the new production-possibilities curve is (outside, inside, the same as) the earlier curve. The opportunity cost of corn has (increased, decreased) as a result of clear-cutting.

7. Study your original production-possibilities curve in Figure 1.2 and decide which of the combinations shown (*U, F, O*) demonstrates each of the following. (*Hint:* Check the answers at the end of the chapter to make sure you have diagrammed the production-possibilities curve in Figure 1.2 correctly.)
   (a) Society is producing at its maximum potential. Combination _____.
   (b) Society has some unemployed or underemployed resources. Combination _____.
   (c) Society cannot produce this combination at this time. Combination _____.
   (d) Society might be able to produce this combination if new resources were found or technology improved, but it cannot produce this combination currently. Combination _____.
   (e) If society produces this combination, some of society's wants will go unsatisfied unnecessarily. Combination _____.

Exercise 3

This exercise requires the understanding of scarcity, opportunity cost and production possibilities. Answer the following questions based on the information on pages 6 through 11 in the text.

_____ 1. In the U.S., the share of total output devoted to military goods:
   (a) Has remained fairly constant since 1940.
   (b) Is currently about 25 percent.
   (c) Is fairly low and results in no opportunity cost.
   (d) Is less than the share of total output devoted to military goods in China.

_____ 2. According to Figure 1.1 in the text, as the mix of output moves from point *C* to point *D*:
   (a) There is an increase in the production of televisions.
   (b) There is no opportunity cost because point *D* represents the optimal mix of output.
   (c) More factors of production are available for both shoes and televisions.
   (d) All of the above are true.

_____ 3. According to the text, the North Korean army:
   (a) Is the largest in the world in terms of number of personnel.
   (b) Absorbs a large share of output because North Korea is such a large country.
   (c) Absorbs approximately 14 percent of the country's resources.
   (d) All of the above are true.

_____ 4. Which of the following is the opportunity cost of maintaining an army in North Korea?
   (a) There is no opportunity cost because North Korea needs a large army to protect its citizens.
   (b) There is no opportunity cost because North Korea is producing the optimal mix of output.
   (c) Only the money spent on military equipment and salaries.
   (d) The food and other consumer goods that must be given up.

_____ 5. According to the text, Russia made the decision to reduce the size of its army, which released "... over 300,000 workers to produce civilian goods and services." This represents:
   (a) A market economy at work.
   (b) The concept of opportunity cost.
   (c) The tradeoff between consumption and investment.
   (d) The tradeoff between food and civilian goods.

Exercise 4

This exercise provides practice in the use of graphs.

Use Figure 1.3 below to answer the following questions.

Figure 1.3

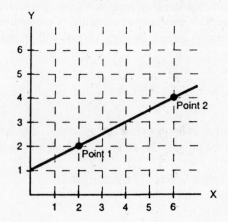

The slope of a line is the rate of change between two points or the vertical change divided by the horizontal change.

1. The vertical distance between the two points equals _____ .

2. The horizontal distance between the two points equals _____ .

3. The slope of the line equals _____ .

4. The slope of the line is (positive, negative) because as one variable increases the other variable (increases, decreases).

5. The line has the same slope at every point implying a (constant, changing) relationship between the two variables.

6. When the slope of a line is the same at every point, the curve is (linear, nonlinear).

Common Errors

The first statement in each "common error" below is incorrect. Each incorrect statement is followed by a corrected version and an explanation.

1. Words mean the same thing in economics that they do in our everyday conversation. WRONG!

   Words used in everyday conversation *very often* have different meanings when they are used in economics. RIGHT!

   You'll have to be very careful here. Words are used with precision in economics. You'll have difficulty if you confuse their everyday meanings with their economic meanings. For example, the term "capital" in economics means simply "man-made instruments of production." In everyday usage it may mean money, machines, a loan, or even the British response to the question "How are you feeling?"

2. Economic models are abstractions from the real world and are therefore useless in predicting and explaining economic behavior. WRONG!

   Economic models are abstractions from the real world and *as a result* are useful in predicting and explaining economic behavior. RIGHT!

   You have to be willing to deal with abstractions if you want to get anything accomplished in economics. By using economic models based on specific assumptions, we can make reasonable judgments about what's going on around us. We try not to disregard any useful information. However, to try to include everything (such as what cereal we like for breakfast) would be fruitless. For example, the production-possibilities frontier is an abstraction. No economist would argue that it is an economy! But it certainly is useful in focusing on public-policy choices, such as the choice between guns and butter.

3. Because economics is a "science," all economists should come up with the same answer to any given question. WRONG!

   Economics is a science, but there is often room for disagreement in trying to answer a given question. RIGHT!

   Economics is a social science, and the entire society and economy represent the economist's laboratory. Economists cannot run the kind of experiments that are done by physical scientists. As a result, two economists may attack a given problem or question in different ways using different models. They may come up with different answers, but since there is no answer book, you cannot say which is right. The solution is, then, to do more testing, refine our models, compare results, and so on. By the way, the recent space probes have given physicists cause to reevaluate much of their theory concerning the solar system, and there is much controversy concerning what the new evidence means. But physics is still a science, as is economics!

4. Increasing opportunity cost results from increasing inefficiency. WRONG!

   Increasing opportunity cost occurs even when resources are being used at their peak efficiency. RIGHT!

   Increasing opportunity cost and inefficiency are confused because both result in a lower amount of output per unit of input. However, inefficiency results from poor utilization or underemployment of resources, while increasing opportunity cost results from the increasing difficulty of adapting resources to production as more of a good is produced. Inefficiency can be represented as a movement inward from the production-possibilities curve, while increasing opportunity cost can be measured in movements along the production-possibilities curve. As the slope becomes steeper because of a movement down the production-possibilities curve, the good on the *x*-axis experiences increasing opportunity cost (a steeper slope). Similarly, a movement up along the production-possibilities curve represents a higher opportunity cost for the good on the *y*-axis – this time in the form of a flatter slope as more of the good on the *y*-axis is produced.

•ANSWERS•

Using Key Terms

Across

1. opportunity cost
3. government failure
6. factors of production
7. microeconomics
11. economics
14. market mechanism
16. ceteris paribus
17. laissez faire

Down

2. production possibilities
4. entrepreneurship
5. macroeconomics
8. mixed economy
9. economic growth
10. market failure
12. capital
13. scarcity
15. efficiency

True or False

1. F   All societies experience the problem of scarcity because human wants for goods and services will always exceed society's ability to produce goods and services.
2. F   Factors of production are required to produce education. These factors could have been used to produce other goods and services. The opportunity cost of education is the value of the best goods and services given up to get education.
3. T
4. F   Efficiency is maximized along a given production-possibilities curve. The production-possibilities curve bows outward because of the law of increasing opportunity costs, i.e., resources are not perfectly transferable from the production of one good to the production of another. Efficiency means "getting the most from what you have."
5. T
6. T
7. F   The economy achieves the greatest efficiency when it is on the curve.
8. F   An economy could produce a combination of goods and services outside its existing curve in the future if technology improves and/or the quantity of resources increase sufficiently.
9. T
10. T

Multiple Choice

1. c	5. d	9. d	13. b	17. d	21. a
2. a	6. c	10. d	14. b	18. a	22. b
3. a	7. c	11. c	15. c	19. d	23. b
4. c	8. b	12. b	16. a	20. a	

Problems and Applications

Exercise 1

1. **Figure 1.1 Answer**

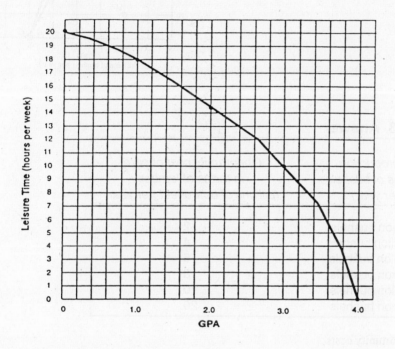

2. 4.5 hours of leisure time.

3. 10 hours of leisure time.

4. Higher grades are harder to get, particularly if the class is graded on a curve, with higher grades being received by a decreasing number of students. The "law" of increasing opportunity cost is evident in the economy and in the classroom.

Exercise 2

1. 2, 1, 2

2. **Figure 1.2 Answer**

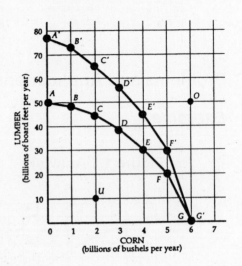

3. **Table 1.3 Answer**

Corn production (billions of bushels per year)	Opportunity cost of corn in terms of lumber (billions of board feet per year)
1st billion bushels	2
2nd billion bushels	4
3rd billion bushels	6
4th billion bushels	8
5th billion bushels	10
6th billion bushels	20

4. Rises, increasing opportunity costs
5. See Figure 1.2 answer; combination *G.*
6. Outside, increased
7. a. *F;* b. *U;* c. *O;* d. *O;* e. *U*

Exercise 3

1. d   3. c   5. b
2. a   4. d

16

Exercise 4

1. 2
2. 4
3. Slope = vertical change/horizontal change = 2/4 = 1/2 or 0.5
4. Positive, increases
5. Constant
6. Linear

CHAPTER 2

The U.S. Economy: A Global View

Quick Review

- The answers to the WHAT, HOW, and FOR WHOM questions in the U.S. economy are a product of both market activity and government intervention. Economic activity is assessed using economic statistics.

- The most frequently used measure of an economy's production is gross domestic product (GDP), which is the monetary value of a nation's output. Real GDP is the measure of output adjusted for inflation. GDP for the United States, at over $10 trillion, is approximately one-fourth of the world's total output.

- The pattern of production in the United States has changed over the last century. At the beginning of the century farming was the dominant sector, then manufacturing, and now services. Service industries currently produce over 70 percent of total output.

- GDP can be classified as consumer goods, investment goods, goods purchased by the government (federal, state, and local levels) and net exports. Consumer goods represent the largest portion of U.S. output.

- Per capita GDP for the United States is more than five times the world's average. Abundant resources, skilled management, an educated work force, and advanced technology have contributed to the high level of output. Factor mobility and capital-intensive production have resulted in high productivity. Economic freedom has also played a significant role in growth for the U.S. economy.

- Government establishes the legal rules of the game under which economic activity takes place. Government provides protection to consumers, labor and the environment through laws and regulations. Sometimes the answers to the WHAT, HOW, and FOR WHOM questions are made worse by government intervention, which is referred to as "government failure."

- GDP can be classified as consumer goods, investment goods, goods purchased by the government (federal, state, and local levels) and net exports. Consumer goods represent the largest portion of U.S. output.

- Income is not distributed equally in the United States. Those in the highest income quintile receive almost half of the total U.S. income.

- In the future, society will demand different answers to the WHAT, HOW, and FOR WHOM questions as new concerns cause us to revise our priorities.

Learning Objectives

After reading Chapter 2 and doing the following exercises, you should:

1. Be able explain why GDP and its components are an answer to the WHAT question.
2. Understand that factors of production differ in quantity, quality, and mobility in the United States and elsewhere.
3. Be able to trace the broad changes in industry structure in the United States from 1900 to the present.
4. Understand the role of government intervention as the economy answers the HOW question.
5. Understand that the economy's answer to the FOR WHOM question lies in the income distribution.
6. Expect that new market signals and government directives will change the answers to the WHAT, HOW, and FOR WHOM questions.

Using Key Terms

Fill in the puzzle on the opposite page with the appropriate term from the list of Key Terms at the end of the chapter in the text.

Across

1. Account for nearly half of all federal government spending but are not part of GDP.
6. Used in Figure 2.6 in the text to divide the population and then rank by income level.
9. The ability of a country to produce a good at a lower opportunity cost than another country.
10. The high level of _____ in the U.S. is explained to some extent by the level of education according to the article in the text titled "The Education Gap Between Rich and Poor Nations."
12. Goods and services bought from other countries.
13. A market situation in which the government intervenes to protect consumers from exploitation.
14. The costs or benefits of a market activity that affect a third party.
15. The resources used to produce goods and services.
16. A high ratio of capital to labor in the production process.

Down

2. Goods and services sold to other countries.
3. The sum of consumption, investment, government expenditure, and net exports.
4. The knowledge and skills possessed by the labor force.
5. An expansion of production possibilities.
7. Used to compare the average living standards in one country versus another according to the text.
8. The value of exports minus imports.
11. Expenditures for plant, machinery, and equipment.

Puzzle 2.1

True or False: *Circle your choice and explain why any false statements are incorrect.*

T F 1. The top 20 percent of U.S. households get nearly 20 percent of all U.S. income.

T F 2. If the economic growth rate exceeds the population growth rate, per capita GDP will increase.

T F 3. Federal government purchases of goods and services make up approximately 20 percent of GDP.

T F 4. Food stamps, medicare, and veterans' benefits are counted as government expenditures in the GDP.

T F 5. Whenever technology improves, an economy can produce more output with existing resources.

T F 6. As a percentage of GDP, output by the U.S. manufacturing sector has declined since World War II.

T F 7. If a business installs outdoor lighting that makes it difficult for you to sleep, this is an externality.

T F 8. The corporation is the dominant form of business organization in the United States in terms of numbers, assets, and sales.

T F 9. In developed countries, the richest quintile of the population gets a smaller proportion of total income than that quintile receives in poor, developing nations.

T F 10. Income transfers are intended to alter the market's answer to the HOW question.

Multiple Choice: *Select the correct answer.*

_____ 1. The economic growth rate of the economy is best measured by:
   (a) The percentage change in the GDP between two points in time.
   (b) The percentage change in per capita GDP between two points in time.
   (c) The sum of the value of the factors of production used to produce output in a country.
   (d) A measure of output divided by a measure of population.

_____ 2. GDP per capita will decline:
   (a) Whenever the GDP falls.
   (b) If the percentage change in per capita GDP rises.
   (c) If the rate of population growth exceeds the rate of economic growth.
   (d) If factor growth exceeds economic growth.

_____ 3. Suppose that during the course of a year, an economy produces $4.8 trillion consumer goods, $1.2 trillion investment goods, $1.4 trillion government services, $0.6 trillion exports, and $0.8 trillion imports. For that economy, GDP would be:
   (a) $8,000 trillion.
   (b) $7,000 trillion.
   (c) $8,800 trillion.
   (d) $7,200 trillion.

_____ 4. Which of the following countries (or regions) annually produces the most output?
   (a) Japan.
   (b) United States.
   (c) China.
   (d) The combined European Union.

5. Since 1900 the change in the relative importance of different sectors in the U.S. economy is best characterized as:
   - (a) Relative growth in farm output share.
   - (b) Relative growth in manufacturing output share.
   - (c) Relative growth in service output share.
   - (d) Relative decrease in service output share.

6. As the United States economy relies more and more heavily on the production of services rather than goods:
   - (a) GDP will decrease since there will be less "real" production.
   - (b) International trade will become more difficult.
   - (c) Mass unemployment will result.
   - (d) None of the above are likely to occur.

7. Which of the following has contributed to the increase in international trade in the United States since the 1920s?
   - (a) Reduced trade barriers.
   - (b) Improved communication systems.
   - (c) The growing share of services in U.S. production.
   - (d) All of the above.

8. Most of the United States GDP is used by:
   - (a) Consumers.
   - (b) Federal, state and local governments.
   - (c) Businesses.
   - (d) Foreign individuals and businesses.

9. Investment goods:
   - (a) Both maintain and expand production possibilities.
   - (b) Maintain production possibilities but do not expand them.
   - (c) Expand production possibilities but do not maintain them.
   - (d) Include consumption goods.

10. Which of the following are included in the GDP?
    - (a) Social security benefits.
    - (b) Net exports.
    - (c) Imports.
    - (d) Welfare checks.

11. Which of the following explains the low productivity of workers in poor, developing countries?
    - (a) Labor intensity of their production processes.
    - (b) The low factor mobility.
    - (c) The low quality of labor as a result of poor education.
    - (d) All of the above.

12. An increase in the level of human capital in an economy, *ceteris paribus*, will have the following effect on the economy's production possibilities curve.
    - (a) Shift the curve inward.
    - (b) Result in a movement from inside the curve to a point on the curve.
    - (c) Shift the curve outward.
    - (d) Result in a movement along the curve.

_____ 13. The primary way to distinguish among corporations, partnerships, and proprietorships is through:
   (a) Their ownership characteristics.
   (b) The size of firms.
   (c) The market share of leading firms.
   (d) The number of firms in each classification.

_____ 14. Which of the following would *not* be a common government activity in the U.S. economy?
   (a) The distribution of goods and services.
   (b) The regulation of water pollution.
   (c) Enforcing child labor laws.
   (d) Requiring producers to label the contents of baby food.

_____ 15. When the production of a good creates external costs:
   (a) Profits for the producer of the good will be lower.
   (b) Production of the good will be lower.
   (c) Society's collective well-being will be lower.
   (d) The level of environment pollution will be lower.

_____ 16. When monopolies exist:
   (a) Prices tend to be lower than in a competitive market.
   (b) Production tends to be higher than in a competitive market.
   (c) Quality tends to be lower than in a competitive market.
   (d) All of the above can occur.

_____ 17. The result of government intervention in the market in the case of market failure is that:
   (a) Society is always better off.
   (b) The production-possibilities curve will always shift outward.
   (c) Society may be worse off.
   (d) Society will always be worse off.

_____ 18. Which of the following statements about the way markets allocate resources is most accurate from society's perspective?
   (a) The market always allocates resources in the best way.
   (b) The market may allocate resources in a way that is not in society's best interest.
   (c) Resource allocation by markets may not be perfect, but it is always better than when the government allocates resources.
   (d) Markets often fail to allocate resources properly, so we must rely on governments to determine the proper use of our resources.

_____ 19. Inequalities in income caused by market forces:
   (a) Are always undesirable.
   (b) Can provide incentives and rewards for achievements.
   (c) Cannot be addressed by government action.
   (d) Do not exist.

_____ 20. According to The Heritage Foundation and Figure 2.5 in the text, highly regulated and taxed economies have:
   (a) Lower per capita GDPs than relatively unregulated, low-taxed economies.
   (b) Higher per capita GDPs than relatively unregulated, low-taxed economies.
   (c) Lower birth rates than relatively unregulated, low-taxed economies.
   (d) Higher birth rates than relatively unregulated, low-taxed economies.

Problems and Applications

Exercise 1

Each year an economic report on the state of the U.S. economy is prepared, called *The Economic Report of the President.* It summarizes the essential features of the economy's performance and describes the policy initiatives that are likely to be undertaken. This exercise uses the kind of information that is developed in this publication. Data was chosen from a specific period of time in order to show particular economic occurrences.

1. Table 2.1 shows the real GDP and the nominal GDP for the years 1990-97.

Table 2.1
Real GDP and nominal GDP, 1990-97

Year	Real GDP (in billions of dollars per year)	Nominal GDP (in billions of dollars per year)	Percentage growth in real GDP	Percentage growth in nominal GDP	U.S. population (in millions)	Real GDP per capita
1990	6,136.3	5,743.8	------------	-----------	249.9	_____
1991	6,079.4	5,916.7	_____	_____	252.6	_____
1992	6,244.4	6,244.4	_____	_____	255.4	_____
1993	6,389.6	6,558.1	_____	_____	258.1	_____
1994	6,610.7	6,947.0	_____	_____	260.6	_____
1995	6,742.1	7,265.4	_____	_____	263.0	_____
1996	6,928.4	7,636.0	_____	_____	265.5	_____
1997	7,191.4	8,083.4	_____	_____	267.9	_____

2. From the information in Table 2.1, calculate the percentage growth in nominal and real GDP for each of the years 1991-97 and insert your answers in the appropriate columns.
Use the following formula:

$$\text{Percentage growth in real GDP} = \frac{\text{real GDP}_t - \text{real GDP}_{t-1}}{\text{real GDP}_{t-1}} \times 100\%$$

where: t = current year

$t - 1$ = previous year

For example, for 1994 real GDP grew by the following percentage:

$$\frac{\text{real GDP}_t - \text{real GDP}_{t-1}}{\text{real GDP}_{t-1}} = \frac{\$6,610.7 - \$6,389.6}{\$6,389.6} \times 100\% = 3.46\% \text{ or } 3.5\%$$

3. T F When nominal GDP grows, real GDP must also grow.

4. By what nominal-dollar amount did nominal GDP grow from 1990 to 1997? $_____

5. By what constant-dollar amount did real GDP grow from 1990 to 1997? $_____

6. The U.S. population for the years 1990–97 is presented in column 6 of Table 2.1. Calculate the real GDP per capita in column 7.

7. T F When real GDP rises, real GDP per capita must also rise.

25

Exercise 2

This problem is designed to help you understand the mix of output in the United States.

1. Calculate the percentage of total output accounted for by each of the expenditure categories in Table 2.2 for 1997. (Your answers may not be exactly the same as the answers in this book due to rounding.) Now compare your answers to Figure 2.3 in the text, and notice the differences in various categories.

Table 2.2
U.S. national-income aggregates, 1997 (billions of dollars per year)

Expenditure categories		Percentage of total output
Consumption goods and services	$5,489	_____
Investment goods	1,238	_____
Exports	959	_____
Imports	1,056	_____
Federal government purchases	525	_____
State and local government purchases	929	_____

2. Which of the categories is the largest percentage of total output? _____

3. Which of the categories is the second largest percentage of total output? _____

4. Are net exports positive or negative in Table 2.2 above? _____

5. T   F   When net exports are negative, an economy uses more goods and services than it produces.

Exercise 3

This exercise focuses on the growth rates for GDP, population, and per capita GDP.

Refer to Table 2.1 in the text to answer questions 1-5.

1. Which country had the highest growth rate of per capita GDP during this time period? _____

2. Which country had the lowest growth rate of per capita GDP during this time period? _____

3. In Nigeria, the growth rate of GDP during this time period was _____ percent and the growth rate of population was _____ percent. When the population growth rate is greater than the GDP growth rate, then per capita GDP must (increase, decrease).

4. In general, the population of high-income countries grew more (rapidly, slowly), which made it easier to raise living standards.

5. T   F   Since the GDP growth rate for Kenya was greater than the GDP growth rate for Venezuela, during this time period, then Kenya experienced a greater increase in per capita GDP than did Venezuela.

Common Errors

The first statement in each "common error" below is incorrect. Each incorrect statement is followed by a corrected version and an explanation.

1. A higher GDP means an increase in the standard of living. WRONG!

    A high per capita GDP is an imperfect measure of the standard of living. RIGHT!

    Many developing countries experience a rise in GDP, but their population grows faster. This means that there is actually less income per person and the standard of living falls! The growth in population must be taken into account in measuring the standard of living, which is the reason that the per capita GDP, not just the GDP, is used. However, even the per capita GDP measure fails to take into account the distribution of income.

2. Investors make an economic investment when they invest in the stock market. WRONG!

    Economic investment occurs only with the *tangible* creation or maintenance of capital goods. RIGHT!

    A distinction must be made between financial investment and economic investment. Common usage usually refers to financial investment, in which individuals purchase a financial security backed by a financial institution. Such an activity is called saving, which is the alternative to immediate consumption. Such saving may eventually be used by financial corporations to make loans that will eventually lead to economic investment. But economists have found that there are a lot of things that can happen to saving before it turns into tangible production of capital goods. Therefore economists analyze saving and investment separately.

3. As the United States imports more, consumption rises and therefore so does the GDP. WRONG!

    Imports replace consumption of goods produced in the United States and lower the GDP. RIGHT!

    The GDP is the sum of consumption, investment, government purchases, and *net exports*. Net exports are computed by *subtracting* imports from exports. So, let's look at the GDP as an equation:
    GDP = consumption + investment + government purchases + exports - imports

    Greater imports mean a lower GDP, *ceteris paribus*! Consumption of foreign goods is not the concept of U.S. consumption used by economists. Economists focus on the output that is actually produced *in the United States* to satisfy U.S. consumers, not all of the expenditures that consumers make.

4. Export goods are not included in the GDP because they are not consumed by Americans. WRONG!

    Export goods are produced in the United States and therefore are included in the GDP. RIGHT!

    The GDP is the sum of consumption, investment, government purchases, and *net exports*. Once again the equation appears as follows:
    GDP = consumption + investment + government purchases + exports - imports

    Larger exports mean a higher GDP! The GDP focuses on the output of the economy and our use of resources to produce that output, regardless of who consumes it.

•ANSWERS•

Using Key Terms

Across

1. income transfers
6. income quintile
9. comparative advantage
10. productivity
12. imports
13. monopoly
14. externalities
15. factors of production
16. capital intensive

Down

2. exports
3. gross domestic product
4. human capital
5. economic growth
7. per capita GDP
8. net exports
11. investment

True or False

1. F The top 20 percent of U.S. households receive nearly 50 percent of all U.S. income.
2. T
3. F Federal government purchases of goods and services only make up approximately 8 percent of GDP.
4. F These are income transfers and are not included in GDP. No good or service is directly provided in exchange for these payments.
5. T
6. T
7. T
8. F The corporation is dominant in sales and assets, but the single proprietorship is the most common form of business structure in the U.S.
9. T
10. F Income transfers alter the market's answer to the FOR WHOM question.

Multiple Choice

1. a	5. c	9. a	13. a	17. c
2. c	6. d	10. b	14. a	18. b
3. d	7. d	11. d	15. c	19. b
4. b	8. a	12. c	16. d	20. d

Problems and Applications

Exercise 1

1. Table 2.1 Answer

Year	Real GDP (in billions of dollars per year)	Nominal GDP (in billions of dollars per year)	Percentage growth in real GDP	Percentage growth in nominal GDP	U.S. population (in millions)	Real GDP per capita
1990	6,136.3	5,743.8	----	----	249.9	24,555
1991	6,079.4	5,916.7	-0.9	3.0	252.6	24,067
1992	6,244.4	6,244.4	2.7	5.5	255.4	24,449
1993	6,389.6	6,558.1	2.3	5.0	258.1	24,756
1994	6,610.7	6,947.0	3.5	5.9	260.6	25,367
1995	6,742.1	7,265.4	2.0	4.6	263.0	25,635
1996	6,928.4	7,636.0	2.8	5.1	265.5	26,096
1997	7,191.4	8,083.4	3.8	5.9	267.9	26,844

2. See Table 2.1 answer, columns 4, 5
3. F
4. $2,339.6 billion

5. $1,055.1 billion
6. See Table 2.1 answer, column 7
7. F

Exercise 2

1. Table 2.2 Answer

Expenditure categories		Percentage of total output
Consumption goods and services	$5,489	67.9
Investment goods	1,238	15.3
Exports	959	11.9
Imports	1,056	13.1
Federal government purchases	525	6.5
State and local government purchases	929	11.5

2. Consumer goods and services
3. Investment goods

4. Negative
5. T

Exercise 3

1. China
2. Ethiopia
3. 2.4, 2.8, decrease
4. Slowly
5. F

CHAPTER 3
Supply and Demand

Quick Review

- Participation in the market by consumers, businesses, and government is motivated by the desire to maximize something: utility for consumers, profits for businesses, and general welfare for the government.

- Interactions in the marketplace involve either the factor market, where factors of production are bought and sold, or the product market, where goods and services are bought and sold.

- The demand curve represents buyer behavior. It slopes downward and to the right, showing that buyers are willing and able to purchase greater quantities at lower prices, *ceteris paribus*. The supply curve represents producer behavior. It slopes upward and to the right, indicating that producers are willing and able to produce greater quantities at higher prices, *ceteris paribus*.

- Movements along a demand curve result from a change in price. Shifts in a demand curve result from a change in a nonprice determinant—tastes, income, other goods, expectations, the number of buyers.

- Movements along a supply curve result from a change in price. Shifts in a supply curve result from a change in a nonprice determinant—technology, factor costs, other goods, taxes and subsidies, expectations, the number of sellers.

- Market demand and market supply summarize the intentions of all those participating on one side of the market or the other.

- Equilibrium price and quantity are established at the intersection of the supply and demand curves. At any price other than the equilibrium price, disequilibrium will occur.

- Price ceilings are set below the equilibrium price and result in shortages; price floors are set above the equilibrium price and result in surpluses. In either case, the market does not clear.

- The market mechanism relies on the forces of demand and supply to establish market outcomes (prices and quantities) in both product and factor markets. The market mechanism thus can be used to answer the WHAT, HOW, and FOR WHOM questions.

Learning Objectives

After reading Chapter 3 and doing the following exercises, you should:

1. Know the basic questions in economics and how the U.S. economy answers the questions.
2. Be able to describe the motivations of participants in the product and resource markets.
3. Understand how a demand schedule represents demand and how a supply schedule represents supply.
4. Be able to define, graph, and interpret supply and demand curves.
5. Know the nonprice determinants of both supply and demand and the direction they shift the curves.
6. Know what causes movements along demand and supply curves.
7. Understand how market-demand and market-supply curves are derived from individual demand and supply curves.
8. Know how equilibrium is established and why markets move toward equilibrium.
9. Understand the consequences of price ceilings and price floors.
10. Understand how the market mechanism provides the answer to the WHAT, HOW, and FOR WHOM questions.

Using Key Terms

Fill in the puzzle on the opposite page with the appropriate term from the list of Key Terms at the end of the chapter in the text.

Across

3.   The result of the price ceiling on electricity set by the California legislature according to the text.
6.   Changes from $20 to $30 in Figure 3.7 in the text.
7.   The willingness and ability to sell various quantities of a good at alternative prices.
10. The willingness and ability to buy a particular good at some price.
12. The assumption by economists that nothing else changes.
15. Where businesses purchase the factors of production.
16. The use of market price and sales to signal desired output.
17. Refers to the inverse relationship between price and quantity.

Down

1.   The result of an income change in Figure 3.3 in the text.
2.   According to the webnote on page 53 in the text, consumers reveal their _____ _____ to Priceline.
3.   The sum of all producers' sales intentions.
4.   The name of the table from which Figure 3.2 in the text is drawn.
5.   Where goods and services are exchanged.
8.   According to Figure 3.6 in the text, at a price of $25 per hour, a _____ exists.
9.   Put in place by the California legislature to control the retail price of electricity according to the text.
11. Explains why the curve in Figure 3.5 in the text is upward sloping.
13. The value of the most desired forgone alternative.
14. The name for the final curve drawn in Figure 3.4 in the text.

Puzzle 3.1

True or False: *Circle your choice and explain why any false statements are incorrect.*

T F 1. The demand curve shows how much of a good a buyer will actually buy at a given price.

T F 2. A change in one of the determinants of demand causes a movement along the demand curve for the good.

T F 3. An increase in the price of one good can cause the demand for another good to increase if the goods are substitutes.

T F 4. Supply curves reflect the potential behavior of the sellers or producers of a good or service, not of the buyers.

T F 5. The "law of supply" has nothing to do with opportunity costs.

T F 6. When the number of suppliers in a market changes, the market supply curve also changes, even if the individual supply curves of original suppliers do not shift.

T F 7. The equilibrium price can be determined through the process of trial and error by both the buyers and the sellers in a market.

T F 8. There are never shortages or surpluses when the price in a market is equal to the equilibrium price for the market.

T F 9. When economists say that the market mechanism provides an "optimal" allocation of resources they mean that all consumer desires are satisfied and business profits are maximized.

T F 10. In a market economy, producers earn profits by producing the goods and services that consumers want the most.

Multiple Choice: *Select the correct answer.*

_____ 1. The goals of the principal actors in the economy are:
   (a) Income for consumers, profits for businesses, and taxes for government.
   (b) Goods and services for consumers, scarce resources for businesses, and resources not used by businesses for government.
   (c) Satisfaction from purchases for consumers, profits for businesses, and general welfare for government.
   (d) Available goods and services for consumers, scarce resources for businesses, and general welfare for government.

_____ 2. Which of the following helps to explain why economic interaction occurs?
   (a) Limited ability to produce what we need.
   (b) Constraints on time, energy, and resources.
   (c) The gains possible from specialization.
   (d) All of the above.

_____ 3. Consumers:
   (a) Provide dollars to the product market.
   (b) Receive dollars from the product market.
   (c) Provide dollars to the factor market.
   (d) Receive goods and services from the factor market.

_____ 4. The law of demand states that:
  (a) As price falls, quantity demanded falls, *ceteris paribus*.
  (b) As price falls, quantity demanded increases, *ceteris paribus*.
  (c) As price falls, demand falls, *ceteris paribus*.
  (d) As price falls, demand increases, *ceteris paribus*.

_____ 5. Which of the following must be held constant according to the *ceteris paribus* assumption in defining a demand schedule?
  (a) The price of the good itself.
  (b) Expectations of sellers.
  (c) Income.
  (d) Technology.

_____ 6. The quantity of a good that a consumer is willing to buy depends on:
  (a) The price of the good.
  (b) The consumer's income.
  (c) The opportunity cost of purchasing that good.
  d) All of the above.

_____ 7. Jon's demand schedule for donuts indicates:
  (a) How much he likes donuts.
  (b) His opportunity cost of buying donuts.
  (c) Why he likes donuts.
  (d) How many donuts he will actually buy.

_____ 8. According to the law of supply, a supply curve:
  (a) Has a negative slope.
  (b) Has a positive slope.
  (c) Is a horizontal, or flat, line.
  (d) Will always be less than the demand curve.

_____ 9. When a seller sells a good, *ceteris paribus*:
  (a) There is no change in supply or the quantity supplied.
  (b) The supply curve shifts to the left, but quantity supplied remains the same.
  (c) The quantity supplied of the good falls, but supply remains unchanged.
  (d) The supply curve shifts to the left, and the quantity supplied falls.

_____ 10. If corn and wheat are alternative pursuits for a farmer, a change in the supply of corn will take place:
  (a) When the price of corn changes.
  (b) When the price of wheat changes.
  (c) When the demand for corn changes.
  (d) When consumers want to buy more corn at the same price.

_____ 11. Suppose the MC Birdhouse Co. announces that they need higher prices than last year to sell the same quantity of birdhouses. We can conclude that there has been:
  (a) An increase in demand.
  (b) A decrease in demand.
  (c) A decrease in the company's supply.
  (d) An increase in the company's supply.

_____ 12. To calculate market supply we:
  (a) Add the quantities supplied for each individual supply schedule horizontally.
  (b) Add the quantities supplied for each individual supply schedule vertically.
  (c) Find the average quantity supplied at each price.
  (d) Find the difference between the quantity supplied and the quantity demanded at each price.

13. In the market for web design services, an increase in the number of people with web designing skills will cause:
    (a) An increase in the equilibrium price and a decrease in the equilibrium quantity.
    (b) A decrease in the equilibrium price and an increase in the equilibrium quantity.
    (c) An increase in the equilibrium price and an increase in the equilibrium quantity.
    (d) A decrease in the equilibrium price and a decrease in the equilibrium quantity.

14. In a market, the equilibrium price is determined by:
    (a) What buyers are willing and able to purchase.
    (b) What sellers are willing and able to offer for sale.
    (c) Both demand and supply.
    (d) The government.

15. A leftward shift in a demand curve and a leftward shift in a supply curve both result in a:
    (a) Lower equilibrium quantity.
    (b) Higher equilibrium quantity.
    (c) Lower equilibrium price.
    (d) Higher equilibrium price.

16. If the number of consumers in a market decreases, this will cause:
    (a) An increase in the equilibrium price and a decrease in the equilibrium quantity.
    (b) A decrease in the equilibrium price and an increase in the equilibrium quantity.
    (c) An increase in the equilibrium price and an increase in the equilibrium quantity.
    (d) A decrease in the equilibrium price and a decrease in the equilibrium quantity.

17. In a market economy, the people who receive the goods and services produced are the people who:
    (a) Need the goods and services.
    (b) Want the goods and services the most.
    (c) Have the most political power.
    (d) Are willing and able to pay the market price.

18. When economists talk about "optimal outcomes" in the marketplace, they mean that:
    (a) The allocation of resources by the market is perfect.
    (b) All consumer desires are satisfied and business profits are maximized.
    (c) The allocation of resources by the market is likely to be the best possible, given scarce resources and income constraints.
    (d) Everyone who wants a good or service can get it.

19. When effective price ceilings are set for a market:
    (a) Quantity supplied will be less than the equilibrium quantity, and price will be less than the equilibrium price.
    (b) Quantity supplied will be less than the equilibrium quantity, and price will be greater than the equilibrium price.
    (c) Quantity supplied will be greater than the equilibrium quantity, and price will be less than the equilibrium price.
    (d) Quantity supplied will be greater than the equilibrium quantity, and price will be greater than the equilibrium price.

_____ 20. One *In the News* article in the text is titled "Californians Pinched by Power Prices." This article best illustrates the concept that:
  (a) An increase in the price of electricity causes the supply of water to decrease.
  (b) A decrease in the supply of electricity causes the price of electricity to increase.
  (c) A decrease in the quantity supplied of electricity causes the price of electricity to increase.
  (d) An increase in the demand for electricity causes the price of electricity to decrease.

Problems and Applications

Exercise 1

This exercise provides practice in graphing demand and supply curves for individual buyers and sellers as well as graphing market demand and market supply curves.

1. Suppose you are willing and able to buy 20 gallons of gasoline per week if the price is $1 per gallon, but if the price is $3 per gallon you are willing and able to buy only the bare minimum of 10 gallons. Complete the demand schedule in Table 3.1.

Table 3.1
Your demand schedule for gasoline

Price (dollars per gallon)	Quantity (gallons per week)
$1	_____
3	_____

2. Use the demand schedule in Table 3.1 to draw the demand curve in Figure 3.1. Assume the demand curve is a straight line.

Figure 3.1
Your demand curve for gasoline.

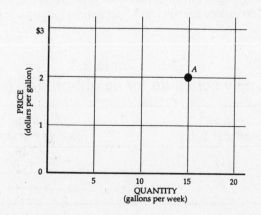

If you have drawn your demand curve correctly, it should go through point *A*.

3. Suppose that 999 other people in your town have demand curves for gasoline that are just like yours in Figure 3.1. Fill out the town's market-demand schedule in Table 3.2 at each price. (Remember to include your own quantity demanded along with everyone else's at each price.)

Table 3.2
Market-demand schedule for gasoline in your town

Price (dollars per gallon)	Quantity (gallons per week)
$1	_____
3	_____

4. Using the market-demand schedule in Table 3.2, draw the market-demand curve for gasoline for your town in Figure 3.2. Assume that the curve is a straight line, and label it D.

Figure 3.2
Market supply and demand curves for gasoline in your town

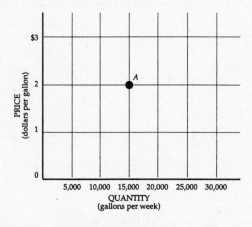

If you have drawn the demand curve correctly, it should pass through point A.

5. Suppose the friendly neighborhood gas station is willing to sell 250 gallons of gasoline per week at $1 per gallon and 1,250 gallons per week at $3 per gallon. Fill in the supply schedule for this gas station in Table 3.3.

Table 3.3
Supply schedule for neighborhood gas station

Price (dollars per gallon)	Quantity (gallons per week)
$1	_____
3	_____

38

6. Graph the supply curve for the gas station in Figure 3.3 using the information in Table 3.3. Assume that the supply curve is a straight line.

Figure 3.3
Supply curve for neighborhood gas station

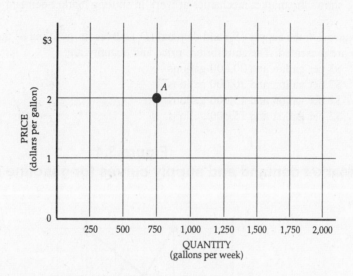

If you have drawn the supply curve correctly, it should pass through point *A*.

7. Suppose that 19 other gas stations in your town have the same supply schedule as your neighborhood gas station (Table 3.3). Fill out the market-supply schedule for gasoline of the 20 gas stations in your town in Table 3.4.

Table 3.4
Market supply schedule for gasoline in your town

Price (dollars per gallon)	Quantity (gallons per week)
$1	_____
3	_____

8. Using the market supply schedule in Table 3.4, draw the market supply curve for gasoline for your town in Figure 3.2. Assume that the market supply curve is a straight line. If you have drawn the curve correctly, it should pass through point *A*. Label the supply curve *S*.

9. The equilibrium price for gasoline for your town's 20 gas stations and 1,000 buyers of gasoline (see Figure 3.2) is:
   (a) Above $2.
   (b) Exactly $2.
   (c) Below $2.

10. At the equilibrium price:
    (a) The quantity demanded equals the quantity supplied.
    (b) There is a surplus.
    (c) There is a shortage.
    (d) There is an excess of inventory.

Exercise 2

This exercise shows the market mechanics at work in shifting market-demand curves.

1. In Figure 3.4, the supply (S_1) and demand (D_1) curves for gasoline as they might appear in your town are presented. The equilibrium price and quantity are:
   (a) $3 per gallon and 20,000 gallons.
   (b) $2 per gallon and 20,000 gallons.
   (c) $1 per gallon and 15,000 gallons.
   (d) $2 per gallon and 15,000 gallons.

Figure 3.4
Market demand and supply curves for gasoline in your town

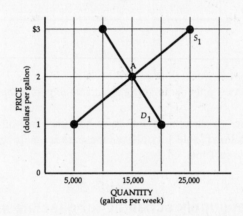

2. Assume that one-half of the people in your town move away. Because of this, suppose that the remaining buyers are willing and able to buy only half as much gasoline at each price as was bought before. Draw the new demand curve in Figure 3.4 and label it D_2.

3. When the number of buyers in a market changes, the market demand curve for goods and services shifts and there is a change in (demand, quantity demanded).

4. When half of the buyers move from your town and the demand curve shifts, the new equilibrium price:
   (a) Is above the old equilibrium price.
   (b) Is below the old equilibrium price.
   (c) Remains the same as the old equilibrium price.
   (*Hint:* See the second demand curve, D_2, in Figure 3.4.)

40

5. Given the new demand curve, if the market price remains at the old equilibrium price of $2 then:
   (a) The quantity demanded will equal the quantity supplied.
   (b) A shortage of gasoline will occur.
   (c) A surplus of gasoline will occur.

6. When there is a surplus in a market:
   (a) Buyers do not wish to buy as much as sellers want to sell.
   (b) Sellers are likely to offer discounts to eliminate expensive excess inventories.
   (c) Buyers who cannot buy commodities at the current market price are likely to make offers to buy at lower prices that sellers will now accept.
   (d) All the above.

7. When there is a leftward shift of the market-demand curve, market forces should push:
   (a) Market prices upward and market quantity downward.
   (b) Market prices upward and market quantity upward.
   (c) Market prices downward and market quantity downward.
   (d) Market prices downward and market quantity upward.

8. Whenever there is a rightward shift of the market demand curve, market forces should push:
   (a) Market prices upward and market quantity upward.
   (b) Market prices upward and market quantity downward.
   (c) Market prices downward and market quantity upward.
   (d) Market prices downward and market quantity downward.

Exercise 3

This exercise gives practice in computing market demand and market supply curves using the demand and supply curves of individuals in a market. It is similar to a problem for chapter 3 in the text.

1. Table 3.5 shows the weekly demand and supply schedules for various individuals. Fill in the total market quantity that these individuals demand and supply.

Table 3.5
Individual demand and supply schedules

Price	$4	$3	$2	$1
Buyers				
Al's quantity demanded	1	3	4	6
Betsy's quantity demanded	2	2	3	3
Casey's quantity demanded	2	2.5	3	3.5
Total market quantity demanded	___	___	___	___
Sellers				
Alice's quantity supplied	5	3	2	0
Butch's quantity supplied	6	5	4	3
Connie's quantity supplied	5	4	3	2
Ellen's quantity supplied	4	3	1	0
Total market quantity supplied	___	___	___	___

Use the data in Table 3.5 to answer questions 2-4.

2. Construct and label market-supply and market-demand curves in Figure 3.5.

3. Identify the equilibrium point and label it *EQ* in Figure 3.5.

4. What is true about the relationship between quantity demanded and quantity supplied at a price of $3 in Figure 3.5? _____

Figure 3.5
Market-supply and market-demand curves for buyers and sellers

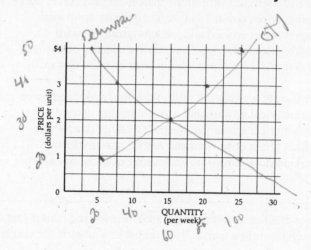

Exercise 4

This exercise provides examples of events that would shift demand or supply curves. It is similar to a problem at the end of the chapter in the text.

Figure 3.6
Shifts of curves

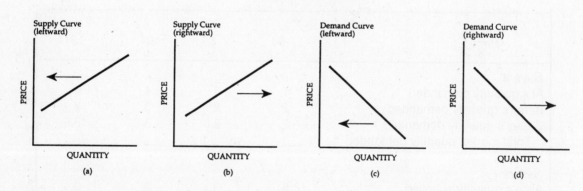

Choose the letter of the appropriate diagram in Figure 3.6 that best describes the shift that would occur in each of the following situations. The shifts are occurring in the market for U.S. defense goods. (*Hint*: Ask yourself if the change first affects buyers or the sellers. Refer to the nonprice determinants for demand and supply listed in the text if necessary.)

42

_____ 1. Because of increased protectionism for steel, steel producers are able to raise the price of specialty steel, which is a key resource in the production of defense goods.

_____ 2. A new process for creating microchips is developed that reduces the cost of materials needed to produce nuclear submarines.

_____ 3. As a result of worldwide terrorist threats, new buyers enter the market to purchase defense goods.

_____ 4. A country that previously bought U.S. defense goods enters into a peace agreement.

_____ 5. A large firm in the defense industry closes down when it loses a defense contract.

Exercise 5

The media often provide information about supply and demand shifts. This exercise uses one of the articles in the text to show the kind of information to look for.

Reread the *In the News* article entitled "Californians Pinched by Power Prices." Then answer the following questions:

1. Which of the four diagrams in Figure 3.6 in the previous exercise best represents the shift in the market for electricity? a   b   c   d   (circle one)

2. The change in the electricity market is referred to as a:
   (a) Change in quantity supplied.
   (b) Change in supply.
   (c) Change in quantity demanded.
   (d) Change in demand.

3. What is the expected change in equilibrium price and quantity in the electricity market?

   _____

Common Errors

The first statement in each "common error" below is incorrect. Each incorrect statement is followed by a corrected version and an explanation.

1. If a large number of people petition the government in order to get something, then there is a large demand for that item. WRONG!

   If a large number of people desire a commodity *and have the ability to pay for it,* then there is a large demand for that item. RIGHT!

   People want something, but there is no "demand" for it unless they are able to pay for it. Economists use the word "demand" in a way that is quite different from normal usage. People who want (desire; have preferences, a taste, or liking for) a commodity are seen as going to a market to purchase the commodity with money. "Demand" does not mean claiming the right to something when a person does not have the ability to buy it.

2. Market price is the same thing as equilibrium price. WRONG!

    The market price moves by trial and error (via the market mechanism) toward the equilibrium price. RIGHT!

    When demand and supply curves shift, the market is temporarily out of equilibrium. The price may move along a demand or supply curve toward the new equilibrium.

3. Since the quantity bought must equal the quantity sold, every market is always in equilibrium by definition. WRONG!

    Although the quantity bought equals the quantity sold, there may be shortages or surpluses. RIGHT!

    Although the quantity actually bought does equal the quantity actually sold, there may still be buyers who are willing and able to buy more of the good at the market price (market shortages exist) or sellers who are willing and able to sell more of the good at the market price (market surpluses exist). If the market price is above the equilibrium price, there will be queues of goods (inventories). Prices will be lowered by sellers toward the equilibrium price. If the market price is below the equilibrium price, there will be queues of buyers (shortages). Prices will be bid up by buyers toward the equilibrium price.

4. The intersection of supply and demand curves determines how much of a good or service will actually be exchanged and the actual price of the exchange. WRONG!

    The intersection of supply and demand curves shows only where buyers and sellers intend and have the ability to exchange the same amount of a commodity. RIGHT!

    Many institutional interferences may prevent the market from ever reaching the equilibrium point, where supply and demand curves intersect. All that can be said is that, given a free market, prices and production will tend to move toward equilibrium levels.

5. A change in price changes the demand for goods by consumers. WRONG!

    A change in price changes the quantity demanded by consumers in a given time period. RIGHT!

    Economists differentiate the terms "quantity demanded" and "demand." A change in the quantity demanded usually refers to a movement along the demand curve as a result of a change in price. A change in demand refers to a shift of the demand curve as a result of a change in incomes, tastes, prices or availability of other goods, or expectations.

6. A change in price changes the supply of goods produced by a firm. WRONG!

    A change in price changes the quantity supplied of a good by a firm in a given time period. RIGHT!

    Economists differentiate the terms "quantity supplied" and "supply." A change in the quantity supplied usually refers to a movement along a supply curve as a result of a change in price or production rate. A change in supply refers to a shift of the supply curve as a result of a change in technology, prices of resources, number of sellers, other goods, expectations, or taxes.

•ANSWERS•

Using Key Terms

Across

3.   market shortage
6.   equilibrium price
7.   supply
10. demand
12. ceteris paribus
15. factor market
16. market mechanism
17. law of demand

Down

1.   shift in demand
2.   demand curve
3.   market supply
4.   demand schedule
5.   product market
8.   market surplus
9.   price ceiling
11. law of supply
13. opportunity cost
14. market demand

True or False

1.   F   The demand curve indicates how much a buyer would like to buy and is able to pay for. How much is actually bought also depends on supply.
2.   F   A change in one of the determinants of demand results in a shift in the demand curve.
3.   T
4.   T
5.   F   The quantity of a good that a producer is willing and able to produce and offer for sale at any price depends on the value of the alternative goods that could have been produced with those same resources, i.e., the opportunity costs.
6.   T
7.   T
8.   T
9.   F   An optimal outcome does not mean that all consumer desires are satisfied and business profits are maximized. It simply means that the market outcome is likely to be the best possible given scarce resources and income constraints.
10. F   In a market economy, producers earn profits by producing the goods and services that consumers demand, i.e., are willing and able to pay for.

Multiple Choice

1. c	5. c	9. a	13. b	17. d
2. d	6. d	10. b	14. c	18. c
3. a	7. b	11. c	15. a	19. a
4. b	8. b	12. a	16. d	20. b

Problems and Applications

Exercise 1

1.   **Table 3.1 Answer**

p	q
$1	20
3	10

2.   **Figure 3.1 Answer**

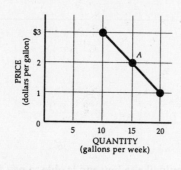

3.   **Table 3.2 Answer**

p	q
$1	20,000
3	10,000

46

4.   See Figure 3.2 Answer, curve D.

Figure 3.2 Answer

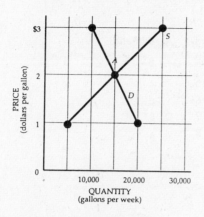

5.   ## Table 3.3 Answer

p	q
$1	250
3	1,250

6.   ## Figure 3.3 Answer

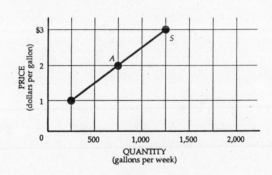

7.   ## Table 3.4 Answer

p	q
$1	5,000
3	25,000

8.   See Figure 3.2 Answer, curve S.

9. c
10. a

Exercise 2

1. d

3. demand
4. b
5. c
6. d
7. c

2. **Figure 3.4 Answer**

8. a

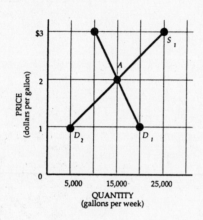

Exercise 3

1. **Table 3.5 Answer**

Price	$4	$3	$2	$1
Buyers Total market quantity demanded	5	7.5	10	12.5
Sellers Total market quantity supplied	20	15	10	5

2. **Figure 3.5 Answer**

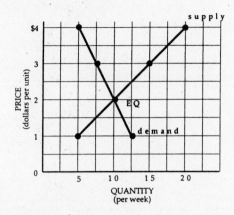

3. See point *EQ* in Figure 3.5.
4. The quantity supplied is greater than the quantity demanded or there is a surplus of 7.5 units (15 minus 7.5.)

Exercise 4

1. a
2. b
3. d
4. c
5. a

Exercise 5

1. a
2. b
3. An increase in equilibrium price and a decrease in equilibrium quantity.

CHAPTER 4
The Public Sector

Quick Review

- Market failure occurs when the market mechanism causes the economy to produce a combination of goods different from the optimal mix of output or results in an inequitable distribution of income. Market failure may prompt the government to intervene.

- There are four specific sources of market failure at the micro level: public goods, externalities, market power, and equity.

- Private goods can be consumed exclusively by those who pay for the goods, but public goods cannot. Public goods, such as national defense, can be consumed jointly by everyone no matter who pays. Because the link between paying and receiving is broken, everyone seeks to be a "free rider" and benefit from purchases made by others. As a result, the market underproduces public goods, and government intervention is necessary to provide these goods.

- Externalities are costs (or benefits) of a market transaction borne by a third party. Externalities cause a divergence between social costs and private costs and lead to suboptimal market outcomes. In the case of externalities such as pollution, which impose costs on society, too much of the polluting good is produced. If the externality produces benefits, too little of the good will be produced by the market alone. Regulations and emission fees are used to reduce the external costs associated with externalities.

- Market power allows producers to ignore the signals generated in the marketplace and produce a suboptimal mix of output. Antitrust policy and laws seek to prevent or restrict concentrations of market power.

- The market mechanism tends to allocate output to those with the most income. The government responds with a system of taxes and transfer payments to ensure a more equitable distribution of income and output.

- Markets may also fail at the macro level. In this case, the problems include unacceptable levels of unemployment, inflation, and economic growth. Government intervention is then necessary to achieve society's goals.

- State and local government activity exceeds that of the federal government and has grown much more rapidly in recent decades. Federal expenditures are supported mainly by personal income taxes and Social Security taxes. State and local governments rely most heavily on sales taxes and property taxes, respectively.

51

- Government intervention that does not improve economic outcomes is referred to as government failure.

Learning Objectives

After reading Chapter 4 and doing the following exercises, you should:

1. Understand that market failure can occur and as a result the government may decide to intervene.
2. Be able to describe the communal nature of public goods and the free-rider dilemma.
3. Know the nature of externalities and how they influence the decisions of producers and consumers.
4. Use the concepts of social cost and private cost to explain the problems associated with externalities.
5. Understand the policy options that can be used to address the problems associated with externalities.
6. Understand how antitrust activity attempts to combat monopoly power.
7. Be familiar with some fundamental antitrust laws.
8. Understand that inequity in income distribution is an example of market failure with respect to the FOR WHOM question.
9. Understand the concept of macro failure.
10. Understand the recent trend in terms of spending at the federal level vs. the state and local levels.
11. Know where government revenues come from and the difference between the different tax structures.
12. Understand that government failure can occur.

Using Key Terms

Fill in the puzzle on the opposite page with the appropriate term from the list of Key Terms at the end of the chapter in the text.

Across

1. The most desired goods and services that are given up in order to obtain something else.
5. An increase in the average level of prices.
8. Referred to as the "invisible hand."
10. The likely outcome of government intervention according to the survey titled "Persistent Doubts about Government Waste" in the text.
14. An industry in which a single firm achieves economies of scale over the entire range of output.
17. State lotteries are categorized in this way according to the article titled "Big Lotteries' Real Losers" in the text.
19. A form of government intervention to address the FOR WHOM question.
20. Theory that emphasizes the role of self-interest in public decision making.
21. The ability to alter the market price of a good or service.
22. The fee paid for the use of a public-sector good or service.
23. A tax system in which the tax rate stays the same as income rises.

Down

2. Labeled as point X in Figure 4.1 in the text.
3. Occurs when people are willing to work but are unable to find jobs.
4. The market failure discussed in the article "The Human Cost of Secondhand Smoke" in the text.
6. A tax system in which tax rates rise as incomes rise.
7. For a _____ _____, consumption by one person excludes consumption by others.
9. Federal grants to state and local governments for specific purposes.
11. Represented by point M in Figure 4.1 in the text.
12. Only one producer in an industry.
13. A good or service that society believes everyone is entitled to a minimal quantity of, such as food.
15. Can be consumed jointly.
16. One who does not pay but still enjoys the benefits.
18. The legislation used to prevent or break up concentrations of market power such as Microsoft.

Puzzle 4.1

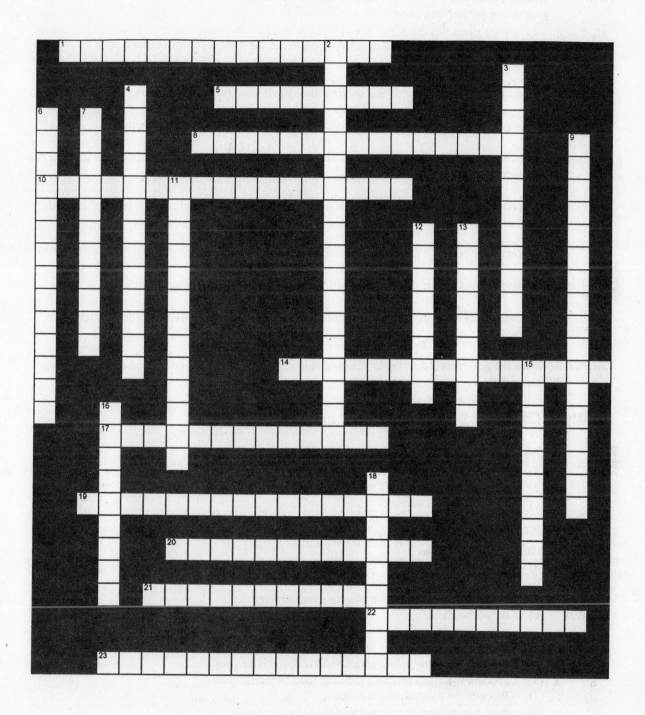

True or False: *Circle your choice and explain why any false statements are incorrect.*

T F 1. Market failure implies that the forces of supply and demand have not led to the best point on the production-possibilities curve.

T F 2. Government intervention is not necessary even when the market mix of output equals the optimal mix of output.

T F 3. The existence of public goods and externalities causes resource misallocations.

T F 4. Police protection is an example of a service that involves the free-rider problem.

T F 5. If you burn garbage in your backyard and the smoke damages a neighbor's health, the damage is considered an externality.

T F 6. Markets will overproduce goods that yield external benefits and underproduce goods that yield external costs.

T F 7. Market power creates a flawed response to an accurate price signal.

T F 8. Monopolies will tend to overproduce goods and charge a higher than competitive price.

T F 9. The federal government in the U.S. economy has grown in both relative and absolute terms since the 1950s.

T F 10. When the government intervenes in the economy, the market mix of goods and services is always improved.

Multiple Choice: *Select the correct answer.*

_____ 1. In a market economy, producers will produce the goods and services:
   (a)   That consumers desire the most.
   (b)   That consumers need the most.
   (c)   That consumers demand.
   (d)   That optimize consumer utility.

_____ 2. Market failure includes:
   (a)   Externalities.
   (b)   Market power.
   (c)   Inequity in the distribution of goods and services.
   (d)   All of the above.

_____ 3. Market failure suggests that the market mechanism, left alone, will:
   (a)   Produce too many public goods and too few private goods.
   (b)   Produce too many private goods and too few public goods.
   (c)   Produce the optimal mix of output.
   (d)   Result in too few resources being allocated to private goods.

_____ 4. The market will sometimes fail to produce society's optimum output because:
   (a) Producers do not always measure the same benefits and costs as society.
   (b) Producers will not produce certain types of important goods and services that cannot be kept from consumers who do not pay.
   (c) When producers have market power, they will tend to underproduce goods and services.
   (d) All of the above are correct.

_____ 5. When the market fails, which of the following is true?
   (a) The mix of goods and services is inside the production-possibilities curve.
   (b) Government intervention will improve the mix of goods and services.
   (c) The mix of goods and services is at the wrong point on the production-possibilities curve.
   (d) All of the above could be true.

_____ 6. Which of the following is most likely a public good?
   (a) Roads.
   (b) A hamburger.
   (c) An automobile.
   (d) Vegetables from a Farmer's market.

_____ 7. When public goods are marketed like private goods:
   (a) Public goods are underproduced.
   (b) Many consumers want to buy the goods.
   (c) Public goods are overproduced.
   (d) Government failure results.

_____ 8. For which of the following goods and services is the government likely to encourage production because of the existence of external benefits?
   (a) Education.
   (b) Health services for the poor.
   (c) A neighborhood renovation project.
   (d) All of the above.

_____ 9. The federal government's role in antitrust enforcement is justified by considerations of:
   (a) Equity in the distribution of goods and services.
   (b) Public goods and externalities.
   (c) Underproduction by firms with market power.
   (d) Macro failure.

_____ 10. The development of market power by a firm is considered to be a market failure because firms with market power:
   (a) Produce more and charge a lower price than what is socially optimal.
   (b) Tend to ignore external costs.
   (c) Produce less and charge a higher price than what is socially optimal.
   (d) Do not respond to consumer demand.

_____ 11. Transfer payments are an appropriate mechanism for correcting:
   (a) Market power.
   (b) Government failure.
   (c) Inflation.
   (d) Inequity in the distribution of goods and services.

_____ 12. Social demand is equal to
    (a) Private demand plus market demand.
    (b) Market demand plus external benefits.
    (c) Private demand.
    (d) Market demand minus external benefits.

_____ 13. The primary function of taxes is to:
    (a) Transfer command over resources from the private sector to the public sector.
    (b) Increase the purchasing power of the private sector.
    (c) Increase private saving.
    (d) Make it possible to sell bonds to finance the U.S. budget deficit.

_____ 14. Government intervention in the market:
    (a) Involves an opportunity cost.
    (b) Never involves an opportunity cost because only market activities result in other goods and services being given up.
    (c) Does not involve an opportunity cost if market outcomes are improved.
    (d) Results in the "free-rider dilemma."

_____ 15. The largest single source of revenue for the federal government is:
    (a) Borrowing (selling government bonds).
    (b) Social security taxes.
    (c) The corporate profits tax.
    (d) The personal income tax.

_____ 16. Which of the following can be classified as a regressive tax?
    (a) The federal corporate income tax.
    (b) The federal personal income tax.
    (c) The state sales tax.
    (d) All of the above.

_____ 17. Which of the following is an example of a progressive tax?
    (a) The excise tax on distilled spirits.
    (b) The federal tax on gasoline.
    (c) The federal personal income tax.
    (d) All of the above.

_____ 18. States receive most of their tax revenues from:
    (a) Sales taxes.
    (b) State income taxes.
    (c) Property taxes.
    (d) User charges.

_____ 19. Reread the article in the text titled "Napster Gets Napped." According to the article an item is a public good if:
    (a) The government produces the good.
    (b) Consumers can be excluded from consumption.
    (c) Consumers must meet certain criteria to consume the good.
    (d) Consumers cannot be excluded from consumption.

_____ 20. Which of the following would *not* support the theory of public choice?
    (a) The governor of the state vetoes a highway bill even though the highway would enhance the value of property he owns.
    (b) The local mayor campaigns in favor of a bond issue for the construction of sewer lines that will raise the value of his property.
    (c) The local police chief fails to give the mayor a speeding ticket because the mayor might fire him.
    (d) A college president asks the board of regents to allow her to remain in office so she can bolster her retirement income, even though she has reached the mandatory retirement age.

Problems and Applications

Exercise 1

Assume point *A* represents the optimal mix of output in Figure 4.1. Determine which letter best represents the following situations. Then answer questions 4-7.

Figure 4.1

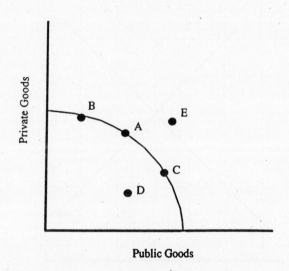

_____ 1. Government failure at the micro level that results in an overproduction of public goods.

_____ 2. Macro failure in the marketplace.

_____ 3. The free-rider dilemma.

4. The market mechanism tends to _____ public goods and _____ private goods.

5. In terms of the production-possibilities curve, _____ failures imply that society is at the wrong point on the curve and _____ failures imply that society is inside the curve.

6. Market failures justify government _____.

7. If government involvement fails to improve market outcomes then there is _____
_____.

Exercise 2

This exercise examines the difference between internal and external costs and the impact on the demand curve.

The market-demand and market-supply curves for a particular good are drawn in Figure 4.2. Assume that the consumption of the good generates external costs equal to $2 per unit.

1. Draw the social demand curve in Figure 4.2 and label it.

Figure 4.2

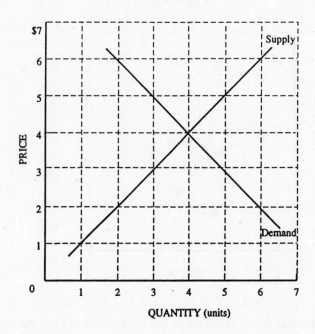

2. Market equilibrium occurs at a price of _____ and a quantity of _____ in Figure 4.3.

3. The socially optimal level of production occurs at a price of _____ and a quantity of _____.

4. External costs cause the market to produce (more, less) of a good than is optimal.

5. T   F   The social demand curve will always be less than the market demand curve if external costs are generated.

58

Exercise 3

This exercise focuses on the changes in public-sector spending in the U.S.

Refer to figure 4.4 in the text titled "Government Growth" to answer questions 1-4.

1. The large increase in total government purchases between 1940 and 1945 was the result of an increase in (only federal, both state and local and federal) government spending.

2. Compared to the level of federal spending in 1960, the level of federal spending for 2000 is (greater, less, the same).

3. Compared to the level of state and local spending in 1960, the level of state and local spending for 2000 is (greater, less, the same).

4. The decrease in total government purchases during the 1990s was primarily due to the decrease in (federal, state and local) purchases.

Exercise 4

This exercise examines progressive, regressive, and proportional tax structures.

Suppose Table 4.1 describes the incomes and taxes for individuals in the countries of Zebot and Dobler.

1. Calculate the following in Table 4.1:
   (a) The percentage of income paid in taxes at each income level for the people of Zebot (column 3).
   (b) The percentage of income paid in taxes at each income level for the people of Dobler (column 5).

Table 4.1 Taxes on income in the countries of Zebot and Dobler

(1) Income	(2) Taxes paid in Zebot	(3) Tax rate	(4) Taxes paid in Dobler	(5) Tax rate
$10,000	$2,000	_____%	$1,000	_____%
40,000	6,400	_____	6,000	_____
75,000	10,500	_____	15,000	_____
125,000	12,500	_____	27,500	_____

2. In Zebot, is the income tax progressive, regressive, or proportional? _____

3. In Dobler, is the income tax progressive, regressive, or proportional? _____

4. Which of the following is the most logical approach if a society wishes to redistribute income to the poor?
   (a) A regressive tax structure.
   (b) A progressive tax structure.
   (c) A proportional tax structure.

5. T   F   A proportional tax structure means that the tax rate is constant regardless of income level.

Common Errors

The first statement in the "common error" below is incorrect. The incorrect statement is followed by a corrected version and an explanation.

1. Fire protection, police protection, education, and other services can be produced more efficiently by the private sector than by the public sector. WRONG!

   The public sector can produce many services more efficiently than the private sector. RIGHT!

   The existence of externalities and the free-rider problem force society to produce some goods and services through public-sector expenditures. Many of the goods and services we take for granted (such as education) would not be produced in sufficient quantities if left to the private sector. And can you imagine trying to provide for your own defense against foreign countries?

2. A public good is only produced by the government sector. WRONG!

   A public good is one whose consumption by one person does not prevent consumption by others. RIGHT!

   A public good can be produced by the private sector or the public sector. The source of production is not what makes it a public good. It is a public good because consumption is not exclusive. The government does provide many of the public goods such as national defense.

•ANSWERS•

Using Key Terms

Across
1. opportunity cost
5. inflation
8. market mechanism
10. government failure
14. natural monopoly
17. regressive tax
19. transfer payments
20. public choice
21. market power
22. user charge
23. proportional tax

Down
2. optimal mix of output
3. unemployment
4. externalities
6. progressive tax
7. private good
9. categorical grants
11. market failure
12. monopoly
13. merit good
15. public good
16. free rider
18. antitrust

True or False

1. T
2. F   Equity considerations may necessitate government intervention.
3. T
4. T
5. T
6. F   Markets will underproduce goods that yield external benefits and overproduce goods that yield external costs.
7. T
8. F   Monopolies will tend to underproduce goods and are therefore able to charge a higher price.
9. F   The federal government has grown in absolute terms since the 1950s but its relative share of production has declined, i.e., it has grown more slowly than the private sector.
10. F   Sometimes government intervention worsens the market mix of goods and services. This is an example of "government failure."

Multiple Choice

1. c	5. d	9. c	13. a	17. c
2. d	6. a	10. c	14. a	18. a
3. b	7. a	11. d	15. d	19. d
4. d	8. d	12. b	16. c	20. a

Problems and Applications

Exercise 1

1. c
2. d
3. b
4. Underproduce, overproduce
5. Micro, macro
6. Intervention
7. Government failure

Exercise 2

1. See Figure 4.2 answer.

Figure 4.2 Answer

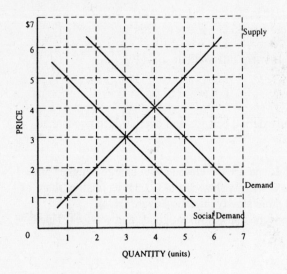

2. $4.00, 4 units
3. $3.00, 3 units
4. More
5. T

Exercise 3

1. Only federal
2. Less
3. Greater
4. Federal

Exercise 4

1. See Table 4.1 Answer.

Table 4.1 Answer

(1) Income	(2) Taxes paid in Zebot	(3) Tax rate	(4) Taxes paid in Dobler	(5) Tax rate
$10,000	$2,000	20.0 %	$1,000	10.0 %
40,000	6,400	16.0	6,000	15.0
75,000	10,500	14.0	15,000	20.0
125,000	12,500	10.0	27,500	22.0

2. Regressive. With greater income, a lower percentage of income goes to taxes (from 20% to 10% in column 3).
3. Progressive. With greater income, a higher percentage of income goes to taxes (from 10% to 22% in column 5).
4. b (A progressive tax is the most logical choice if society wants to redistribute income to the poor.)
5. T

CHAPTER 5

National-Income Accounting

Quick Review

- National-income accounting is used to measure a nation's economic activity. It provides information about the strength of an economy and can be used to evaluate economic policy.

- The most often used economic aggregate is gross domestic product (GDP)—the total market value of all final goods and services produced within a nation's borders during a year. Only transactions involving goods and services that are sold for final consumption are included. Intermediate goods are not included in GDP in order to avoid double counting.

- GDP focuses on goods and services produced within a country's borders while gross national product (GNP) focuses on goods and services produced by a country's factors of production, regardless of where the factors are located. GDP per capita is the average GDP per person.

- GDP is not a perfect measure of a country's output because nonmarket activities and unreported income are not captured in the statistic.

- The standard of living is based on real goods and services, so a distinction is made between real GDP and nominal GDP. Nominal GDP is measured in current dollars and can increase because prices go up, because quantities go up, or both. Real GDP is measured in constant dollars and is used for comparing the output of different economies and changes in the output of a single economy over time.

- GDP can be calculated as the sum of all expenditures by the market participants—consumption, investment, government expenditures, and net exports.

- Depreciation is the value of capital that is consumed in the production process. The net domestic product (NDP) is calculated as GDP minus depreciation and is a good measure of the future production possibilities for an economy.

- NDP minus indirect business taxes plus net foreign factor income results in national income (NI). NI reflects the payments to the factors of production used to produce the nation's output. In order to determine how much of the income earned is actually received, personal income (PI) and disposable income (DI) are calculated. DI represents the dollars consumers have available to spend after personal taxes are taken out.

- Expenditures made by one market participant become income for another market participant. This income is then spent again and the circular flow continues.

Learning Objectives

After reading Chapter 5 and doing the following exercises, you should:

1. Know the purposes of national-income accounting.
2. Understand the significance of GDP as a measure of output.
3. Understand the difference between GDP and GNP and the meaning of GDP per capita.
4. Be able to explain the measurement problems associated with GDP.
5. Know the difference between real GDP and nominal GDP and be able to calculate each.
6. Understand the importance of NDP and depreciation.
7. Know the definitions and how to calculate the various national-income aggregates.
8. Understand the circular flow nature of the economy.

Using Key Terms

Fill in the puzzle on the opposite page with the appropriate term from the list of Key Terms at the end of the chapter in the text.

Across

1. Calculated as nominal GDP divided by the price index.
3. Equal to GDP minus depreciation and indirect business taxes.
4. Total investment expenditure in a given time period.
9. Alternative combinations of goods and services that can be produced with the available resources and technology.
10. Equal to $0.12 in the first stage of production according to Table 5.2 in the text.
11. Equal to disposable income minus consumption.
13. The reduction in the value of plant and equipment.
16. The amount of output that can be consumed without reducing a country's capital stock.
18. The income received by households before the payment of taxes.
19. Equal to $6,990 billion in Table 5.6 in the text.
20. Used as a measure of the relative standard of living.

Down

2. Equal to $9,963 billion according to Table 5.6 in the text.
3. The measurement of aggregate economic activity.
5. Persistent increases in the price level.
6. Goods purchased for use as input in further stages of production.
7. Equal to real GDP in 1996 according to Figure 5.1 in the text.
8. Expenditures on new plant, equipment and structures plus changes in inventories.
12. Gross investment minus depreciation.
14. Goods and services purchased from other countries.
15. The basis for indexing price changes.
16. Equal to exports minus imports.
17. Goods and services sold to other countries.

64

Puzzle 5.1

True or False: *Circle your choice and explain why any false statements are incorrect.*

T F   1. Without prices, it would be impossible to add up the outputs produced in different sectors of the economy in a meaningful way.

T F   2. Intermediate goods are not counted in GDP because their value is included in the value of the final product.

T F   3. If drugs that are now illegal in the U.S. were legalized (e.g., marijuana), U.S. GDP would increase, *ceteris paribus*.

T F   4. Per capita GDP provides information about the distribution of GDP within a country.

T F   5. If real per capita GDP increases, everyone in the nation is better off.

T F   6. In a period of rising prices, real GDP will rise more rapidly than nominal GDP.

T F   7. NDP provides information about future production possibilities because it measures gross investment.

T F   8. According to the expenditures approach to calculating GDP, GDP equals Consumption + Gross Investment + Government Expenditures + (Exports - Imports).

T F   9. State and local government expenditures on goods and services are *not* included in GDP because to do so would result in double counting.

T F 10. The total value of market incomes must equal the total value of final output, or GDP.

Multiple Choice: *Select the correct answer.*

_____ 1. A basic function of the national-income accounting system is to:
 (a)   Identify economic problems.
 (b)   Evaluate economic policy.
 (c)   Provide a framework for policy.
 (d)   All of the above.

_____ 2. GDP can be found by:
 (a)   Adding up the spending by business, government, households, and foreigners, and subtracting imports.
 (b)   Adding up the value added at every stage of production in the economy.
 (c)   Adding up all the receipts of households, government, and business.
 (d)   All of the above.

_____ 3. Suppose that a friend of yours claims that he is helping the economy by throwing trash on the street rather than in trash cans because the extra expenditures necessary to clean up the streets will increase GDP. Your friend is:
 (a)   Wrong. GDP will not be affected because nothing new is being produced.
 (b)   Right. GDP will increase because the dollars spent to clean up the trash will increase government spending, *ceteris paribus*.
 (c)   Wrong. GDP will not be affected because this is not a socially desirable use of resources and will therefore not be included in GDP.
 (d)   Wrong. GDP will decline because cleaning the streets will take resources away from more productive work.

4. If the real U.S. GDP was $7,500 billion in 2000 and the U.S. population was 280 million, the per capita real GDP would have been closest to:
    (a) $140,000 per person.
    (b) $21,000 per person.
    (c) $26,786 per person.
    (d) $3,733 per person.

5. A housewife takes over the job of a deceased family member in running the family business and hires help to clean house and baby-sit. As a result, the GDP of the economy, *ceteris paribus:*
    (a) Remains unchanged, since the amount of productive activity remains unchanged.
    (b) Rises by the amount paid to house cleaners and baby-sitters.
    (c) Falls by the amount of household work left undone by the house cleaners and baby-sitters.
    (d) Falls by the amount of income generated previously by the deceased family member.

6. The underground economy exists because:
    (a) People wish to avoid taxes.
    (b) Illegal activities are often highly profitable.
    (c) It is difficult to trace transactions in the underground economy.
    (d) All of the above are reasons.

7. A manufacturer sells assembled Palm Pilots for $250 each. If the manufacturer pays $100 for components in each Palm Pilot, the value added to each Palm Pilot by manufacturing is:
    (a) $250.
    (b) $100.
    (c) $350.
    (d) $150.

8. Which of the following is *not* a final good or service?
    (a) A printing press purchased by a publishing company.
    (b) Automobile tires purchased by an auto manufacturing company.
    (c) Gasoline purchased for personal use by a car owner.
    (d) The preparation of your tax return by a CPA.

9. The difference between real GDP and nominal GDP is that:
    (a) Nominal GDP is the value of output measured in constant prices.
    (b) Real GDP is the value of output measured in constant prices.
    (c) Real GDP is the value of output measured in current prices.
    (d) Real GDP can give a distorted view of economic activity because of price level changes.

10. Real GDP measures changes in:
    (a) Prices.
    (b) Production.
    (c) Prices and production.
    (d) Wages.

11. Suppose that the total market value of all the final goods and services produced in the country of GDPLAND was $15 billion in 2001 (measured in 2001 prices) and $20 billion in the year 2002 (measured in 2002 prices). Which of the following statements is definitely correct?
    (a) Production increased in GDPLAND between 2001 and 2002.
    (b) Average price levels increased in GDPLAND between 2001 and 2002.
    (c) Nominal GDP increased in GDPLAND between 2001 and 2002.
    (d) All of these statements are definitely correct.

_____ 12. If depreciation exceeds gross investment, then:
   (a) Net investment exceeds depreciation.
   (b) Gross investment is negative.
   (c) The difference between GDP and NDP is smaller than gross investment.
   (d) The nation's capital stock is being depleted.

_____ 13. The stock of capital in the United States can grow only if:
   (a) Depreciation is positive.
   (b) Gross investment minus depreciation is positive.
   (c) GDP minus NDP is positive.
   (d) All of the above.

_____ 14. An increase in business inventories during some time period, _ceteris paribus_, will:
   (a) Decrease GDP during that period.
   (b) Increase GDP during that period.
   (c) Not affect GDP during that period but will increase GDP in later periods when the inventory is sold.
   (d) Never affect GDP because changes in inventories are not included in the calculation of GDP.

_____ 15. Which of the following types of government spending is included in the calculation of GDP?
   (a) Federal government spending only.
   (b) Federal, state and local government spending for any purpose.
   (c) Federal, state and local government spending on goods and services only.
   (d) Federal, state and local spending on transfer payments only.

_____ 16. In calculating GDP:
   (a) Imports are subtracted from exports because they represent the value of production and resources absorbed in foreign economies.
   (b) Imports are added to exports because both represent purchases of final goods.
   (c) Imports are subtracted from exports to obtain gross exports.
   (d) Imports are subtracted from exports and included in gross investment.

_____ 17. _DI_ is the most practical way to:
   (a) Measure how much income households can spend and save.
   (b) Measure how much output can be consumed on a sustainable basis.
   (c) Make international comparisons of the standard of living.
   (d) Analyze the growth rate of the economy over time.

_____ 18. Net exports are equal to:
   (a) Exports plus imports.
   (b) Imports minus exports.
   (c) Exports minus imports.
   (d) Exports plus imports minus depreciation.

_____ 19. The value of total output must equal the value of total income in an economy because:
   (a) One person's expenditures on goods and services is another person's income.
   (b) Income earned is spent on goods and services, which creates additional production.
   (c) Of the circular nature of the economy.
   (d) All of the above are reasons.

_____ 20. The social well-being of a country:
   (a) Is best measured by per capita GDP.
   (b) Always increases when real GDP increases.
   (c) Decreases when real GDP decreases.
   (d) Is measured by more than changes in real GDP.

Problems and Applications

Exercise 1

This exercise demonstrates the concept of value added. It is similar to a problem in the text.

Assume that orange juice production involves the following steps.

Step 1: A juice company grows its own oranges to reduce costs.
Step 2: The juice company sells a jug of orange juice to the grocery store for $1.85.
Step 3: The grocery store sells the jug of juice to the consumer for $3.25.

1. The value added from step 1 to step 2 is equal to _____.

2. The value added from step 2 to step 3 is equal to _____.

3. If the juice company bought the oranges from a farmer, the oranges would be considered a (an) (intermediate, final) good.

4. What is the total contribution to GDP because of the production of one jug of orange juice?
    _____

Exercise 2

This exercise demonstrates how to calculate real GDP and emphasizes the difference between nominal and real GDP.

Table 5.1 GDP Data

	Nominal GDP (billions of dollars per year)	Price index	Real GDP (billions of dollars per year)
Year 1	$3,400	100	_____
Year 2	$3,500	103	_____
Year 3	$3,700	111	_____
Year 4	$4,000	120	_____

1. Calculate real GDP in Table 5.1. Use the formula:

$$\text{Real GDP} = \frac{\text{Nominal GDP}}{\text{Price index}} \times 100$$

2. According to Table 5.1, in which year is the real level of output greatest? _____

3. The measurement of goods and services produced, without the impact of price level changes, is referred to as _____.

4. The best measure of physical changes in output in Figure 5.1 above is (nominal, real) GDP.

5. In Figure 5.1 in the text, nominal GDP rises more rapidly than real GDP because nominal GDP includes _____.

Exercise 3

This exercise provides practice in calculating GDP and other national income accounts. (The chart below can be referred to as you work this exercise.)

Flow chart 5.1

Add items in this column to get the next account	National income account	Subtract items in this column to get the next account
	GDP	
		Depreciation
	NDP	
Net Foreign Factor Income		Indirect Business Taxes
	NI	
Transfer Payments		Corporate Taxes
Net Interest		Retained Earnings
		Social Security Taxes
	PI	
		Personal Income Taxes
	DI	
		Consumption
	Saving	

Table 5.2 National Income Data

Consumption	$300 billion
Depreciation	10 billion
Exports	30 billion
Corporate Taxes	15 billion
Personal Income Taxes	60 billion
Gross Investment	30 billion
Indirect Business Taxes	5 billion
Retained Earnings	10 billion
Imports	35 billion
Government Purchases	80 billion
Social Security Taxes	15 billion
Transfer Payments	30 billion
Net Interest	5 billion
Net Foreign Factor Income	2 billion

Use the information in Table 5.2 to make the following calculations.

1. GDP   _____

2. NDP   _____

3. NI   _____

4. PI   _____

5. DI   _____

6. Savings   _____

7. Net investment _____

8. Which of the accounts above is equal to the total income earned by the factors of production?
    _____.

9. Which of the accounts above is the best indicator of future production possibilities? _____

Common Errors

The first statement in each "common error" below is incorrect. Each incorrect statement is followed by a corrected version and an explanation.

1. Income and output are two entirely different things. WRONG!

    Income and output are two sides of the same coin. RIGHT!

    This is fundamental. Every time a dollar's worth of final spending takes place, the seller must receive a dollar's worth of income. It could not be otherwise. Remember, profits are used as a balancing item. Don't confuse the term "income" with the term "profit." Profits can be negative, whereas output for the economy cannot.

2. Comparisons of per capita GDP between countries tell you which population is better off. WRONG!

    Comparisons of per capita GDP between countries are only indicators of which population is better off. RIGHT!

    Simple comparisons of per capita GDP ignore how the GDP is distributed. A country with a very high per capita GDP that is unequally distributed may well provide a standard of living that is below that of another country with a lower per capita GDP, which is more equally distributed. There are other problems with comparisons of per capita GDP between countries because of exchange-rate distortions, differences in mix of output in two countries, and how the economy is organized. GDP per capita is an indicator only of the amount of goods and services each person could have, not what each person does have.

3. Value added is a measure of a firm's profit. WRONG!

    Value added includes all factor payments to land, labor, and capital in addition to the residual (profit) that goes to the entrepreneur for taking risks. RIGHT!

    In computing value added, a firm subtracts *from* total revenue the cost of items sold to the firm. There are additional cost items that normally would be subtracted to calculate "profit," which are not subtracted in the computation of value added. Those items include the cost of capital, land, and labor. When value added for all economic units is combined, the total of payments to capital (interest), land (rent), labor (wages), and risk taking (profits) will equal the total gross domestic product.

Using Key Terms

Across
1. real GDP
3. national income
4. gross investment
9. production possibilities
10. value added
11. saving
13. depreciation
16. net domestic product
18. personal income
19. disposable income
20. GDP per capita

Down
2. gross domestic product
3. national income accounting
5. inflation
6. intermediate goods
7. nominal GDP
8. investment
12. net investment
14. imports
15. base period
16. net exports
17. exports

True or False

1. T
2. T
3. T
4. F GDP per capita is simply a statistical average and tells us nothing about the way GDP is distributed.
5. F Real per capita GDP is an average. When real per capita GDP rises, the living standard for the country as a whole increases. Some individuals are better off, but some individuals could be worse off.
6. F Nominal GDP is affected by inflation and will increase faster than real GDP. Real GDP is not affected by changing price levels.
7. F NDP provides information about future growth potential because it measures net investment.
8. T
9. F State and local government expenditures on goods and services are included in GDP. These expenditures measure additional production beyond the goods and services the federal government consumes so there is no double counting.
10. T

Multiple Choice

1. d	5. b	9. b	13. b	17. a
2. d	6. d	10. b	14. b	18. c
3. b	7. d	11. c	15. c	19. d
4. c	8. b	12. d	16. a	20. d

Problems and Applications

Exercise 1

1. $1.85
2. $1.40
3. Intermediate
4. $3.25

Exercise 2

1.
Table 5.1 Answer

	Nominal GDP (billions of dollars per year)	Price index	Real GDP (billions of dollars per year)
Year 1	$3,400	100	$3,400
Year 2	$3,500	103	$3,398
Year 3	$3,700	111	$3,333
Year 4	$4,000	120	$3,333

2. Year 1
3. Real GDP
4. Real
5. An increase in the price level or inflation.

Exercise 3

1. $405 billion
2. $395 billion
3. $392 billion
4. $387 billion
5. $327 billion
6. $27 billion
7. $20 billion
8. NI
9. NDP

73

CHAPTER 6
Unemployment

Quick Review

- The labor force is defined as those who are working for pay and those who are looking for work. Only about half of the U.S. population is included in the labor force.

- Since labor is one of the four factors of production, an increase in the size of the labor force causes an increase in the production-possibilities curve and can result in economic growth.

- The institutional production-possibilities curve allows for limits imposed on resources and technology and social constraints on their use. It lies inside the production-possibilities curve. One reason why the labor force is less than the total population is because of institutional constraints such as compulsory education and child labor laws.

- The unemployment rate equals the number of unemployed persons divided by the labor force.

- The macroeconomic cost of unemployment is loss of output. According to Okun's Law, each one percentage point increase in the unemployment rate leads to a two percentage point reduction in GDP. Unemployment imposes other costs on society such as alcoholism, suicide, divorce, and crime.

- The unemployment rate varies by a number of socioeconomic variables—race, age, sex, and education. Discouraged workers are not part of the unemployment rate.

- The four kinds of unemployment are frictional (short-term unemployment between jobs), seasonal (unemployment that varies with the seasons), structural (caused by a mismatch of available labor with skill requirements or job locations), and cyclical (caused by deficient aggregate demand). There will always be some unemployment so the natural rate of unemployment is considered to be 4 to 6 percent.

- To keep the unemployment rate from increasing, the output level must increase at least as fast as the labor force increases.

- The U.S. economy has experienced periods of high unemployment (25% during the Great Depression) and periods of low unemployment (1.2% during World War II).

- In order to achieve full employment in the future we will have to address the structural unemployment that typically occurs with economic growth. Education and training programs can be used to reduce the skills gap.

Learning Objectives

After reading Chapter 6 and doing the following exercises, you should:

1. Know who is included in the labor force.
2. Understand the relationship between the labor force and economic growth.
3. Know the difference between the physical production possibilities and institutional production possibilities.
4. Be able to calculate the unemployment rate.
5. Understand the various costs associated with unemployment and the loss of output that results.
6. Understand that the unemployment rate varies with age, sex, education, and race.
7. Be able to explain what is meant by discouraged workers and phantom unemployment.
8. Be able to distinguish the nature and causes of cyclical, frictional, structural, and seasonal unemployment.
9. Know the meaning of "full employment."
10. Know the dimensions, causes and cures of the emerging "skills gap."

Using Key Terms

Fill in the puzzle on the opposite page with the appropriate term from the list of Key Terms at the end of the chapter in the text.

Across

1. Calculated as the number of unemployed people divided by the size of the labor force.
6. Unemployment experienced by people moving between jobs.
7. The percentage of the population working or seeking work.
11. Education and training can be used to narrow the _____ _____, which reduces structural unemployment.
13. Unemployment due to seasonal changes.
14. An individual who is not looking for a job but would accept a job if one were available.
15. Situation in which people work at jobs below their capacity.
16. Can be represented by a rightward shift of the production-possibilities curve.

Down

2. The rate of unemployment that prevails in the long run.
3. Alternative combinations of goods and services that can be produced with available resources and technology.
4. The type of unemployment most often experienced by teenagers with few job skills and an inadequate education.
5. Unemployment that occurs when there are not enough jobs.
8. Quantifies the relationship between the shortfall in output and unemployment.
9. The lowest rate of unemployment compatible with price stability.
10. Includes everyone sixteen and older who is working for pay or looking for a job.
12. The inability of labor-force participants to find jobs.

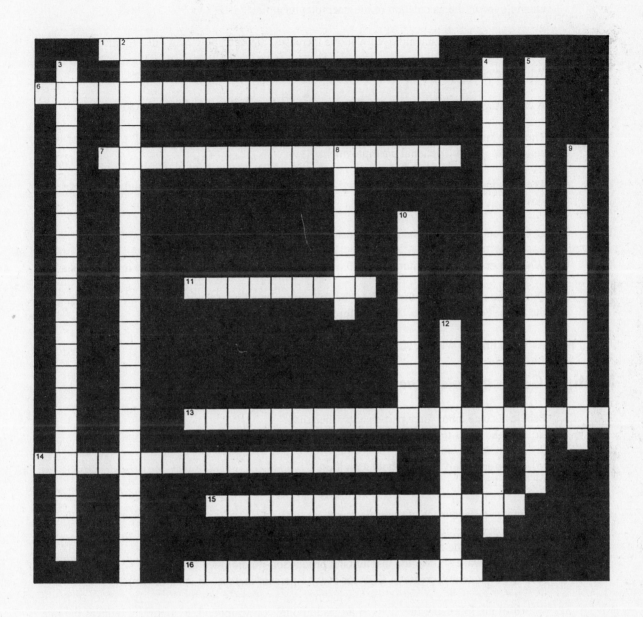

True or False: *Circle your choice and explain why any false statements are incorrect.*

T F 1. Juan says he would like to have a job but hasn't applied for a job in 6 months. Juan is included as unemployed in the calculation of the unemployment rate.

T F 2. When the number of unemployed workers increases, the unemployment rate will always rise.

T F 3. When the economy is growing, the average duration of unemployment declines.

T F 4. A discouraged worker is one who is tired of his job and sees no possibility for advancement.

T F 5. The transition from manufacturing to service industries has accompanied GDP growth, but it has also led to greater frictional unemployment.

T F 6. Teenage unemployment is high because of teenagers' lack of job experience and marketable skills.

T F 7. Cyclical unemployment stems from insufficient aggregate demand.

T F 8. When an economy is producing at full employment, everyone willing and able to work has a job.

T F 9. One of the main reasons for revising the full-employment goal during the 1980s was a change in the age-sex composition of the labor force.

T F 10. As the skills gap widens, structural unemployment increases, *ceteris paribus.*

Multiple Choice: *Select the correct answer.*

_____ 1. People become labor force participants when they:
   (a) Take a full-time job.
   (b) Go back to school.
   (c) Return solely to household activities.
   (d) Retire.

_____ 2. The macro consequence of unemployment is:
   (a) Lost output for the economy.
   (b) Lost income for the individual worker.
   (c) A leftward shift in the institutional production-possibilities curve.
   (d) A 4 percent decrease in GDP for every 1 percent increase in unemployment.

_____ 3. Which of the following functions as an institutional constraint and, in doing so, reduces the rate of economic growth?
   (a) Child labor laws.
   (b) Restrictions on the usage of natural resources.
   (c) Restrictions on the usage of technology.
   (d) All of the above.

_____ 4. As economic output increases and an economy moves toward full employment:
   (a) Production moves closer to the institutional production-possibilities curve, but not beyond it.
   (b) Production moves beyond the physical production-possibilities curve.
   (c) The institutional production-possibilities curve shifts outward but not the physical production-possibilities curve.
   (d) The physical production-possibilities curve shifts outward but not the institutional production-possibilities curve.

5. When the labor force participation rate increases in an economy, *ceteris paribus*:
   (a) Production moves closer to the institutional production-possibilities curve, but not beyond it.
   (b) Production moves beyond the physical production-possibilities curve.
   (c) The institutional production-possibilities curve shifts outward.
   (d) The physical production-possibilities curve shifts outward but not the institutional production-possibilities curve.

6. When the growth rate of the labor force is more rapid than the growth rate of the unemployed, then it is certain that:
   (a) The unemployment rate is rising.
   (b) The labor-force participation rate is rising.
   (c) The percentage of the labor force that is employed is rising.
   (d) The labor-force participation rate is falling.

7. When an economy enters a recession, then:
   (a) The duration of unemployment rises.
   (b) The number of discouraged workers rises.
   (c) The unemployment rate rises.
   (d) All of the above.

8. According to Okun's Law, a two percent decrease in unemployment will result in a:
   (a) Two percent increase in real output.
   (b) Four percent increase in real output.
   (c) One percent increase in real output.
   (d) Four percent decrease in real output.

9. Individuals who are working part-time while seeking full-time employment are classified as:
   (a) Unemployed.
   (b) Underemployed.
   (c) Discouraged workers.
   (d) Phantom unemployed.

10. The official unemployment statistics may exaggerate the significance of unemployment by including the:
    (a) Underemployed.
    (b) Phantom unemployed.
    (c) Discouraged workers.
    (d) All of the above.

11. Which of the following are considered possible side effects of increased unemployment?
    (a) Suicides, homicides, and other crimes.
    (b) Heart attacks and strokes.
    (c) Admissions to mental hospitals.
    (d) All of the above.

12. When a person who mowed lawns all summer seeks employment during the winter, the unemployment rate goes up. This situation is an example of:
    (a) Seasonal unemployment.
    (b) Frictional unemployment.
    (c) Structural unemployment.
    (d) Cyclical unemployment.

_____ 13. Frictional unemployment goes up when:
  (a)   A student quits work to return to school at the end of the summer.
  (b)   A corporation transfers a worker to another city.
  (c)   A worker quits one job in order to search for another.
  (d)   There is inadequate demand for labor.

_____ 14. Which of the following is believed to have contributed to an increase in the level of structural unemployment during the 1970s and 1980s?
  (a)   More youth and women in the labor force.
  (b)   Increased transfer payments.
  (c)   Structural changes in demand.
  (d)   All of the above.

_____ 15. In terms of the musical chairs analogy in the text, which of the following is a description of cyclical unemployment?
  (a)   There are too many chairs.
  (b)   There are enough chairs, but it takes time to find one.
  (c)   There are enough chairs, but some are not the right size.
  (d)   There are too few chairs.

_____ 16. Which of the following government programs would be most appropriate to counteract cyclical unemployment?
  (a)   Those which stimulate economic growth.
  (b)   Those that provide additional health services.
  (c)   Those that provide job placement services.
  (d)   Those that provide job training.

_____ 17. The Employment Act of 1946:
  (a)   Committed the government to pursue a goal of "maximum" employment.
  (b)   Implied that the economy should avoid cyclical and structural unemployment.
  (c)   Implied that frictional unemployment should be kept within a reasonable level.
  (d)   All of the above.

_____ 18. Which of the following groups would be the most likely to qualify for unemployment benefits?
  (a)   People who quit their last jobs.
  (b)   People who lose their jobs due to increased foreign competition and are looking for work.
  (c)   Mothers who have not worked recently.
  (d)   People who are fired from one of the three part-time jobs that they have been working.

_____ 19. During which one of the following decades did unemployment levels first rise significantly above the 4 percent level as the result of increasing proportions of both teenagers and women entering the labor force?
  (a)   1960s.
  (b)   1970s.
  (c)   1980s.
  (d)   1990s.

_____ 20. As the gap between the skills required for emerging jobs and the skills of workers widens:
  (a)   Only those workers entering the job market are affected.
  (b)   Structural unemployment decreases.
  (c)   Structural unemployment increases.
  (d)   Cyclical unemployment increases.

Problems and Applications

Exercise 1

The following exercise provides practice in categorizing the population according to labor force participation, employment, and unemployment.

Suppose the population of a country is 1.6 million and the labor force is 1 million, of whom 920,000 are employed. Assume that the full-employment level occurs at a 5 percent unemployment rate and at a real GDP of $100 billion. Answer the indicated questions on the basis of this information:

1. What is the unemployment rate? _____

2. Assume "full employment" is equal to 5 percent unemployment. How many more members of the labor force must find jobs for the economy to achieve full employment? _____

3. On the basis of the information above and the revised version of Okun's Law stated in the text, how much potential GDP has been lost because the economy is not at full employment?

   _____

4. On the basis of the information above and the revised version of Okun's Law, what is the GDP of the economy? _____

Exercise 2

This exercise shows how to calculate the unemployment rate and indicates the relationship between the unemployment rate and the growth rate of GDP. Data from 1981-1995 is used to demonstrate both expansionary and contractionary economic situations.

1. Compute the unemployment rate based on the information in Table 6.1, and insert it in column 4.

Table 6.1
Unemployment and real GDP, 1981-1995

Year	(1) Noninstitutional population	(2) Civilian labor force (thousands of persons 16 and over)	(3) Unemployment (thousands of persons 16 and over)	(4) Unemployment rate (percent)	(5) Percentage change in real GDP
1981	170,130	108,670	8,273	_____	2.5
1982	172,271	110,204	10,678	_____	-2.1
1983	174,215	111,550	10,717	_____	4.0
1984	176,383	113,544	8,539	_____	6.8
1985	178,206	115,461	8,312	_____	3.7
1986	180,587	117,834	8,237	_____	3.0
1987	182,753	119,865	7,425	_____	2.9
1988	184,613	121,669	6,701	_____	3.8
1989	186,393	123,869	6,528	_____	3.4
1990	188,049	124,787	6,874	_____	1.3
1991	189,765	125,303	8,426	_____	-1.0
1992	191,576	126,982	9,384	_____	2.7
1993	193,550	128,040	8,734	_____	2.2
1994	196,814	131,056	7,996	_____	3.5
1995	198,584	132,304	7,404	_____	2.0

2. In Figure 6.1 graph both the unemployment rate (column 4 of Table 6.1) and the percentage
    change in real GDP (column 5.)

Figure 6.1

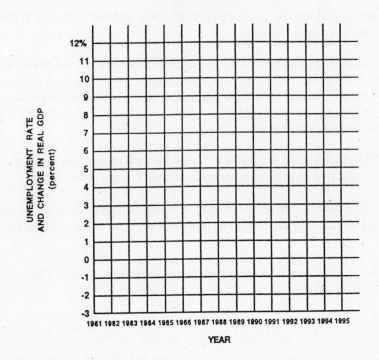

3. The relationship between the unemployment rate and the percentage change in the real GDP is best
    characterized as:
    (a)   A direct relationship (the two indicators go up and down together.)
    (b)   An inverse relationship (the two indicators move in opposite directions.)

4. Which indicator seems to change direction first as time passes?
    (a)   Percentage change in real GDP.
    (b)   The unemployment rate.

5. Which of the following types of unemployment had the largest impact on the unemployment rate
    from 1981 to 1982 in Figure 6.1?
    (a)   Structural unemployment.
    (b)   Seasonal unemployment.
    (c)   Frictional unemployment.
    (d)   Cyclical unemployment.

6. If "full employment" is defined as an unemployment rate of 4-6 percent, in what years was full
    employment achieved between 1981 and 1995? _____

Exercise 3

This exercise shows the relationship between unemployment and population. It is similar to the problem at the end of the chapter.

Suppose the data in Table 6.2 describe a nation's situation.

Table 6.2
Employment and unemployment

	Year 1	Year 2
Population	500 million	550 million
Labor force	300 million	325 million
Unemployment rate	___ percent	___ percent
Number of unemployed	_____	_____
Number of employed	276 million	276 million

1. Fill in the blanks in Table 6.2 to show the number of unemployed and the unemployment rate.

2. When the population grows and the labor force grows, but the number employed remains constant, the unemployment rate (rises, remains the same, falls).

3. If both the population and the number employed remain constant, but a larger percentage of the population passes through to retirement, the unemployment rate should (rise, remain the same, fall), *ceteris paribus*.

4. The people who immigrate to the United States are generally young and of working age compared to the existing population of the United States. As greater immigration rates are permitted and if the unemployment rate stays constant, the number employed would (rise, remain the same, fall), *ceteris paribus*.

5. Assume each employed person contributes $35,000 worth of goods and services to GDP. If the unemployment rate falls from 8 percent to 6 percent in Year 1, by how much will GDP increase? _____

Exercise 4

The following exercise provides practice in categorizing the various types of unemployment. Identify each of the following cases as an example of seasonal, frictional, structural, or cyclical unemployment.

1. An executive quits her current job and takes several months to find a new job. _____

2. The economy is in a recession and one-fourth of the labor force is without work. _____

3. There is a shortage of workers to fill positions in high-tech industries, while many unskilled workers are unemployed. _____

4. A snowplow driver is unemployed during the summer months. _____

Common Errors

The first statement in each "common error" below is incorrect. Each incorrect statement is followed by a corrected version and an explanation.

1. The government should eliminate all unemployment. WRONG!

    The government must reduce unemployment at the same time that it accomplishes other goals. RIGHT!

    Under the Full Employment and Balanced Growth Act of 1978, the government set an unemployment goal for itself, but this goal is well short of a zero unemployment rate. If it lowers unemployment too much, an economy may have to sacrifice other goals. In addition, it is very difficult and even undesirable to eliminate frictional or seasonal unemployment.

2. A rise in the unemployment rate of 0.1 or 0.2 percent for a month is bad. WRONG!

    Monthly changes in the unemployment rate may not have any significant economic implications. RIGHT!

    Small changes in the unemployment rate tell us nothing about what is happening in the labor force; large changes in seasonal or frictional unemployment are not necessarily bad and could not be easily remedied even if they were.

3. Everyone who is counted as unemployed qualifies for unemployment benefits. WRONG!

    To qualify for unemployment benefits, certain conditions must be met. RIGHT!

    Many of those who are counted as unemployed do not qualify for unemployment benefits. Those who are new entrants to the labor force, those who have not worked at their last job for an extended period, and those who quit their last job are ineligible in many states. In addition some who are among the "seasonally unemployed" may not qualify for benefits.

4. Unemployment only occurs during recessions. WRONG!

    Unemployment can occur anytime, but it increases during a recession. RIGHT!

    There are several types of unemployment. Seasonal, frictional, and structural unemployment occur for reasons other than changes in the business cycle. Only cyclical unemployment occurs because of changes in the business cycle or a recession.

•ANSWERS•

Using Key Terms

Across

1. unemployment rate
6. frictional unemployment
7. participation rate
11. skills gap
13. seasonal unemployment
14. discouraged worker
15. underemployment
16. economic growth

84

Down

2. natural rate of unemployment
3. production possibilities
4. structural unemployment
5. cyclical unemployment
8. Okun's Law
9. full employment
10. labor force
12. unemployment

True or False

1. F   Ed is counted as being out of the labor force because he is not actively looking for a job.
2. F   When the number of unemployed workers increases, the unemployment rate will rise only if the labor force increases at a slower rate (or decreases).
3. T
4. F   A discouraged worker is someone who does not have a job and sees no prospect of getting one, thus he has dropped out of the labor force.
5. F   This transition has led to greater structural unemployment.
6. T
7. T
8. F   Full employment does not imply a zero unemployment rate. It is usually defined as between 4 and 6 percent unemployment.
9. T
10. T

Multiple Choice

1.	a	5.	c	9.	b	13.	c	17.	d
2.	a	6.	c	10.	b	14.	d	18.	b
3.	d	7.	d	11.	d	15.	d	19.	b
4.	a	8.	b	12.	a	16.	a	20.	c

Problems and Applications

Exercise 1

1. The unemployment rate is found as follows:

$$\text{Unemployment rate} = \frac{\text{Unemployed}}{\text{Labor force}} = \frac{(\text{Labor force minus employed})}{\text{Labor force}}$$

$$= \frac{(1,000,000 - 920,000)}{1,000,000} = 8\%$$

2. 30,000. The unemployment rate is 8 percent, which is 3 percent above full employment. Multiplying 3 percent by the labor force of 1 million gives 30,000.

3. Unemployment is 3 percentage points above the full employment level. Okun's Law suggests that each percentage point costs the economy 2 percent of full employment GDP. Multiplying 3 percent unemployment times 2 equals 6 percent. Then multiplying 6 percent times $100 billion equals $6 billion.

4. Full employment GDP = $100 billion. Lost output = $6 billion. Thus, GDP = $94 billion.

Exercise 2

1. **Table 6.1 Answer**

Year	(4) Unemployment rate (percent)
1981	7.6
1982	9.7
1983	9.6
1984	7.5
1985	7.2
1986	7.0
1987	6.2
1988	5.5
1989	5.3
1990	5.5
1991	6.7
1992	7.4
1993	6.8
1994	6.1
1995	5.6

2. **Figure 6.1 Answer**

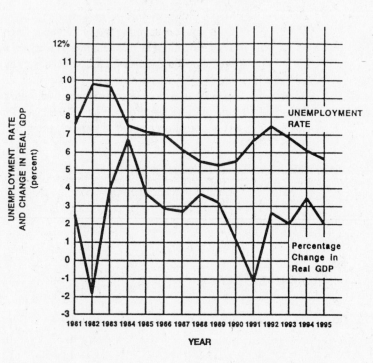

3. b
4. a   After a dramatic rise in real GDP, it takes several years for the unemployment rate to reach the lowest level.
5. d
6. 1988, 1989, 1990, 1995

Exercise 3

1. **Table 6.2 Answer**

	Year 1	Year 2
Population	500 million	550 million
Labor force	300 million	325 million
Unemployment rate	8 percent (= 24 ÷ 300)	15 percent
Number of unemployed	24 million (= 300 – 276)	49 million
Number of employed	276 million	276 million

2. Rises
3. Fall
4. Rise
5. $210 billion (With an additional 2 percent (8 percent – 6 percent) of the labor force now employed, there are 6 million more people employed (= 2 percent x 300 million in the labor force). Each worker can produce an average of $35,000 a year in GDP for a total of $210 billion (= 6 million x $35,000) in GDP.

Exercise 4

1. Frictional
2. Cyclical
3. Structural
4. Seasonal

CHAPTER 7

Inflation

Quick Review

- Inflation is defined as an increase in the average level of prices, but not all prices rise during a period of inflation. Some prices may be falling while the *average* increases.

- During an inflationary period, the prices of some goods rise faster than the average. Incomes may not rise as fast as the rate of inflation, and some forms of wealth may lose value. The price, income, and wealth effects spawned by the increase in average prices cause a redistribution of income and wealth.

- At the macro level, inflation leads decision makers to shorten their time horizons, diverts resources to speculative activities, and can cause a phenomenon known as bracket creep because the tax bill is calculated in nominal terms.

- Inflation is typically measured using the Consumer Price Index (CPI), a weighted average of prices paid by consumers at the retail level. The inflation rate is the percentage change in the CPI from one year to the next. Other indexes—the Producer Price Index (PPI) and the GDP deflator—can be used to answer questions about inflation too.

- In the United States, the goal for price stability is an inflation rate of less than 3 percent, which reduces the conflict with full employment and allows for quality improvements.

- Inflation can result from excessive pressure on the demand side of the economy, known as demand-pull inflation, and from cost increases on the supply side, known as cost-push inflation.

- Inflationary problems experienced in the 1980s led to the development of some practical protective measures such as cost-of-living-adjustment (COLA) clauses in various contractual arrangements and adjustable-rate mortgages (ARMs) for lenders, both of which are tied to the CPI.

- Data indicate that countries with the lowest rates of inflation are also the ones with the lowest rates of unemployment. This makes sense if we consider that inflation interferes with the ability of prices to provide information about relative scarcity in the market.

Learning Objectives

After reading Chapter 7 and doing the following exercises, you should:

1. Understand that inflation is measured as an increase in the *average* level of prices.
2. Understand the difference between average prices and relative prices.
3. Be able to describe how price, income, and wealth effects accomplish redistributions in the economy.
4. Understand that some members of society are subject to money illusion.
5. Be able to explain why the inflationary process causes uncertainty and shortened time horizons, and diverts resources to speculative activity.
6. Understand what a price index is and the difference in the CPI, PPI, and the GDP deflator.
7. Understand that the goal of price stability does not necessarily mean zero inflation.
8. Know that when quality improvements occur, the CPI will overstate the rate of inflation.
9. Know that inflation can originate on both the demand side and the supply side of the economy.
10. Be able to discuss some of the protective mechanisms that reduce the redistributive effects of inflation.

Using Key Terms

Fill in the puzzle on the opposite page with the appropriate term from the list of Key Terms at the end of the chapter in the text.

Across

1. The price of apples compared to the price of other fruit.
5. Computed by the Bureau of Labor Statistics as the average price of consumer goods.
7. The nominal interest rate minus the anticipated rate of inflation.
8. The inflation adjusted value of output.
11. The increase in the average price level over a particular time period.
12. Used to express the purchasing power of income.
13. A decrease in average prices.
14. The price index that refers to all final goods and services.
15. Used in lease and wage agreements to protect real income from inflation.
16. Established at a rate of less than 3 percent inflation in the Full Employment and Balanced Growth Act of 1978.
17. The current dollar value of output.
18. The process in which inflation pushes people into higher tax brackets.
19. The use of nominal dollars, instead of real dollars, to gauge changes in income or wealth.

Down

2. A home loan used to protect the lender during inflationary periods.
3. The time period used for comparative analysis.
4. The situation discussed in the article in this chapter of the text about the Weimar Republic.
6. The percentage of a typical consumer budget spent on a good; used to compute inflation indexes.
9. Results in a redistribution of income and wealth.
10. Income received in a given time period measured in current dollars.

Puzzle 7.1

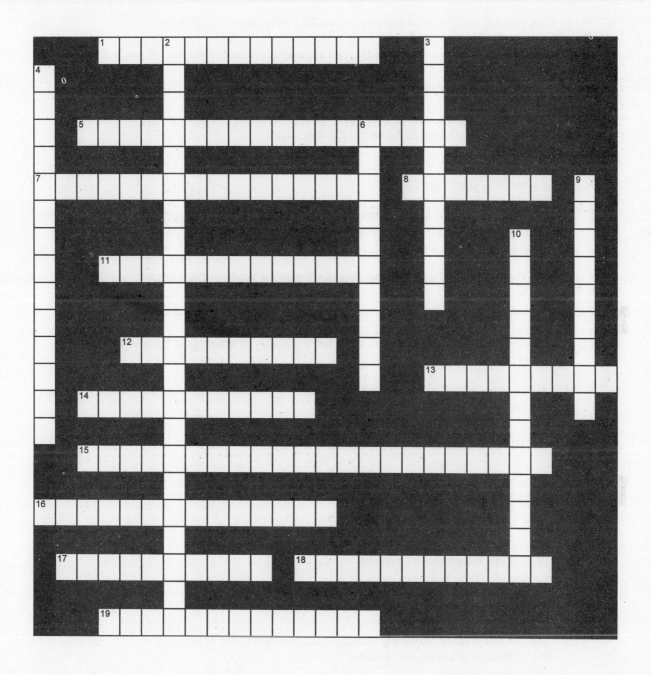

True or False: *Circle your choice and explain why any false statements are incorrect.*

T   F   1.   It is possible for individual prices to rise or fall during periods of inflation.

T   F   2.   Relative price changes are a desirable and essential ingredient of the market mechanism.

T   F   3.   Inflation only affects the poor.

T   F   4.   When doctors' fees rise faster than aspirin prices, real income falls for people who visit a doctor relative to those who prescribe aspirin for themselves.

T   F   5.   If the prices of things you buy do not increase, but the inflation rate is 10 percent, then your real income falls, *ceteris paribus*.

T   F   6.   If all individuals were able to anticipate inflation correctly and make appropriate adjustments in their market behavior, there would be no redistribution of real income or real wealth as a result of inflation.

T   F   7.   The Consumer Price Index usually increases before the Producer Price Index.

T   F   8.   The official goal set by Congress for inflation in the U.S. is three percent.

T   F   9.   The CPI overstates the rate of inflation when the quality of the items in the market basket improves.

T   F   10.   A COLA contributes to the redistribution caused by inflation by adjusting real income based on the rate of inflation.

Multiple Choice: *Select the correct answer.*

_____   1.   If the price of computers falls 10 percent during a period when the level of average prices falls 5 percent, the relative price of computers compared with other goods:
(a)   Stays the same.
(b)   Increases.
(c)   Decreases.
(d)   More information is required.

_____   2.   When an economy experiences a zero rate of inflation, which of the following statements is definitely true?
(a)   Real incomes improve.
(b)   There is no redistribution of income and wealth because of inflation.
(c)   Relative prices do not change.
(d)   All of the above.

_____   3.   As a result of inflation:
(a)   Morale improves.
(b)   The crime rate decreases.
(c)   Tension between labor and management increases.
(d)   Tension between individuals and the government decreases.

_____ 4. Which of the following is a micro consequence of inflation?
   (a) A price effect.
   (b) An income effect.
   (c) A wealth effect.
   (d) All of the above.

_____ 5. If actual inflation is greater than anticipated inflation in an economy:
   (a) Borrowers would experience an increase in real income.
   (b) Lenders would experience an increase in real income.
   (c) All workers would experience a decrease in real income.
   (d) The wealth effect would redistribute purchasing power to people on fixed incomes.

_____ 6. Which of the following groups is likely to lose as a result of unanticipated inflation?
   (a) Borrowers who have loans at fixed interest rates.
   (b) Fixed-income groups.
   (c) Workers under multi-year contracts with COLAs.
   (d) Mortgage lenders who make adjustable-rate mortgages.

_____ 7. Suppose you get a 10 percent raise during a year in which the price level rises by 10 percent. Then over the year:
   (a) Your real income falls, but your nominal income remains unchanged.
   (b) Your real and nominal income both fall.
   (c) Your real income remains unchanged, but your nominal income rises.
   (d) Your real income remains unchanged, but your nominal income falls.

_____ 8. Which of the following best describes the impact of uncertainty caused by inflation?
   (a) Short-run economic decisions become easier to make because people know prices are going to increase.
   (b) Long-run economic decisions become easier to make because people know prices are going to increase.
   (c) Investment decisions are more difficult to make because of the uncertain but rising costs.
   (d) All of the above.

_____ 9. Which of the following characterizes consumers' or businesses' reactions to the uncertainties caused by inflation?
   (a) Consumers cut back on consumption because they fear that future cost increases will make it difficult to make payments on what they consume.
   (b) Consumption increases as consumers try to buy products before their prices rise.
   (c) Businesses decrease investment spending in an attempt to avoid being caught with unprofitable plant and equipment.
   (d) All of the above.

_____ 10. Which of the following is a macro consequence of inflation?
   (a) Increased uncertainty.
   (b) Lengthened time horizons.
   (c) The wealth effect.
   (d) The price effect.

_____ 11. Speculation during periods of inflation can result in:
   (a) People buying resources for resale later rather than using the resources for current production.
   (b) A movement inside the institutional production-possibilities curve.
   (c) People buying gold, silver, jewelry, etc. instead of capital for production.
   (d) All of the above.

_____ 12. At the beginning of 1960 the CPI was 29.6. At the beginning of 2000 it was approximately 170.8. Which of the following most closely approximates the forty-year rate of inflation?
    (a)   141 percent
    (b)   477 percent
    (c)   350 percent
    (d)   550 percent

_____ 13. If you were interested in charting "price changes" for all goods and services produced, which of the following would be the most appropriate to use?
    (a)   The CPI.
    (b)   The PPI.
    (c)   The GDP deflator.
    (d)   The COLA.

_____ 14. The reason that policy makers are reluctant to force the economy to a zero percent inflation rate is that:
    (a)   Unacceptable levels of unemployment might result.
    (b)   Businesses would not be able to raise prices.
    (c)   Real incomes would fall.
    (d)   Businesses would postpone production decisions.

_____ 15. If the CPI doesn't adjust for product quality improvements, then the CPI tends to:
    (a)   Understate the inflation rate.
    (b)   Overstate the inflation rate.
    (c)   Understate economic growth.
    (d)   Be artificially low.

_____ 16. Which one of the following statements about inflation in the U.S. is correct?
    (a)   Prior to World War II, the U.S. experienced periods of both deflation and inflation.
    (b)   The U.S. experienced inflation virtually every year since 1800.
    (c)   Since World War II, the U.S. has consistently met its inflation goal of 3 percent or lower.
    (d)   Prior to World War II, the U.S. experienced deflation virtually every year; since World War II, the U.S. has consistently experienced inflation.

_____ 17. COLAs are desired because:
    (a)   The real value of wages can be maintained, since COLAs correct for the effects of inflation.
    (b)   COLAs help reduce the rate of inflation.
    (c)   COLAs help stimulate employment.
    (d)   All of the above.

_____ 18. For an economy in which nominal interest rates are equal to real interest rates, which of the following statements is definitely true?
    (a)   Anticipated inflation was greater than actual inflation.
    (b)   Actual inflation was greater than anticipated inflation.
    (c)   Inflation was anticipated.
    (d)   No inflation occurred.

_____ 19. The most fundamental function of prices in a market economy is to provide:
    (a)   The data necessary to calculate rates of inflation.
    (b)   The basis for the calculation of sales tax.
    (c)   Information about the relative scarcities of resources and goods and services.
    (d)   Maximum profits to producers.

_____ 20. The most desirable inflation rate is the rate that:
   (a)   Equals the official goal of 3 percent.
   (b)   Least affects the behavior of companies, investors, consumers and workers.
   (c)   Maximizes the "wealth effect" of inflation.
   (d)   Coincides with an unemployment rate of zero percent.

Problems and Applications

Exercise 1

This exercise emphasizes the redistribution of inflation and deflation.

1. During a period of inflation, a person owns no assets and has no COLA to protect his/her income. This is likely to result in a (negative, positive) (wealth, income) effect.

2. During a period of inflation, a family has a COLA that protects their income, but their rent payment rises more rapidly than the rate of inflation. This family experiences a (negative, positive) (price, wealth) effect.

3. During a period of inflation, a person owns stock which increases in value at a rate less than the rate of inflation. This person experiences a (negative, positive) (wealth, price) effect.

4. During a period of deflation, a person's nominal income remains constant. This results in a (positive, negative) (price, income) effect.

5. During a period of deflation, a person owns a home that decreases in value at a rate less than the rate of deflation. The result of this situation is a (positive, negative) (wealth, income) effect.

Exercise 2

This exercise emphasizes the calculation of real GDP, real income, and the real interest rate.

Use the information in Table 7.1 to answer questions 1-6. Assume 1999 is the base period.

Table 7.1

	Nominal GDP (billions of dollars)	Maria's nominal income	GDP deflator	CPI	Nominal interest rate
1999	$3,200	$28,000	100	100	7%
2000	3,500	31,000	105	108	10%
2001	3,700	35,000	112	114	12%

1. Calculate real GDP for 2000. Use the formula:

$$\text{Real GDP for 2000} = \frac{\text{Nominal GDP}_{2000}}{\text{GDP deflator}_{2000}} \times 100$$

_____

2. Calculate real GDP for 2001. _____

3. Calculate Maria's real income for 2001. Use the formula:

$$\text{Real income for 2001} = \frac{\text{Nominal income}_{2001}}{\text{CPI}_{2001}} \times 100$$

_____

4. By what percentage did consumer prices rise from 1999 to 2000? _____

5. By what percentage did consumer prices rise from 1999 to 2001? _____

6. Use the Consumer Price Index as a measure of the anticipated rate of inflation. Calculate the real interest rate for 2001. (The formula is in the text.) _____

Exercise 3

This exercise focuses on the causes of inflation and the different impacts on the economy.

1. When consumers seek to buy more goods than the economy can produce, the result is _____ inflation.

2. When production costs rise for numerous industries, the result is _____ inflation.

Figure 7.1

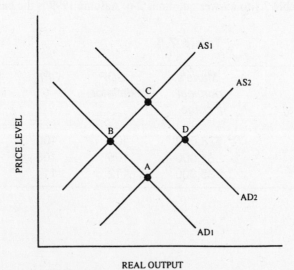

3. Assume the economy is in equilibrium at point A in Figure 7.1. As a result of cost-push inflation, the economy would move to point _____. The price level would (increase, decrease) and the level of output would (increase, decrease).

4. Assume the economy is in equilibrium at point B in Figure 7.1. As a result of demand-pull inflation, the economy would move to point _____. The price level would (increase, decrease) and the level of output would (increase, decrease).

Exercise 4

This exercise will help you see the impact of different inflation rates on the value of money held for different periods of time.

1. Use Table 7.6 in the text to determine the impact of a period of inflation at a particular inflation rate. Calculate the value of $1000 held for:
   a. Four years' time at an inflation rate of 8%. _____
   b. Five years' time at an inflation rate of 4%. _____
   c. Eight years' time at an inflation rate of 4%. _____
   d. Ten years' time at an inflation rate of 2%. _____
   e. Six years' time at an inflation rate of 10%. _____

2. In which of the two cases above does the $1000 come closest to being worth the same amount? _____

3. In which case above is the $1000 worth the least amount?_____

4. Would you lose more money if you placed $1000 under your mattress for ten years at 2% inflation or if you placed $1000 in a cookie jar for four years at 8% inflation?_____ _____

Common Errors

The first statement in each "common error" below is incorrect. Each incorrect statement is followed by a corrected version and an explanation.

1. When the price of a product rises, there is inflation. WRONG!

   When the average level of prices rises, there is inflation. RIGHT!

   The price of a single product may rise while an average of prices of all products falls. Such adjustments in relative prices are essential to the most *efficient* distribution of goods and services through the market. When the average of all prices is rising, however, distribution may not be efficient and capricious redistributions of income may occur.

2. As long as price increases do not exceed the inflation rate, they do not contribute to inflation. WRONG!

   Every price increase contributes to a rise in the inflation rate. RIGHT!

Since the inflation rate is an average of all price increases, the increase in any price by any amount raises the average. Firms that buy commodities from other firms that raise prices will, in turn, attempt to pass the increase on to their own customers; an increased price may have indirect effects in raising the inflation rate.

3. Indexation, such as a COLA clause in a contract, protects the *economy* against the effects of inflation. WRONG!

A COLA clause protects an individual against the effects of inflation. RIGHT!

Indexation can protect the real incomes of specific groups for which indexation is applied. In other words, it can address some of the micro consequences of inflation. However, if everyone's income is not indexed, then even the micro consequences may not be adequately addressed. In fact, indexation can lead to dramatic changes in relative prices. Furthermore, indexation may lead to anticipation of higher rates of inflation; high current inflation rates may guarantee higher future rates as a result of indexation.

•ANSWERS•

Using Key Terms

Across

1. relative price
5. consumer price index
7. real interest rate
8. real GDP
11. inflation rate
12. real income
13. deflation
14. GDP deflator
15. cost-of-living adjustment (COLA)
16. price stability
17. nominal GDP
18. bracket creep
19. money illusion

Down

2. adjustable rate mortgage
3. base period
4. hyperinflation
6. item weight
9. inflation
10. nominal income

True or False

1. T
2. T
3. F — Inflation affects everyone, although the poor and those on fixed incomes tend to be more adversely affected.
4. T

5. F   If your purchasing power does not change, then your real income hasn't changed.
6. T
7. F   The PPI measures changes in average prices at the producer level, which typically occurs before changes in the CPI.
8. T
9. T
10. F   A COLA counteracts the income effect of inflation by adjusting nominal income based on the rate of inflation.

Multiple Choice

1.	c	5.	a	9.	d	13.	c	17.	a
2.	b	6.	b	10.	a	14.	a	18.	d
3.	c	7	c	11.	d	15.	b	19.	c
4.	d	8.	c	12.	b	16.	a	20.	b

Problems and Applications

Exercise 1

1. Negative, income
2. Negative, price
3. Negative, wealth
4. Positive, income
5. Positive, wealth

Exercise 2

1. $3,333.33 billion
2. $3,303.57 billion
3. $30,701.75 billion
4. 8 percent
5. 14 percent
6. −2 percent

Exercise 3

1. Demand-pull
2. Cost-push
3. B, increase, decrease
4. D, increase, increase

Exercise 4

1. a. $735
   b. $822
   c. $731
   d. $820
   e. $564
2. b and d
3. e
4. $1000 in a cookie jar for four years at 8% inflation

CHAPTER 8

The Business Cycle

Quick Review

- Business cycles are alternating periods of growth and contraction in the economy. The cycle is measured by changes in the nation's real GDP. The cycles vary in length and intensity. The worst contraction experienced was the Great Depression of the 1930s. Despite the ups and downs, the economy has had an average annual growth rate of approximately 3 percent since 1929.

- Macroeconomic theory attempts to explain the business cycle while macroeconomic policy tries to control the cycle.

- The primary outcomes of the macroeconomy include output (GDP), prices, jobs, growth, and international balances. These outcomes result from the interplay of internal market forces, external shocks, and policy levers.

- The aggregate demand curve slopes downward to the right and the aggregate supply curve slopes upward to the right. The intersection of the aggregate demand and supply curves defines the macro equilibrium.

- The equilibrium may be undesirable because it may not provide the optimal level of employment and output.

- Even if the equilibrium is desirable, it may be unstable and not last for long because the forces behind the equilibrium can change. Shifts in aggregate demand and/or aggregate supply can lead to unemployment, inflation, or, worse yet, stagflation—a combination of the two.

- The aggregate-demand and aggregate-supply framework provides a convenient way to compare various theories about how the economy works. The theories can be classified as demand-side, supply-side, or eclectic.

- It is also useful to separate the short run from the long run. In the long run, the aggregate supply curve becomes vertical at the "natural" rate of output.

- Specific policy approaches include: Fiscal policy—changes in taxes and government spending; monetary policy—the use of money and credit controls; supply-side policy—favors tax cuts and other policies to increase incentives for producers. The classical approach calls for a laissez-faire policy of nonintervention by the government.

Learning Objectives

After reading Chapter 8 and doing the following exercises, you should:

1. Understand how economic growth is measured and the long term goal for growth.
2. Have a historical perspective on the business cycle from the Great Depression to the present.
3. Understand why the aggregate supply curve slopes upward to the right, and why the aggregate demand curve slopes downward to the right.
4. Recognize that a given macro equilibrium may not be desirable, and that it may also be unstable.
5. Be able to distinguish the different macro theories about how the economy works.
6. Understand the different macro policies—demand-side, supply-side, and eclectic.

Using Key Terms

Fill in the puzzle on the opposite page with the appropriate term from the list of Key Terms at the end of the chapter in the text.

Across

2. The value of final output produced in a given period, adjusted for changing prices.
3. The idea that whatever is produced by suppliers will always be sold.
9. The output level represented by point Q_F in Figure 8.8 in the text.
12. The use of tax cuts and government deregulation to shift the aggregate supply curve.
13. The portion of the business cycle when total output decreases.
14. The macro failure in Figure 8.8 in the text because the equilibrium price level exceeds the desired price level.
15. The concept of nonintervention by government in the market mechanism.

Down

1. A situation in which the economy grows but at a very slow rate.
4. States that an increase in price causes a decrease in quantity demanded of a good.
5. The upward sloping curve in Figure 8.7 in the text.
6. Represented by point E in Figure 8.7 in the text.
7. The area of study that focuses on output, jobs, prices, and growth for the entire economy.
8. The use of money and credit controls to shift the aggregate demand curve.
9. The use of government spending and taxes to shift the aggregate demand curve.
10. Occurs as a result of shifts in aggregate demand and aggregate supply.
11. The curve drawn in Figure 8.5 in the text.

Puzzle 8.1

True or False: *Circle your choice and explain why any false statements are incorrect.*

T F 1. Business cycles are measured by changes in nominal GDP.

T F 2. During the business cycle, unemployment and production typically move in opposite directions.

T F 3. In the classical view of the economy, the product market is brought into equilibrium by flexible prices, the labor market is brought into equilibrium by flexible wages.

T F 4. Business cycles result from shifts of the aggregate supply and aggregate demand curves.

T F 5. The U.S. economy has grown at a steady pace since 1930.

T F 6. The economy cannot possibly be in a recession if real GDP is increasing.

T F 7. The full-employment GDP is the same as the equilibrium GDP.

T F 8. Keynes believed that unemployment could exist for long periods of time if aggregate demand was inadequate.

T F 9. Both Keynesian and monetarist theories focus on shifting the aggregate supply curve.

T F 10. Supply-side theorists believe the unwillingness of producers to supply more goods and services at existing prices can prolong an economic downturn.

Multiple Choice: *Select the correct answer.*

_____ 1. Determinants of macro performance include:
    (a) Internal market forces.
    (b) External shocks.
    (c) Policy levers.
    (d) All of the above.

_____ 2. Business cycles in the United States:
    (a) Are remarkably similar in length but vary greatly in intensity.
    (b) Vary greatly in length, frequency, and intensity.
    (c) Are similar in frequency and intensity.
    (d) Are similar in length, frequency, and intensity.

_____ 3. Which of the following is inherent in the classical view of a self-adjusting economy?
    (a) Flexible wages and prices.
    (b) Inflexible wages and prices.
    (c) Schiller's Law.
    (d) Instability.

_____ 4. Keynesian theory became important when classical economic theory did not adequately explain:
    (a) A prolonged period of both inflation and unemployment.
    (b) A prolonged growth recession.
    (c) A depression.
    (d) A prolonged period of inflation.

_____ 5. In the aggregate demand-aggregate supply diagram:
   (a) More than one equilibrium can occur.
   (b) The horizontal axis measures the average price level.
   (c) The intersection of the two curves marks the macro equilibrium.
   (d) The equilibrium level of output is always at the full employment level.

_____ 6. Which of the following is a reason for a downward-sloping aggregate demand curve?
   (a) The real-balances effect.
   (b) The price effect.
   (c) The inter-state trade effect.
   (d) The savings effect.

_____ 7. The difference between market demand and aggregate demand is:
   (a) Market demand applies to all individuals, and aggregate demand does not.
   (b) Aggregate demand applies to a specific good, and market demand does not.
   (c) Policy levers work only through market demand.
   (d) Market demand applies to a given market while aggregate demand applies to the entire economy.

_____ 8. The foreign-trade effect helps explain the downward slope of the aggregate demand curve because as:
   (a) The U.S. price level falls, people in the United States tend to purchase more imports.
   (b) The U.S. price level falls, people tend to purchase more U.S. produced goods.
   (c) Foreign prices rise, people tend to purchase more U.S. produced goods.
   (d) Foreign prices rise, people in the United States tend to purchase more imports.

_____ 9. When the average price level falls in our economy, consumers tend to:
   (a) Buy more imported goods and fewer domestic goods, _ceteris paribus_.
   (b) Buy more imported goods and more domestic goods, _ceteris paribus_.
   (c) Buy fewer imported goods and more domestic goods, _ceteris paribus_.
   (d) Buy fewer imported goods and fewer domestic goods, _ceteris paribus_.

_____ 10. Which of the following is a reason why the aggregate supply curve is upward sloping?
   (a) Profit effect.
   (b) Interest rate effect.
   (c) Real-balances effect.
   (d) Foreign trade effect.

_____ 11. The cost effect implies:
   (a) That greater output results in increasingly higher costs.
   (b) A curved, upward-sloping aggregate supply curve.
   (c) That higher costs are reflected in higher average prices.
   (d) All of the above.

_____ 12. In macro equilibrium:
   (a) Aggregate quantity demanded equals aggregate quantity supplied.
   (b) The equilibrium price level and rate of output are both stable.
   (c) Both buyers' and sellers' intentions are satisfied.
   (d) All of the above.

_____ 13. When aggregate supply exceeds aggregate demand, what will happen to the price level?
   (a) Prices will rise.
   (b) Prices will remain the same.
   (c) Prices will fall.
   (d) Prices may either rise or fall depending on the business cycle.

_____ 14. Which of the following combination of shifts of aggregate demand and supply curves would definitely result in higher unemployment?
(a) Demand shifts to the left and supply shifts to the right.
(b) Demand shifts to the left and supply shifts to the left.
(c) Demand shifts to the right and supply shifts to the right.
(d) Demand shifts to the right and supply shifts to the left.

_____ 15. Controversies between Keynesian, monetarist, supply-side, and eclectic theories focus on:
(a) The shape and sensitivity of aggregate demand and aggregate supply curves.
(b) The existence or nonexistence of the aggregate supply curve.
(c) The importance of international balances to the economy.
(d) All of the above.

_____ 16. According to Keynes, policy makers should respond to a downturn in the business cycle by:
(a) Cutting taxes and increasing government spending.
(b) Cutting taxes and reducing government spending.
(c) Raising taxes and increasing government spending.
(d) Raising taxes and reducing government spending.

_____ 17. The eclectic approach to macroeconomic policy relies on:
(a) Demand-side policy.
(b) A laissez-faire approach.
(c) Supply-side policy.
(d) Any or all of the above approaches.

_____ 18. Which of the following is _not_ typically used to shift the aggregate demand curve or the aggregate supply curve?
(a) Monetary policy.
(b) International trade policy.
(c) Fiscal policy.
(d) A laissez-faire approach.

_____ 19. If equilibrium GDP is less than full employment GDP, an appropriate fiscal policy lever would be to:
(a) Increase AD by increasing income taxes.
(b) Increase AD by increasing government spending.
(c) Increase AS by reducing government regulations.
(d) Reduce AS by tightening air pollution standards in order to improve air quality.

_____ 20. If an economy is suffering from excessively high rates of inflation, an appropriate monetary policy lever would be to:
(a) Decrease AS by decreasing the money supply.
(b) Decrease AD by increasing interest rates.
(c) Decrease AD by increasing income taxes.
(d) Increase AS by increasing the money supply.

Problems and Applications

Exercise 1

This exercise examines the effects of fiscal policy using aggregate supply and demand curves.

Assume the aggregate demand curve (D_1) and aggregate supply curve (S_1) are those shown in Figure 8.1. Then suppose the government increases spending, which causes the quantity of output demanded in the economy to rise by $1 trillion per year at every price level. Decide whether the change shifts aggregate demand or aggregate supply from its initial position.

Figure 8.1

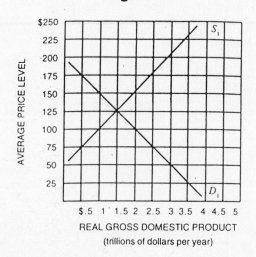

1. Draw the new aggregate demand curve (label it D_2) or aggregate supply curve (label it S_2) in Figure 8.1.

2. What is the new equilibrium average price? _____

3. What is the new equilibrium output level? _____

4. Which school of thought would be most likely to prescribe the use of fiscal policy in this way?
   _____

5. The shift that occurred in question 1 (above) is consistent with:
   (a) Inflation and a higher unemployment rate.
   (b) Inflation and a lower unemployment rate.
   (c) Deflation and a higher unemployment rate.
   (d) Lower inflation and a lower unemployment rate.

Exercise 2

This exercise will help to explain why the aggregate demand curve slopes downward.

1. Suppose you have $1000 in savings at the beginning of the year and the price level is 100. If inflation pushes the price level up by 10 percent to 110 during the year, what will be the real value of your savings at year-end? (*Hint:* Refer to the formula in the text for the real value of savings.) _____

2. The change in purchasing power in question 1 above, because of a change in the price level, is one explanation for the downward slope of the aggregate demand curve. This explanation is referred to as the _____.

3. The impact of the change in purchasing power in question 1 above would cause a (movement up, leftward shift in) the aggregate demand curve.

Exercise 3

This exercise will demonstrate the impact of shifts in demand and aggregate supply. Answer choices for questions 1-4 are "AD", "AS", or "both AD and AS."

Use Figure 8.2 to answer questions 1-4.

Figure 8.2

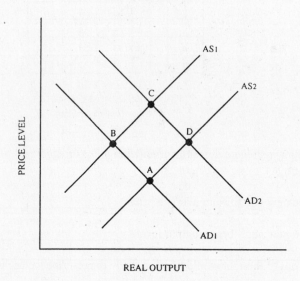

1. Assume the economy is initially in equilibrium at point B in Figure 8.2. Which curve would need to shift in order for a new equilibrium to occur at point C? _____

2. Assume the economy is initially in equilibrium at point D in Figure 8.2. Which curve would need to shift in order for a new equilibrium to occur at point C? _____

3. Assume the economy is initially in equilibrium at point B in Figure 8.2. Which curve would need to shift in order for a new equilibrium to occur at point A? _____

4. Assume the economy is initially in equilibrium at point A in Figure 8.2. Which curve would need to shift in order for a new equilibrium to occur at point C? _____

5. Which policy option might be used to achieve the shift in question 1 above?

   _____

6. Which policy option might be used to achieve the shift in question 3 above?

   _____

Exercise 4

This exercise focuses on the long-run aggregate supply curve and the impact of fiscal policy.

Use Figure 8.3 to answer questions 1-7.

Figure 8.3

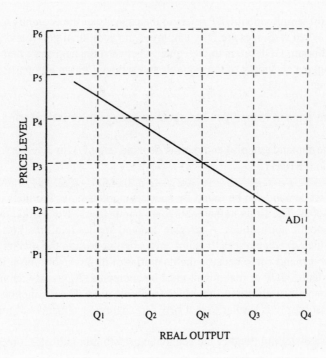

1. In Figure 8.3, aggregate demand is given as AD_1. Draw the long-run aggregate supply curve according to the classical/monetarist view of long-run stability. The equilibrium level of output should occur at Q_N. Label the curve AS. Label the equilibrium point E_1.

2. T F $\quad$ Q_N represents the long-run equilibrium output level.

3. What is the equilibrium price level in Figure 8.3, given the long-run aggregate supply curve and AD_1? _____

4. Suppose the government uses fiscal policy to shift the aggregate demand curve in Figure 8.3 to the right. Draw the new aggregate demand curve and label it AD_2. Label the new equilibrium point E_2.

5. The fiscal policy action in question 4 above caused the price level to (rise, fall, stay the same).

6. The fiscal policy action in question 4 above caused the level of real output to (rise, fall, stay the same).

7. T F $\quad$ With a vertical long-run aggregate supply curve, fiscal policy is effective in changing the level of real output.

Common Errors

The first statement in each "common error" below is incorrect. Each incorrect statement is followed by a corrected version and an explanation.

1. The full-employment GDP is the same as the equilibrium GDP. WRONG!

    The full-employment GDP is not necessarily the same as the equilibrium GDP. RIGHT!

    The full-employment GDP refers to the capacity of the economy to produce goods and services. When resources are fully employed, no additional goods and services can be produced. The equilibrium GDP refers to the equality between the aggregate demand for goods and services and the aggregate supply of those goods and services, not to any particular level of resource employment.

2. Aggregate demand (supply) and market demand (supply) are the same. WRONG!

    Aggregate demand (supply) and market demand (supply) involve very different levels of aggregation. RIGHT!

    Market demand can be found for specific markets only. Products in that market must be homogeneous. The firms in that market are competitors. The market demand is used for microeconomic applications. Aggregate demand applies to all markets within the economy and involves their average prices. It is not even possible to sum the market demand curves to find the aggregate demand curve because the quantities of different commodities cannot be measured in the same units; GDP or real output must be computed. Aggregate demand is used for macroeconomic applications, not microeconomic ones. The distinction between aggregate supply and market supply is similar to that between aggregate demand and market demand.

3. A downward-sloping trend of the economic growth rate indicates a recession. WRONG!

    A downward-sloping trend of the real GDP indicates a recession. RIGHT!

    The economic growth rate is measured by the *percentage change* in the real GDP. A recession occurs whenever that percentage change is negative for two quarters. By contrast, in a graph of the real GDP, without any computation of year-to-year changes, it is necessary to look for a downward dip in the real GDP to spot a recession. Three rules for the relationship between the levels and percentage changes of the real GDP should always be remembered when either graph is being examined:
    1.   Whenever there is a downward slope to a graph of the real GDP, there will be a negative percentage change in real GDP.
    2.   Whenever the graph of the real GDP flattens, the percentage change in the real GDP will approach zero.
    3.   Whenever there is an upward slope to a graph of the real GDP, there will be a positive percentage change in real GDP.

•ANSWERS•

Using Key Terms

Across

2. real GDP
3. Say's Law
9. full employment GDP
12. supply-side policy
13. recession
14. inflation
15. laissez-faire

Down

1. growth recession
4. law of demand
5. aggregate supply
6. equilibrium macro
7. macroeconomics
8. monetary policy
9. fiscal policy
10. business cycle
11. aggregate demand

True or False

1. F   Business cycles are measured by changes in real GDP.
2. T
3. T
4. T
5. F   The U.S. economy has grown at an unsteady pace, with many peaks and troughs in the business cycle.
6. F   If real GDP increases but at a rate below the long term trend, this is known as a growth recession.
7. F   Equilibrium GDP does not guarantee full employment. Equilibrium GDP can be greater than, less than, or equal to full employment GDP.
8. T
9. F   These are demand-side theories that focus on shifting the aggregate demand curve.
10. T

Multiple Choice

1. d	5. c	9. c	13. c	17. d
2. b	6. a	10. a	14. b	18. d
3. a	7. d	11. d	15. a	19. b
4. c	8. b	12. d	16. a	20. b

Problems and Applications

Exercise 1

1. See Figure 8.1 Answer, D_2

Figure 8.1 Answer

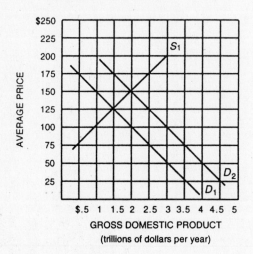

2. $150
3. $2 trillion
4. Keynesian
5. b

Exercise 2

1. $1000/(110/100) = $1000/(1.1) = $909.09
2. Real-balances effect
3. Movement up

Exercise 3

1. AD
2. AS
3. AS
4. Both AD and AS
5. Fiscal or monetary policy
6. Supply-side policy

Exercise 4

Figure 8.3 Answer

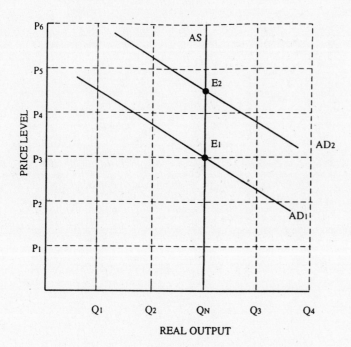

1. See AS and E_1 in Figure 8.3 Answer
2. T
3. P_3
4. See AD_2 and E_2 in Figure 8.3 Answer
5. Rise
6. Stay the same
7. F

Aggregate Spending

Quick Review

- John Maynard Keynes challenged the classical approach of laissez faire. He asserted that the economy was inherently unstable and that government intervention was necessary at times.

- The four components of aggregate demand are consumption (C), investment (I), government spending (G), and net exports ($X - IM$).

- Disposable income must be divided into two parts—that which is spent and that which is saved. Consumption refers to all household spending on goods and services. It can be determined using the consumption function of the form $C = a + bY_D$, where a is referred to as "autonomous spending" and bY_D is the income dependent portion of spending.

- The MPC represents the change in consumption because of a change in income and is the slope of the consumption function. In the function above, the MPC is represented by b.

- Any change in the level of autonomous consumption will shift the consumption function up or down, which will in turn shift the aggregate demand curve to the right or left.

- Investment refers to spending by businesses on new plant and equipment and net changes in inventory. It is dependent on interest rates, expectations, and innovation but *not* on current income.

- Government spending includes expenditure on goods and services at the federal, state, and local levels. Decisions on how much to spend are independent of the level of real income.

- Foreign buyers purchase exports from the U.S. economy, and Americans gladly purchase imports from foreign countries. Net exports is the difference between spending on exports and spending on imports.

- Even if the economy is currently in equilibrium at full employment, this may not last if aggregate demand changes. A decrease in spending can push the economy into a recessionary GDP gap, which causes cyclical unemployment. If demand becomes too great the economy may experience an inflationary GDP gap, which results in demand-pull inflation. Either way the economy misses the goals of full employment and price stability.

Learning Objectives

After reading Chapter 9 and doing the following exercises, you should:

1. Know the Keynesian theory of aggregate demand.
2. Understand that equilibrium may not occur at full employment.
3. Know the four components of aggregate demand.
4. Be able to interpret the consumption function.
5. Know how to find the average and marginal propensities to consume.
6. Understand how a shift in the consumption function leads to a shift in aggregate demand.
7. Be able to describe the determinants of C, I, G, and $(X - IM)$.
8. Know that the intersection of aggregate supply and aggregate demand determines the equilibrium level of income.
9. Be able to graph a recessionary or an inflationary GDP gap and describe the economic implications.

Using Key Terms

Fill in the puzzle on the opposite page with the appropriate term from the list of Key Terms at the end of the chapter in the text.

Across

1. A change in consumers' spending caused by a change in the value of assets owned by consumers.
5. The upward-sloping curve in Figure 9.1 in the text.
7. The difference between equilibrium GDP and full employment GDP in Figure 9.11 in the text.
9. Equal to 0.75 in Figure 9.4 in the text.
10. The combination of price level and real output that is compatible with both aggregate demand and aggregate supply.
12. Provides a basis for predicting how changes in income will affect consumer spending.
14. The negative saving discussed in the article titled "Livin' Large" in the text.
16. The difference between full employment GDP and equilibrium GDP associated with demand-pull inflation in Figure 9.10 in the text.
17. After-tax income of consumers.
18. Unemployment because of an inadequate level of aggregate demand.
19. Alternating periods of expansions and contractions in economic activity.
20. The price level situation demonstrated on the right-hand side of Figure 9.10 in the text.

Down

2. The downward-sloping curve in Figure 9.1 in the text.
3. The proportion of total disposable income spent on consumption.
4. The potential GDP for an economy is the same thing as _____ _____ GDP.
6. Equal to 1 - MPC.
8. The value of total output produced at macro equilibrium.
11. Equal to the difference between the consumption function and the 45-degree line at a disposable income greater than $200 in Figure 9.4 in the text.
13. The largest component of aggregate demand.
15. Determined by expectations, interest rates, and technology.

Puzzle 9.1

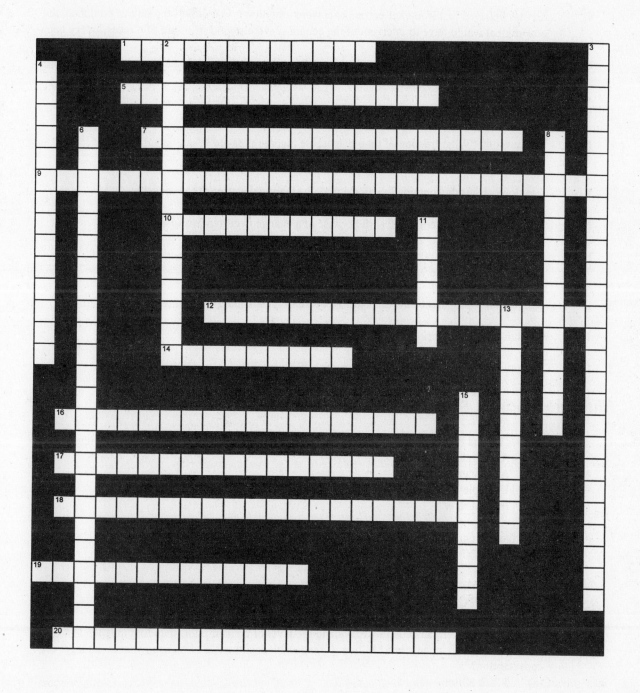

True or False: *Circle your choice and explain why any false statements are incorrect.*

T F 1. Keynes believed that if market participants were unwilling to buy all of the output produced, the government would have to intervene if the economy were to pull itself out of a recessionary gap.

T F 2. The four components of aggregate demand are consumption, investment, government spending, and net exports.

T F 3. The largest component of aggregate demand is government spending.

T F 4. The question "What fraction of total disposable income is saved?" can be answered by calculating the marginal propensity to save.

T F 5. The slope of the consumption function equals the marginal propensity to consume.

T F 6. The consumption function will shift because of a change in current disposable income.

T F 7. If disposable income is constant, a sudden increase in saving results in a lower level of consumption for society, *ceteris paribus*.

T F 8. Cyclical unemployment can result from a decrease in spending by businesses and government.

T F 9. Investment depends primarily upon the current level of income.

T F 10. If people become overly confident in the economy, an inflationary GDP gap can result.

Multiple Choice: *Select the correct answer.*

_____ 1. Keynes argued that the level of economic activity is predominantly determined by the level of:
(a) Aggregate supply.
(b) Aggregate demand.
(c) Unemployment.
(d) Interest rates.

_____ 2. If, in the aggregate, consumers spend 90 cents out of every extra dollar received:
(a) The *APC* is 1.11.
(b) The *APC* is 0.90.
(c) The *MPS* is 0.10.
(d) The *MPC* is 0.10.

_____ 3. Suppose the MPC in an economy is 0.8 and the level of consumption spending independent of current disposable income is $1 billion. If disposable income is $14 billion, what is the level of consumption?
(a) $11.2 billion.
(b) $12.2 billion.
(c) $8.0 billion.
(d) $12.0 billion.

_____ 4. Which of the following is a part of aggregate demand?
(a) The purchase of athletic shoes for your child.
(b) The purchase of a new forklift by a hardware store.
(c) The purchase of a computer by the federal government.
(d) All of the above.

_____ 5. A change in autonomous consumption would correspond to:
- (a) A shift of both the consumption function and the aggregate demand curve.
- (b) A shift of the consumption function and a movement along the aggregate demand curve.
- (c) A movement along the consumption function and a shift of the aggregate demand curve.
- (d) A movement along both the consumption function and the aggregate demand curve.

_____ 6. In the consumption function $C = a + bY_D$, the value of a is determined in part by:
- (a) Disposable income.
- (b) The level of imports.
- (c) Consumer confidence.
- (d) All of the above.

_____ 7. The line described by the consumption function $C = a + bY_D$ will change its slope when:
- (a) The MPC changes.
- (b) Consumer confidence changes.
- (c) Disposable income changes.
- (d) The MPS is greater than 1.0.

_____ 8. The marginal propensity to consume is the:
- (a) Average consumption per dollar of income.
- (b) Additional consumption because of additional income.
- (c) Additional consumption per dollar paid in taxes.
- (d) Additional dollar amount of consumption because of inflation.

_____ 9. An increase in interest rates would result in:
- (a) A decrease in both aggregate demand and the consumption function.
- (b) A decrease in aggregate demand and an increase in aggregate supply.
- (c) An increase in both aggregate demand and the consumption function.
- (d) An increase in both aggregate demand and aggregate supply.

_____ 10. With respect to the aggregate demand curve, improved consumer confidence would:
- (a) Shift the curve rightward.
- (b) Shift the curve leftward.
- (c) Move the economy down along the curve.
- (d) Move the economy up along the curve.

_____ 11. Determinants of consumption include the:
- (a) Level of wealth.
- (b) Availability of credit.
- (c) Tax rate.
- (d) All of the above.

_____ 12. The terrorist attacks on the World Trade Center and The Pentagon in September 2001 helped push the U.S. economy toward a recession because:
- (a) The decrease in consumer confidence caused the consumption function to shift downward and aggregate demand to decrease.
- (b) The increase in government spending to fight terrorism was primarily in the form of foreign expenditure.
- (c) A decrease in the cost of airline travel caused more people to spend money on flying.
- (d) A decrease in the average price level caused an increase in the aggregate quantity demanded.

_____ 13. Which of the following is included in investment spending?
  (a)   The purchase of a new share of stock issued by IBM.
  (b)   The purchase of a previously owned home.
  (c)   The purchase of a used Sears delivery van by a small business.
  (d)   The purchase of a new computer by a local merchant.

_____ 14. Which of the following causes a movement along the investment demand curve?
  (a)   A change in expenditures.
  (b)   A change in technology.
  (c)   A change in the rate of interest.
  (d)   The current level of income.

_____ 15. The growth in the value of the U.S. stock market in the 1990s caused aggregate demand to increase primarily because of:
  (a)   The price effect.
  (b)   The wealth effect.
  (c)   Increased income.
  (d)   The interest rate effect.

_____ 16. Aggregate demand can shift due to changes in expectations on the part of:
  (a)   U.S. consumers.
  (b)   U.S. businesses.
  (c)   Foreign consumers.
  (d)   All of the above.

_____ 17. Dissaving:
  (a)   Is not possible because that would mean saving is less than zero.
  (b)   Is the result of an inflationary GDP gap.
  (c)   Can be financed with savings from a prior period.
  (d)   Occurs when consumption is greater than real GDP.

_____ 18. If aggregate demand is too great:
  (a)   Equilibrium will still occur at full employment GDP.
  (b)   Cyclical unemployment will occur.
  (c)   There will be an inflationary GDP gap.
  (d)   All of the above.

_____ 19. When consumers, government, businesses, and the foreign sector do not buy all of the output that is produced, then:
  (a)   Inventories accumulate.
  (b)   There is an inflationary GDP gap.
  (c)   The economy will sustain itself at its potential GDP.
  (d)   The aggregate expenditure line should decrease.

_____ 20. When aggregate demand falls below the full-employment level of output, which of the following types of unemployment is most likely to increase?
  (a)   Cyclical.
  (b)   Seasonal.
  (c)   Frictional.
  (d)   Structural.

_____ 21. In graphs with output on the horizontal axis and aggregate expenditures on the vertical axis, a 45-degree line represents:
   (a) The potential growth path for consumption.
   (b) A line marking where aggregate demand and supply intersect for equilibrium (macro).
   (c) The points on which aggregate expenditure equals output.
   (d) Points where consumption equals saving.

_____ 22. Equilibrium (macro) occurs at the output at which:
   (a) The aggregate expenditure curve intersects the 45-degree line.
   (b) The aggregate demand curve intersects the aggregate supply curve.
   (c) Desired expenditure equals the value of output.
   (d) All of the above.

_____ 23. The amount by which the desired rate of total expenditure at full employment is less than full-employment output is the:
   (a) GDP gap.
   (b) Recessionary gap.
   (c) Inflationary gap.
   (d) Budget deficit.

Problems and Applications

Exercise 1

This exercise emphasizes the relationship between consumption and disposable income.

1. Complete columns 4, 5, and 7 in Table 9.1, and then compute the average propensity to consume and the marginal propensity to consume in columns 3 and 6.

Table 9.1
Marginal and average propensity to consume
(billions of dollars per year)

_(1)_ Disposable income	_(2)_ Total consumption	_(3)_ Average propensity to consume	_(4)_ Change in consumption	_(5)_ Change in income	_(6)_ Marginal propensity to consume	_(7)_ Saving
$ 0	$100	----	----	----	----	$_____
1,000	1000	_____	$900	$1000	_____	_____
2,000	1900	_____	_____	_____	_____	_____

2. What is the level of consumption if disposable income increases to $3,000? _____

3. Write the consumption function based on the information in Table 9.1. _____

Exercise 2

This exercise provides practice in using the consumption function and in distinguishing shifts of the consumption function from movements along it.

1. Assume the following consumption function:

$$C = \$200 \text{ billion} + 0.75Y_D$$

In Table 9.2, compute a consumption schedule from the formula.

Table 9.2
Computation of a consumption schedule
(billions of dollars per year)

Disposable income (Y_D)	Autonomous consumption (a)	+	Income-dependent consumption (bY_D)	=	Total consumption (C)
$ 0	___		___		$___
400	___				
1,200	200		0.75 x 1,200		1,100

2. Using the consumption schedule in Table 9.2, draw the consumption function in Figure 9.1 and label it 1. The curve should pass through point *B* if it is correctly drawn.

3. In Table 9.3, fill in the schedule for the consumption function $C = \$300 \text{ billion} + 0.75Y_D$.

4. What is the marginal propensity to consume in Table 9.3? _____

Table 9.3
Consumption function shift
(billions of dollars per year)

Disposable income (Y_D)	Autonomous consumption (a)	+	Income-dependent consumption (0.75 x Y_D)	=	Total consumption (C)
$ 0	$300		___		$___
400	300		___		___
800	300		___		___
1,200	300		___		___

5. Using the schedule in Table 9.3, graph the consumption function in Figure 9.1 (label it 2) and draw a 45-degree line from the origin.

6. T F   In Figure 9.1, the shift in the consumption function from curve 1 to curve 2 shows that at any given level of disposable income, consumption will be greater and savings will be less.

Figure 9.1
Consumption functions

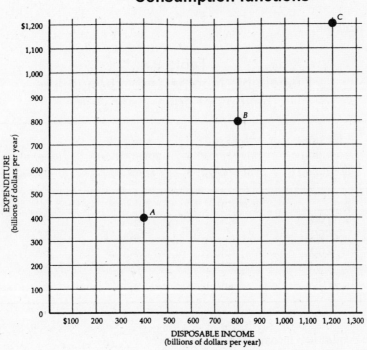

Exercise 3

Choose the diagram (a or b) in Figure 9.2 that best represents the shift in the consumption function that accompanies each of the events described in questions 1-4. Then, try to decide what impact each shift in the consumption function would have on the aggregate demand curve (c or d) for the economy. Place your answers in the blanks provided.

Figure 9.2

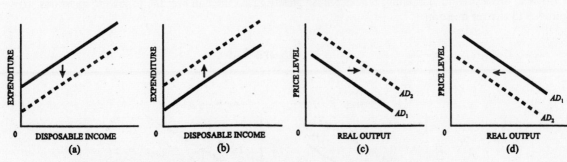

1. Consumer confidence falters as a recession becomes more likely. ____ ____

2. Many U.S. households receive a tax refund, which they promptly spend. ____ ____

3. Congress passes new, strict regulations on the distribution and use of credit cards. ____ ____

4. Consumer interest rates are reduced to stimulate the economy. ____ ____

123

Exercise 4

This examines the relationship between the components of aggregate expenditure (consumption, investment, government spending, and net exports) and the level of income.

1. Complete Table 9.4.

Table 9.4
Disposable income and expenditures
(billions of dollars per year)

At an output of	Desired consumer spending	Desired investment spending	Desired government spending	Net export spending	Aggregate expenditure
$1000	$ _____	$ 350	$ 400	$ 50	$ 1750
2000	1700	350	400	50	_____
3000	2450	_____	400	50	3250
4000	3200	350	400	50	_____
5000	_____	350	400	50	4750
6000	4700	350	400	_____	5500

2. What is the equilibrium income level in Table 9.4? _____

3. What is the MPC from Table 9.4? _____

4. If full-employment output occurs at $6000 billion, there is a _____ gap and aggregate demand is (less than, greater than) the full employment level of output.

5. If full-employment output occurs at $2000 billion, there is a _____ gap and aggregate demand is (less than, greater than) the full employment level of output.

Exercise 5

The media continually present information about events that shift aggregate demand for the U.S. economy. This exercise uses one of the articles in the text to show the kind of information to look for. Reread the article in the text entitled "Falling Stocks Smash Nest Eggs." Then answer the following questions. Use Figure 9.3 to answer question 1.

Figure 9.3

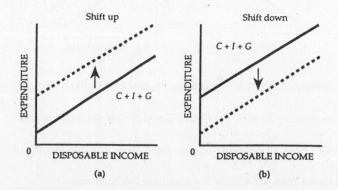

(a)   (b)

1. Which diagram in Figure 9.3 best represents the shift in consumption spending that the article is describing? _____

2. What should happen to the aggregate demand curve as a result of the change described in the article? _____

3. What happened that encouraged consumers to spend so much? _____
_____

4. What phrase indicates how consumers have responded to the recent change in the stock market?
_____

Common Errors

The first statement in each "common error" below is incorrect. Each incorrect statement is followed by a corrected version and an explanation.

1. The economy can spend no more than its income. WRONG!

   The economy *can* spend more than its income. RIGHT!

   The economy can spend more than its income by drawing down inventories of both public and private goods or by consuming capital (allowing it to depreciate) without replacing it. If the economy consumes more than its income, it will actually dissave and experience negative investment.

2. When a person invests in stocks, investment expenditure is increased. WRONG!

   The purchase of stocks has only an indirect relationship to investment expenditure in the economy. RIGHT!

   Investment expenditure refers to purchases of new capital goods (plant, machinery, and the like), inventories, or residential structures. A purchase of stock represents a transfer of ownership from one person to another. Sometimes such purchases are called "financial investments," but they do not represent economic investment.

3. The marginal propensity to consume is consumption divided by income. WRONG!

   The average propensity to consume is consumption divided by income. RIGHT!

   There is a big difference between total consumption and a change in consumption. While the average propensity to consume involves total consumption and total income, the marginal propensity to consume involves changes in consumption and changes in income.

4. Aggregate demand rises when people buy more imports. WRONG!

   Aggregate demand falls when people buy more imports, *ceteris paribus*. RIGHT!

   Students often think of imports as expenditures and therefore believe that increased spending on imports will have the same effect on the economy as an increase in consumption. Expenditures on imports, however, do not generate domestic income. If imports increase, they do so at the expense of purchases of U.S. goods, meaning fewer jobs in the United States. Because employment declines, there is less income with which to purchase goods; consumption falls and so does aggregate spending.

5. If the economy is in macroeconomic equilibrium, the economy must be operating at full employment. WRONG!

   If the economy is in macroeconomic equilibrium, unemployment can still exist. RIGHT!

   There is always a macro equilibrium because equilibrium occurs where aggregate demand and aggregate supply intersect. This equilibrium point may occur at the full-employment level of output, but it can also occur at a level other than full employment.

[CHAPTER 9 APPENDIX COMMON ERRORS]

6. The aggregate expenditure curve is the same as the aggregate demand curve. WRONG!

   The aggregate expenditure curve and aggregate demand curve are related to each other only indirectly. RIGHT!

   The aggregate expenditure curve and aggregate demand curve are two quite different concepts. They have different units on the axes; aggregate expenditure represents the intended expenditures at each *income* level; aggregate demand represents quantity demanded at each average price level for all goods and services.

7. Dissaving is the difference between the 45-degree line and aggregate expenditure curve. WRONG!

   Dissaving is the difference between a curve representing the consumption function and the 45-degree line. RIGHT!

   Both saving and dissaving are defined as the difference between disposable income and consumption. The 45-degree line shows the points at which expenditure equals income. So, when consumption expenditure equals income (the consumption function intersects the 45-degree line), there is zero saving. When the consumption expenditure exceeds income (the consumption function is above the 45-degree line), there will be dissaving.

•ANSWERS•

Using Key Terms

Across

1. wealth effect
5. aggregate supply
7. recessionary GDP gap
9. marginal propensity to consume
10. equilibrium
12. consumption function
14. dissaving
16. inflationary GDP gap
17. disposable income
18. cyclical unemployment
19. business cycle
20. demand-pull inflation

126

Down

2. aggregate demand
3. average propensity to consume
4. full employment
6. marginal propensity to save
8. equilibrium GDP
11. saving
13. consumption
15. investment

True or False

1. T
2. T
3. F   Consumption is the largest component of aggregate spending.
4. F   The marginal propensity to save measures the fraction of additional disposable income that is saved.
5. T
6. F   There is a movement along a given consumption function when disposable income changes.
7. T
8. T
9. F   Investment changes a business's future capacity to produce, so expectations about future sales (i.e., income) are more relevant than current income.
10. T

Multiple Choice

1. b	5. a	9. a	13. d	17. c	21. c
2. c	6. c	10. a	14. c	18. c	22. d
3. b	7. a	11. d	15. b	19. a	23. b
4. d	8. b	12. a	16. d	20. a	

Problems and Applications

Exercise 1

1. **Table 9.1 Answer**

(1) Disposable income	(2) Total consumption	(3) Average propensity to consume	(4) Change in consumption	(5) Change in income	(6) Marginal propensity to consume	(7) Saving
$ 0	$100	----	----	----	----	$ -100
1000	1000	1.00	$900	$1000	0.9	0
2,000	1900	0.95	900	1000	0.9	100

2. $2800
3. $C = 100 + .9Y_D$

Exercise 2

1. **Table 9.2 Answer**

Disposable income (Y_D)	Autonomous consumption (a)	+	Income-dependent consumption (bY_D)	=	Total consumption (C)
$ 0	200		0		$ 200
400	200		0.75 x 400		500
1,200	200		0.75 x 1,200		1,100

2. **Figure 9.1 Answer**

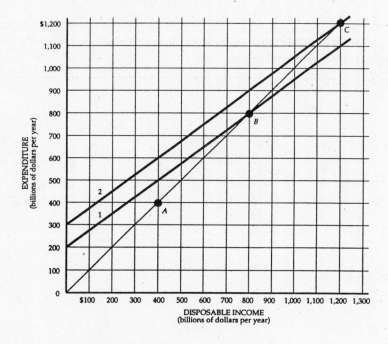

3. **Table 9.3 Answer**

Disposable income (Y_D)	Autonomous consumption (a)	+	Income-dependent consumption (0.75 x Y_D)	=	Total consumption (C)
$ 0	$300		0		$ 300
400	300		0.75 x 400		600
800	300		0.75 x 800		900
1,200	300		0.75 x 1200		1200

4. 0.75. The marginal propensity to consume is the change in consumption (e.g., $600 - $300 billion per year) divided by the corresponding change in income ($400 - $0 billion per year).
5. See Figure 9.1 Answer, line 2
6. T

Exercise 3

1. a, d
2. b, c
3. a, d
4. b, c

Exercise 4

1. **Table 9.4 Answer**

At an output of	Desired consumer spending	Desired investment spending	Desired government spending	Net export spending	Aggregate expenditure
1000	<u>950</u>	350	400	50	1750
2000	1700	350	400	50	<u>2500</u>
3000	2450	<u>350</u>	400	50	3250
4000	3200	350	400	50	<u>4000</u>
5000	<u>3950</u>	350	400	50	4750
6000	4700	350	400	<u>50</u>	5500

2. $4,000 billion
3. MPC = 0.75
4. Recessionary GDP, less than
5. Inflationary GDP, greater than

Exercise 5

1. b
2. Aggregate demand should shift to the left.
3. The soaring value of the U.S. stock market and increased home values contributed to the so-called "wealth effect."
4. "Many of the . . . big ticket purchases Americans would have made . . . are on hold."

CHAPTER 10

Self-Adjustment or Instability?

Quick Review

- In the Keynesian view of a market-driven economy, macro equilibrium may not occur at a desirable rate of output.

- Consumer saving is a leakage from the flow of income as are business saving, imports, and taxes. There are several injections, including investment, government purchases, and exports.

- Imbalances between leakages and injections result in an aggregate expenditure imbalance. This imbalance can cause demand-pull inflation or cyclical unemployment. If leakages and injections are not equal at full employment GDP, the economy experiences either a recessionary or an inflationary gap.

- Classical economists believed interest rates and prices would change in response to an imbalance between leakages and injections, and this would bring the economy to a full-employment equilibrium.

- Keynes argued that an initial spending imbalance will be multiplied as it works its way through the economy. If output is greater than desired spending, inventories will accumulate and producers will reduce output. This will cause a decrease in income, which will reduce consumer spending. The spending decrease will lead to further cutbacks in production, more lost income, and still less consumption. This process is known as the multiplier effect.

- The multiplier is calculated as $1/(1-MPC)$. It is used to determine the cumulative change in total expenditure because of an initial change in spending.

- A change in spending will shift the aggregate demand curve. Since the aggregate supply curve is upward sloping, any change in aggregate demand will affect both output and the price level. The result is a tradeoff between inflation and unemployment.

- The recessionary GDP gap is the amount by which equilibrium GDP falls short of the full-employment GDP.

- The inflationary gap, measured at full employment, is the amount by which equilibrium GDP exceeds full-employment GDP. In this case inventories are drawn down, prices rise, more people are hired, wages rise, there is an attempt to expand capacity, and interest rates rise.

- Because a change in spending patterns can move the economy away from full-employment equilibrium, the economy is vulnerable to continual booms and busts known as the business cycle.

Learning Objectives

After reading Chapter 10 and doing the following exercises you should:

1. Understand that equilibrium may not occur at a desirable output level.
2. Know the different leakages and injections and how they impact the circular flow.
3. Be able to distinguish between the Keynesian and classical views of the adjustment process in a market-driven economy.
4. Understand the critical distinction between desired investment and actual investment.
5. Be able to describe the multiplier process and calculate the multiplier.
6. Understand the possible divergence between equilibrium GDP and full-employment GDP.
7. Be able to describe how the economy responds to a recessionary GDP gap and an inflationary GDP gap.
8. Be able to describe and demonstrate price and output effects and the inflation-unemployment tradeoff in an AS-AD framework.

Using Key Terms

Fill in the puzzle on the opposite page with the appropriate term from the list of Key Terms at the end of the chapter in the text.

Across
1. Equal to 4 in Table 10.1 in the text.
3. The difference between Q_F and Q_E in Figure 10.7 in the text.
4. The rate of real output at which aggregate demand equals aggregate supply.
5. The lowest rate of unemployment compatible with price stability.
7. The difference between Q_F and Q_E in Figure 10.9 in the text.
10. Equal to depreciation allowances and retained earnings.
11. Unemployment because of a recessionary gap.

Down
1. The fraction of additional income spent by consumers.
2. The situation that results in Figure 10.9 in the text because of excessive aggregate demand.
6. The downward-sloping curve in Figure 10.2 in the text.
7. An addition of spending to the circular flow of income.
8. Income diverted from the circular flow.
9. The value of total output produced at full-employment.

Puzzle 10.1

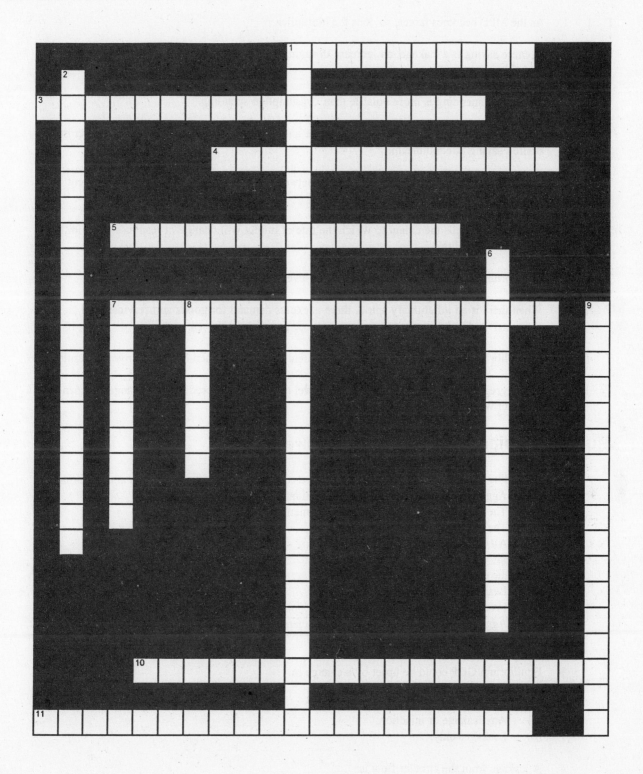

True or False: *Circle your choice and tell why any false statements are incorrect.*

T F 1. As the MPC becomes larger, so does the multiplier.

T F 2. Because saving is a leakage, an increase in saving results in lower equilibrium income for society, *ceteris paribus.*

T F 3. Investment spending is more volatile than consumption spending.

T F 4. If saving and investment are the only leakage and injection, desired investment is greater than desired saving at equilibrium.

T F 5. In a purely private economy, the difference between desired saving and desired investment measures the undesired change in inventory.

T F 6. The multiplier tells the extent to which the rate of output will change in response to an initial change in spending.

T F 7. Equilibrium GDP is always the most desired level of GDP for an economy.

T F 8. When there is an inflationary spiral, there is excess demand for goods and services, and consumers bid up prices by competing for those goods and services.

T F 9. If equilibrium GDP is less than full-employment GDP, then structural unemployment results.

T F 10. The aggregate supply-aggregate demand model can be used to predict how changes in spending behavior will affect output and prices.

Multiple Choice: *Select the correct answer.*

_____ 1. According to the Keynesian view of the macro economy, when the economy is at equilibrium:
   (a) Aggregate supply equals aggregate demand.
   (b) The economy is always at full employment.
   (c) The price level is always stable.
   (d) All of the above are true.

_____ 2. When the economy is at equilibrium:
   (a) Leakages equal injections.
   (b) Inventories are at desired levels.
   (c) Aggregate supply equals aggregate demand.
   (d) All of the above are true.

_____ 3. Equilibrium GDP could be upset by a change in:
   (a) Investment only.
   (b) Injections only.
   (c) Any leakage or injection.
   (d) Leakages only.

_____ 4. A leakage from the circular flow is:
   (a) An export from the economy.
   (b) A decline in the capacity of the economy to produce goods.
   (c) A diversion of income from spending on output.
   (d) A decrease in aggregate supply.

5. When an economy is at full employment and consumption spending decreases, if all other levels of spending remain constant:
    (a) Increased unemployment results.
    (b) Any GDP gap disappears.
    (c) Inventory levels are less than desired until a new equilibrium is reached.
    (d) Changes in consumption spending have no impact on GDP.

6. Given $C = 100 + 0.80Y$, the multiplier is:
    (a) 0.20.
    (b) 5.
    (c) 4.
    (d) 8.

7. If actual investment exceeds desired investment then:
    (a) Inventories are increasing.
    (b) Output will increase as a result.
    (c) Demand-pull inflation exists.
    (d) Inventories are being depleted.

8. Keynes emphasized that because there is no automatic adjustment back to full employment:
    (a) Equilibrium GDP might be less than full-employment GDP.
    (b) A long-term recessionary gap could occur.
    (c) Cyclical unemployment could persist.
    (d) All of the above.

9. Suppose that as a result of higher interest rates, desired investment and aggregate demand decrease. Additional decreases in aggregate demand will be the result of:
    (a) Decreases in consumption.
    (b) Decreases in induced expenditures.
    (c) The multiplier effect.
    (d) All of the above.

10. Assuming an upward-sloping aggregate supply curve, when aggregate demand increases:
    (a) Unemployment decreases and the price level decreases.
    (b) Unemployment decreases and the price level increases.
    (c) Unemployment increases and the price level decreases.
    (d) Unemployment increases and the price level increases.

11. Suppose that an economy has an upward-sloping aggregate supply curve and a GDP gap equal to $45 billion. If aggregate demand increases by a total of $45 billion:
    (a) The GDP gap will be eliminated.
    (b) The resulting equilibrium GDP will be lower than full employment GDP because some of the additional spending will drive up prices instead of increasing output.
    (c) The resulting equilibrium GDP will be greater than full employment GDP because of demand-pull inflation.
    (d) Any of the above could occur depending on the size of the multiplier.

_____ 12. Using a consumption function of the form $C = a + bY_D$, which of the following would best measure the total impact on output of a change in autonomous spending?

(a) $\dfrac{1}{MPS}$

(b) $\dfrac{1}{1 - b}$

(c) $\dfrac{1}{1 - MPC}$

(d) All of the above.

_____ 13. When output exceeds desired spending, which of the following is included in the Keynesian adjustment process?
(a) Producers cut output and employment.
(b) Lost income causes a decline in consumer spending.
(c) Lower consumer spending results in additional loss of income.
(d) All of the above.

_____ 14. Because the aggregate supply curve rises more steeply as the economy approaches full employment:
(a) Inflation tends to accelerate.
(b) The GDP gap becomes larger.
(c) Aggregate demand shifts to the left.
(d) The multiplier effect becomes greater.

_____ 15. In which of the following cases would cyclical unemployment tend to increase, _ceteris paribus_?
(a) Undesired inventory depletion.
(b) Total value of goods supplied exceeds the total value of goods demanded.
(c) A period of significant inflation.
(d) Desired investment exceeds desired saving.

_____ 16. If the equilibrium level of output is less than full employment, to achieve a full-employment equilibrium the AD curve must shift to the right by an amount:
(a) Equal to the GDP gap.
(b) Less than the GDP gap because the spending increase causes the multiplier process to occur.
(c) Greater than the GDP gap because the spending increase raises the price level.
(d) Less than the GDP gap because the spending increase raises output and prices.

_____ 17. In an inflationary GDP gap situation:
(a) Savings dollars are readily available and interest rates fall.
(b) There are sufficient resources available and wages tend to decrease.
(c) There is excess demand for goods and consumers bid up prices.
(d) All of the above.

_____ 18. A rightward shift in the aggregate demand curve will cause:
(a) Both higher prices and higher output if the aggregate supply curve is upward sloping.
(b) Higher prices and lower output if the aggregate supply curve is upward sloping.
(c) No change in prices, but higher output, if the aggregate supply curve is upward sloping.
(d) Lower prices and higher output if the aggregate supply curve is upward sloping.

_____ 19. With an MPC of 0.50, an increase of $2 billion in autonomous consumption would cause:
(a) An initial increase of $1 billion in income.
(b) $500 million in multiplier effects.
(c) Income to change by a total of $4 billion.
(d) Income to change by a total of $2 billion.

136

_____ 20. A basic conclusion of Keynesian analysis is that:
  (a) The economy is vulnerable to abrupt changes in spending behavior.
  (b) The economy does not self adjust to reach full employment or stable price levels.
  (c) Equilibrium GDP may not be consistent with full employment or price stability.
  (d) All of the above.

Problems and Applications

Exercise 1

This exercise focuses on a recessionary GDP gap caused by a change in investment spending.

Assume the economy is initially in equilibrium on AD_3 in Figure 10.1 and full-employment GDP occurs at Q_3. Use Figure 10.1 to answer questions 1-7.

Figure 10.1

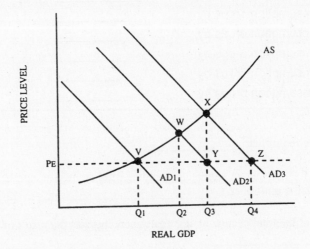

1. Suppose the rate of investment decreases and aggregate demand shifts initially to AD_2. The new equilibrium real GDP occurs at _____.

2. The decline in investment spending causes a (decrease, increase) in household income and consumption. Aggregate demand shifts to the (right, left) to (AD_1, AD_3). The final equilibrium is at a real GDP level of _____.

3. T   F   The real GDP gap is equal to the distance $Q_3 - Q_1$.

4. If equilibrium output is less than full-employment, there is a (recessionary, inflationary) GDP gap.

5. When equilibrium output is less than full-employment output, at the full-employment level actual investment is (less than, greater than, equal to) desired investment because undesired inventories are (less than, greater than, equal to) zero.

6. When aggregate expenditure is (less than, greater than, equal to) the full-employment level of output, a recessionary GDP gap exists.

7. A recessionary GDP gap causes (seasonal, structural, cyclical, frictional) unemployment.

137

Exercise 2

The following exercise shows how the multiplier works and how to calculate it.

1. Suppose the economy was at full employment but suddenly experienced a $100 billion decrease in business expenditures because of a decrease in the value of corporate stocks. Follow the impact of this sudden change through the economy by completing Table 10.1. (Refer to Table 10.1 in the text.) Assume the marginal propensity to consume is 0.80. (Hint: Consumption will decrease in each round by the "change in spending in the previous cycle" times the MPC.) Then use Table 10.1 to answer questions 2-7.

Table 10.1

Spending cycles	Decrease in expenditure	Change in spending (billions of dollars per year)	Cumulative decrease in aggregate spending (billions of dollars per year)
First cycle:	GDP gap emerges	$100	$100
Second cycle:	consumption drops by	_____	_____
Third cycle:	consumption drops by	_____	_____
Fourth cycle:	consumption drops by	_____	_____
Fifth cycle:	consumption drops by	_____	_____
Sixth cycle:	consumption drops by	_____	_____
Seventh cycle:	consumption drops by	_____	_____

2. Compute the multiplier. _____

3. What is the total change in aggregate spending after an infinite number of cycles? (Multiply $100 billion times the multiplier.) _____

4. How much of the total change in aggregate spending was the result of a change in investment?

   _____

5. How much of the total change in aggregate spending was the result of a change in consumption?

   _____

6. T   F   A large portion of the change in aggregate spending in question 3 was due to the multiplier effect.

Exercise 3

This exercise emphasizes the short-run trade-off between unemployment and inflation.

Assume the economy is initially on AD_1. The full-employment level of output is Q_1 and the desired price level is P_2. Use Figure 10.2 to answer questions 1-3.

Figure 10.2

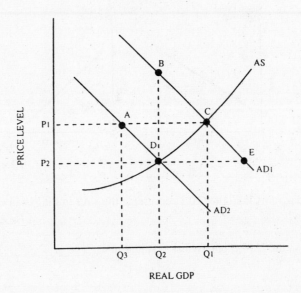

1. Assume price level P_1 is considered inflationary. If the AD curve is shifted to AD_2 to reduce the price level, the result is a _____ in the level of output and an _____ in the level of unemployment.

2. If AD is shifted back to the right to AD_1, output returns to the full-employment level, but the price level _____.

3. Because the AS curve is _____ sloping, any shift in AD will cause a trade-off between _____.

Exercise 4

This exercise focuses on an inflationary GDP gap situation.

1. Figure 10.9 in the text illustrates an inflationary gap situation. An increase in investment caused AD to shift to _____ and the resulting multiplier effects caused AD to shift again to _____.

2. When AD shifts to the right, the price level _____.

3. In the situation in question 2, actual investment is (less than, greater than, equal to) desired investment and _____ are being depleted.

4. Producers will respond to the increased demand by (increasing, decreasing) production.

5. The resulting economic situation is referred to as _____ inflation.

Exercise 5

Reread the article in the text titled "U.S. Slowdown Helps Derail Asia." Then answer questions 1-4.

Figure 10.3

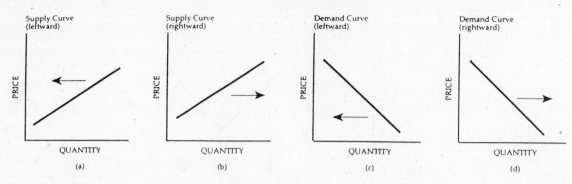

1. Which of the diagrams in Figure 10.3 represents the shift in the Asian economy because of the U.S. slowdown?

2. The downturn in the U.S. economy has resulted in a _____ in demand for Asian exports.

3. How have U.S. manufacturers responded to the downturn? _____

_____

4. The slowdown in the U.S. economy causes a decrease in demand for Asian exports, which causes a decrease in demand for U.S. exports in Asia. This is called the _____ _____ effect.

Common Errors

The first statement in each "common error" below is incorrect. Each incorrect statement is followed by a corrected version and an explanation.

1. Since saving and investment must be the same by definition, a closed economy must be at expenditure equilibrium because investment equals saving. WRONG!

   Intended investment equals intended saving at expenditure equilibrium in a closed economy. RIGHT!

   If there are excess inventories or if people are forced to save because they cannot spend on desired goods and services, then the income level may be different from equilibrium income. Do not confuse actual investment and actual saving with intended investment and intended saving.

2. If consumers save more, interest rates will fall and investment will rise. WRONG!

   When consumption falls as a result of increased saving, investment may be discouraged. RIGHT!

   Interest rates *may* fall because of increased saving. However, Keynes showed that businesses may invest less when they expect to sell less. The lower consumption that results from increased saving may actually cause businesses to reduce investment.

3. Expenditure equilibrium and full-employment GDP are always the same. WRONG!

   Expenditure equilibrium and full-employment GDP are determined in different ways. RIGHT!
   Expenditure equilibrium occurs where the aggregate expenditure curve and the 45-degree line intersect. The full-employment GDP occurs at the GDP level where the market supply and

market demand curves for labor are in equilibrium. For most purposes, we can consider the two levels to be independent of each other.

Be careful! While it is possible to determine the expenditure equilibrium or income level by glancing at the aggregate spending curve and the 45-degree line, it is not possible to determine full-employment GDP this way. Full-employment GDP is shown simply as a vertical line.

•ANSWERS•

Using Key Terms

Across
1. multiplier
3. recessionary GDP gap
4. equilibrium GDP
5. full employment
7. inflationary GDP gap
10. gross business saving
11. cyclical unemployment

Down
1. marginal propensity to consume
2. demand-pull inflation
6. aggregate demand
7. injection
8. leakage
9. full-employment GDP

True or False
1. T
2. T
3. T
4. F   At equilibrium, leakages must equal injections. In a closed private economy, the only leakages and injections are saving and investment.
5. T
6. F   The multiplier tells how much total spending will change in response to an initial change in spending. Whenever the AS curve is upward sloping, the total change in output will be less than the total change in spending.
7. F   Equilibrium GDP does not necessarily mean that the economy is experiencing full employment or stable price levels.
8. T
9. F   Cyclical unemployment results.
10. T

Multiple Choice

1. a	5. a	9. d	13. d	17. c
2. d	6. b	10. b	14. a	18. a
3. c	7. a	11. b	15. b	19. c
4. c	8. d	12. d	16. c	20. d

Problems and Applications

Exercise 1

1. Q_2
2. Decrease, left, AD_1, Q_1
3. T
4. Recessionary
5. Greater than; greater than
6. Less than
7. Cyclical

Exercise 2

1. **Table 10.1 Answer**

Spending cycles	Amount	Cumulative decrease in aggregate spending
First cycle:	$100.00	$100.00
Second cycle:	80.00	180.00
Third cycle:	64.00	244.00
Fourth cycle:	51.20	295.20
Fifth cycle:	40.96	336.16
Sixth cycle:	32.77	368.93
Seventh cycle:	26.22	395.15

2. Multiplier = 1/(1-MPC) = 1/(1-0.8) = 5
3. $500 billion
4. $100 billion
5. $400 billion
6. T

Exercise 3

1. Decrease, increase
2. Increases
3. Upward sloping; inflation and unemployment

Exercise 4

1. AD_5; AD_6
2. Increases
3. Less than; inventories
4. Increasing
5. Demand-pull

Exercise 5

1. c
2. Decrease
3. Lay-offs, decreased production
4. International multiplier

CHAPTER 11

Fiscal Policy

Quick Review

- Keynes concluded that the macroeconomy would not automatically correct spending imbalances. He said government intervention was necessary to shift the economy's aggregate demand in the appropriate direction.

- The primary tools of fiscal policy are changes in taxes, government spending on goods and services and income transfers.

- Fiscal expansion can be accomplished with an increase in government spending. The required increase in AD does not come completely from government purchases. Successive rounds of spending, kicked off by the initial government purchases, ripple through the economy through the multiplier process.

- The aggregate demand curve must shift by more than the GDP gap because some of the shift is felt in a price level change. The fiscal stimulus required to get the economy to full employment can be calculated by the following:

    Desired fiscal stimulus = (AD shortfall/the multiplier)

    The same thing can be accomplished with a tax cut, which is calculated in two steps. First determine the desired fiscal stimulus and then determine the desired tax cut using:

    Desired tax cut = (desired fiscal stimulus/MPC)

- A tax cut of a given size will be less expansionary than a spending increase of the same size because part of the tax cut leaks into saving before the first private-sector spending takes place.

- Fiscal restraint can be accomplished with cuts in government spending, increased taxes, or reduced income transfers. The desired fiscal restraint is the same as the fiscal stimulus except it causes a decrease in AD.

- Greater borrowing by government might crowd out an equal amount of private spending. Tax cuts can go to businesses or households and favor investors or consumers. Either way, the mix of output is affected. Changes in transfers lead to a different mix of output also.

Learning Objectives

After reading Chapter 11 and doing the following exercises, you should:

1. Understand that government intervention may be necessary to achieve full employment.
2. Know the tools of fiscal policy.
3. Understand how fiscal stimulus and fiscal restraint can be used to stabilize the economy.
4. Be able to explain why tax cuts are less expansionary than increases in government purchases of an equal size.
5. Understand that any fiscal policy initiative will be multiplied through the economy.
6. Understand that the AD curve must shift by more than the GDP gap to close the gap.
7. Be able to calculate the AD shortfall or excess, the multiplier, and the desired fiscal stimulus or restraint.
8. Be able to explain how fiscal stimulus can be offset by the "crowding out" of private expenditure.
9. Understand how fiscal policy can change the mix of output for an economy.

Using Key Terms

Fill in the puzzle on the opposite page with the appropriate term from the list of Key Terms at the end of the chapter in the text.

Across

2. The use of fiscal policy to reduce aggregate demand.
5. The use of the federal government budget to change macroeconomic outcomes.
9. Personal income minus personal taxes.
10. The downward-sloping curve in Figure 11.2 in the text.
11. Government spending in the form of Social Security, welfare, and unemployment benefits.
12. Occurs at an output level of $5.6 trillion in Figure 11.2 in the text.
13. The difference between full-employment GDP and equilibrium GDP.

Down

1. The change in consumption divided by the change in disposable income.
2. Tax cuts or spending increases intended to shift aggregate demand to the right.
3. The upward-sloping curve in Figure 11.2 in the text.
4. A decrease in private-sector borrowing caused by increased government borrowing.
6. The amount aggregate demand must increase to achieve full-employment, after allowing for price-level changes.
7. Equal to $1/(1-MPC)$.
8. Equal to $400 billion in Figure 11.6 in the text.

144

Puzzle 11.1

True or False: *Circle your choice and indicate why any false statements are incorrect.*

T F 1. Fiscal policy works principally through shifts of the aggregate supply curve.

T F 2. From a Keynesian perspective, the way out of a recession includes an increase in government spending, a tax cut, or an increase in transfer payments.

T F 3. If the AS curve is horizontal (i.e., flat), the GDP gap is equal to the desired fiscal stimulus (or restraint).

T F 4. Increasing government expenditures by the amount of the AD shortfall will achieve full employment.

T F 5. Fiscal policy involves changes in government spending and taxes.

T F 6. When there is excess aggregate demand, desired fiscal restraint equals the desired AD reduction divided by the multiplier.

T F 7. A tax cut contains less stimulus to the economy than an increase in government spending of the same size because some of the tax cut is saved.

T F 8. Both government purchases of goods and services and government transfer payments are part of AD.

T F 9. Every dollar of new government spending has a multiplied impact on aggregate demand.

T F 10. Crowding out is the idea that an increase in government spending may cause a reduction in private-sector spending.

Multiple Choice: *Select the correct answer.*

_____ 1. Fiscal policy works principally through shifts of:
  (a) The aggregate supply curve.
  (b) The aggregate demand curve.
  (c) The full-employment output line.
  (d) The 45-degree line.

_____ 2. Which of the following is a tool of fiscal policy?
  (a) Increasing government purchases of goods and services.
  (b) Increasing taxes.
  (c) Increasing income transfers.
  (d) All of the above.

_____ 3. In a diagram of aggregate demand and aggregate supply curves, the GDP gap is measured:
  (a) As the vertical distance between the equilibrium price and the price at which the aggregate demand would intersect aggregate supply at full employment.
  (b) As the horizontal distance between the equilibrium output and the full employment output.
  (c) As the horizontal distance between the aggregate demand and the aggregate supply curves at the equilibrium price.
  (d) As the amount of the AD shortfall or excess.

_____ 4. If the economy is operating below full employment, which of the following policies will increase aggregate spending but will not increase the size of the government?
   (a) Increase government spending and leave taxes unchanged.
   (b) Increase government spending and taxes by the same amount.
   (c) Leave government spending unchanged and decrease taxes.
   (d) Decrease government spending and leave taxes unchanged.

_____ 5. The GDP gap will differ from the AD shortfall when:
   (a) The aggregate supply curve slopes upward.
   (b) The multiplier effect raises spending.
   (c) The budget is balanced.
   (d) All of the above.

_____ 6. To eliminate the AD shortfall of $100 billion when the economy has an _MPC_ of 0.80, the government should increase its purchases by:
   (a) $20 billion.
   (b) $100 billion.
   (c) $500 billion.
   (d) $800 billion.

_____ 7. Assuming an _MPC_ of 0.75, the change in total spending for the economy as a result of a $100 billion new government spending injection would be:
   (a) $40 billion.
   (b) $75 billion.
   (c) $750 billion.
   (d) $400 billion.

_____ 8. $1 \div (1 - MPC)$ multiplied by a new spending injection gives the:
   (a) _MPC_.
   (b) Multiplier.
   (c) Total change in income generated from the new spending.
   (d) First-round income that is gained from the new spending.

_____ 9. An _MPS_ of 0.10 means a $100 tax increase ultimately causes:
   (a) Spending to fall by $1000.
   (b) Spending to fall by $900.
   (c) Spending to rise by $90.
   (d) Spending to rise by $100.

_____ 10. Suppose the consumption function is $C=100+.5Y$. If the government stimulates the economy with $100 billion in increased income transfers, aggregate expenditure would rise ultimately by:
   (a) $50 billion.
   (b) $80 billion.
   (c) $200 billion.
   (d) $400 billion.

_____ 11. When the government tries to correct for an aggregate demand shortfall in the economy, it must take into account that:
   (a) The total change in spending equals the government's spending and the multiplier effects of that spending.
   (b) The desired stimulus should be set at the AD shortfall divided by the multiplier.
   (c) Prices will rise unless the AS curve is horizontal.
   (d) All of the above.

_____ 12. The desired fiscal stimulus that will eliminate an AD shortfall should equal the:
   (a)   Desired AD increase ÷ the multiplier.
   (b)   Desired tax cut × *MPC*.
   (c)   Desired income transfer × *MPC*.
   (d)   All of the above.

_____ 13. The desired tax cut necessary to close an AD shortfall is given by:
   (a)   Desired fiscal stimulus ÷ multiplier.
   (b)   Desired fiscal stimulus ÷ *MPC*.
   (c)   (Desired fiscal stimulus ÷ multiplier) ÷ *MPC*.
   (d)   Desired fiscal stimulus times MPC.

_____ 14. For the balanced-budget multiplier to equal 1, the budget:
   (a)   Need not be balanced, but the changes in taxes and spending must be equal.
   (b)   Must be balanced before the changes in taxes and spending take place.
   (c)   Must be balanced and the change in spending must equal the change in taxes.
   (d)   Must be balanced, but the changes in taxes and spending may be unequal amounts.

_____ 15. Which of the following is most powerful in shifting the aggregate demand curve?
   (a)   A increase in Social Security payments of $10 billion.
   (b)   A reduction in personal income taxes of $10 billion.
   (c)   An increase in defense spending of $10 billion.
   (d)   All of the changes above affect aggregate demand equally.

_____ 16. The initial, or first round, increase in consumption because of a tax cut is equal to:
   (a)   *MPC* x the amount of the tax cut.
   (b)   *MPC* x (multiplier x the amount of the tax cut).
   (c)   Amount of the tax cut/MPS.
   (d)   Multiplier x the amount of the tax cut.

_____ 17. If the desired fiscal restraint is $10 billion and the desired AD decrease is $100 billion, we can conclude that the desired tax:
   (a)   Increase is $11.11 billion.
   (b)   Increase is $10 billion.
   (c)   Cut is $11.11 billion.
   (d)   Cut is $10 billion.

_____ 18. Crowding out occurs when the government:
   (a)   Increases taxes, thus causing a decrease in consumption.
   (b)   Issues debt, thus making it more difficult for the private sector to issue debt.
   (c)   Prints money, which displaces currency.
   (d)   Does all of the above.

_____ 19. Which of the following are factors which may limit the effectiveness of fiscal policy in the real world?
   (a)   The crowding out effect.
   (b)   Time lags between the recognition of a macro problem and the implementation of corrective measures.
   (c)   Political considerations that could alter the content and timing of fiscal policy.
   (d)   All of the above are factors.

_____ 20. The federal government approves a new highway that injects $100 million of new spending into the economy during the first year of the project. *Ceteris paribus*, if the consumption function for this economy is given by the equation $C = 500 + 0.75Yd$, how much is the increase in spending for the second round of the multiplier process?
  (a) $400 million.
  (b) $100 million.
  (c) $75 million.
  (d) $56.25 million.

Problems and Applications

Exercise 1

This exercise shows how to use the aggregate demand and supply curves to analyze macro equilibrium, the AD shortfall, excess AD, and the GDP gap.

Table 11.1
Aggregate demand and supply*

Price Index (1)	Aggregate Supply (Qs) (2)	Aggregate Demand (Qd) Full Employment (3)	Aggregate Demand (Qd) AD1 (4)	Aggregate Demand (Qd) AD2 (5)
2.6	24	-	-	-
2.2	23	0	-	14
1.8	22	6	0	22
1.0	18	18	8	-
0.8	16	21	10	-
0.6	12	24	12	-
0.4	4	27	14	-

(* Quantity is measured in billions of units in columns 2 through 5.)

1. Use the first two columns in Table 11.1 to draw the aggregate supply curve for an economy in Figure 11.1. Then use columns 1 and 3 to draw the aggregate demand curve at full employment. Label the aggregate supply curve *AS* and the aggregate demand curve at full employment AD_F.

Figure 11.1
Aggregate demand and supply

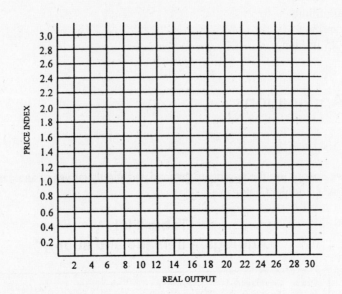

2. When macro equilibrium is achieved at full employment, the full-employment real output is
    _____. The corresponding full-employment price index is _____.

3. Now draw the aggregate demand curve corresponding to columns 1 and 4 labeling it AD_1. For
    this aggregate demand curve, the equilibrium real output is _____. The corresponding
    equilibrium price index is _____.

4. Assume the economy is on AD_1. In Figure 11.1 indicate the GDP gap, which is _____
    billion units of output, and the AD (excess, shortfall), which is _____ billion units of
    output.

5. Which of the following government policies could be used to shift AD to full employment?
    (a) The government increases taxes.
    (b) The government provides tax incentives to encourage more saving.
    (c) The government eliminates investment tax credits, which results effectively in higher
         taxes on investment goods.
    (d) A trade agreement is approved, which suddenly results in U.S. exports rising faster than
         imports.
    (e) Foreign governments place limits on imports from the U.S.
    (f) Government cuts back on its expenditures.

6. Now draw the aggregate demand curve corresponding to columns 1 and 5 labeling it AD_2. For
    this aggregate demand curve, the equilibrium real output is _____. The corresponding
    equilibrium average price index is _____.

7. Assume the economy is on AD_2. In Figure 11.1 indicate the GDP gap, which is _____ units
    of output, and the AD (excess, shortfall), which is _____ units of output.

8. Which of the following government policies could be used to shift AD to full employment?
   (a) The government lowers interest rates.
   (b) The government cuts taxes.
   (c) The government cuts its expenditures.
   (d) The government raises tariffs, which increases the cost of imports.
   (e) The government subsidizes exports to help domestic firms sell abroad.
   (f) The government eliminates IRAs and other instruments that encourage saving, which results in greater autonomous consumption.

Exercise 2

This exercise emphasizes the impact of various fiscal policies on total spending.

Assume the economy can be described by the consumption function: $C = \$400$ billion $+ 0.8Y$.

1. Calculate the cumulative change in total spending if the government increases purchases of goods and services by $100 million. _____

2. Calculate the cumulative change in total spending if the government reduces taxes by $100 million. _____

3. Calculate the cumulative change in total spending if the government increases transfer payments by $100 million. _____

4. The $100 million increase in government spending on goods and services had a (smaller, larger) impact on total spending than the $100 million decrease in taxes because there is a savings (leakage, injection) out of the tax change.

5. Calculate the cumulative change in total spending if the government increases purchases of goods and services by $100 million and at the same time increases taxes by $100 million to finance the spending. _____

6. The situation described in question 5 represents a _____ _____ expenditure.

Exercise 3

The media often provide information on multiplier effects in the economy. This exercise will use one of the articles in the text to show the kind of information to look for.

Reread the article "Economy Is Already Feeling the Impact of Federal Government's Spending Cuts" in the text. Then answer the following questions:

1. Which passages indicate the cause of the change in the economy? _____
   _____

2. The change in the economy is (more, less) of a/an (injection, leakage).

3. What statement indicates the estimated impact of the "belt tightening" on GDP? _____
   _____

4. What evidence of secondary changes in income are reported? _____
   _____

Exercise 4

This exercise shows how the multiplier works to eliminate a GDP gap.

Refer to Figure 11.2 to answer questions 1-4. Assume the MPC equals 0.90 and the current level of aggregate demand is equal to AD_1.

Figure 11.2

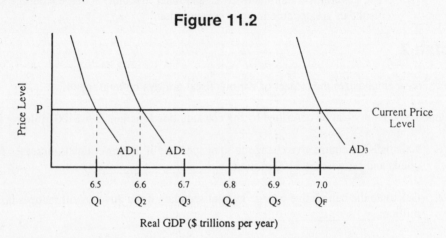

Real GDP ($ trillions per year)

1. What is the equilibrium level of real GDP if aggregate demand is equal to AD_1? _____

2. What is the full employment level of real GDP? _____

3. What is the size of the GDP gap? _____

4. What is the value of the multiplier? _____

5. An increase in government spending of $50 billion would cause consumption to increase by $ _____ billion in the second spending cycle.

6. An increase in government spending of $50 billion would cause a cumulative increase in aggregate demand equal to $ _____ billion and would result in an equilibrium real GDP equal to $ _____ trillion.

Common Errors

The first statement in each "common error" below is incorrect. Each incorrect statement is followed by a corrected version and an explanation.

1. Government deficits always lead to inflation. WRONG!

   Government deficits may result from government spending to reach full employment with price stability. RIGHT!

   You should focus on what is happening to aggregate supply and demand, not just deficits, when looking for the sources of inflation. By looking at the deficit, you cannot tell if there is adequate aggregate demand in the economy. If there is a shortfall in aggregate demand, government spending and resulting deficits may restore full employment with price stability! If there is an excess aggregate demand, demand-pull inflation can result from increased consumption, investment, or export expenditures, just as much as from increased government spending. It is all too easy to point the finger at the government and forget the contribution to inflation of all the other sectors of the economy.

2. If the government increases spending and taxes by the same amount, there will be no effect on income. WRONG!

Income increases by the amount of government spending, even if taxes are increased by the same amount. RIGHT!

The full impact of the increased government spending turns into income for the people who provide goods and services to the government. Part of the increased taxes, however, comes from people's savings, which had been leakages from the economy. So consumption decreases by less than the loss of taxes. This in turn means that income generated by consumption spending is not cut back by the amount of taxes. Therefore, the economy experiences a smaller cutback in incomes as a result of increased taxes than from stimulus from increased government spending.

•ANSWERS•

Using Key Terms

Across

2. fiscal restraint
5. fiscal policy
9. disposable income
10. aggregate demand
11. income transfer
12. equilibrium macro
13. real GDP gap

Down

1. marginal propensity to consume
2. fiscal stimulus
3. aggregate supply
4. crowding out
6. AD shortfall
7. multiplier
8. AD excess

True or False

1. F Fiscal policy works through shifts in the AD curve.
2. T
3. F If the AS curve is horizontal (i.e., flat), the GDP gap is equal to the AD shortfall (or excess).
4. F The effect of the multiplier must be taken into account even when AS is flat. In this case, government expenditures should be increased by an amount equal to the AD shortfall divided by the multiplier.
5. T
6. T
7. T
8. F Only government purchases of goods and services are part of AD. Government transfer payments are not part of AD because they do not represent a direct purchase of goods and services.
9. T
10. T

Multiple Choice

1. b	5. a	9. b	13. b	17. a
2. d	6. a	10. c	14. a	18. b
3. b	7. d	11. d	15. c	19. d
4. c	8. c	12. d	16. a	20. c

Problems and Applications

Exercise 1

1. See Figure 11.1 Answer, AS and AD_F.

Figure 11.1 Answer

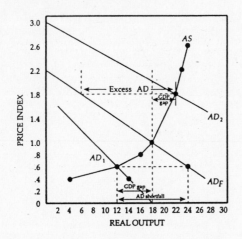

2. At full employment, the price index is 1.0 at an output of 18 units.
3. See Figure 11.1 Answer, AD_1. At AD_1, the price index is 0.6 at an output of 12 units.
4. See Figure 11.1 Answer. GDP gap = 6.0 units; AD shortfall = 12 units.
5. d   We are looking for more of an injection or less of a leakage, and we find higher United States exports, which is more of an injection.
6. See Figure 11.1 Answer, AD_2. At AD_2, the price index is 1.8 at an output of 22 units.
7. See Figure 11.1 Answer. GDP gap = -4.0 units; excess AD = 16 units.
8. c   We are looking for more of a leakage or less of an injection, and we find lower government expenditures, which is less of an injection.

Exercise 2

1. $500 million increase
2. $400 million increase [($100 million x 0.8) x multiplier = $80 million x 5]
3. $400 million increase
4. Larger, leakage
5. $100 million increase
6. Balanced budget

154

Exercise 3

1. "Skeptical about the federal government's pledge to tighten its belt?" and "Federal purchases of goods and services dropped 3.3% in 1992 . . . " tell us that *G* has been reduced.
2. Less, injection
3. ". . . cuts in purchases by the federal government knocked as much as 0.5 percentage point off the gross domestic product last year . . . "
4. 400,000 jobs were lost in 1992 and the same was expected for the next year.

Exercise 4

1. 6.5 trillion
2. 7.0 trillion
3. $7 trillion - $6.5 trillion = $500 billion
4. Multiplier = 1/(1-MPC) = 1/(1-0.9) = 10
5. $45 billion
6. 10 x $50 billion = $500 billion; $7.0 trillion

CHAPTER 12

Surpluses, Deficits, and Debt

Quick Review

- When the federal government's revenues fall short of its expenditures in any fiscal year, there is a budget deficit. The U.S. Treasury issues IOUs (e.g., Treasury bonds) and sells them to cover the difference. If revenues are greater than expenditures, there is a budget surplus.

- Policy makers distinguish between "cyclical deficits," which are related to economic conditions, and the "structural deficit," which is the deficit that would result if the economy were at full employment. The cyclical deficit widens automatically when unemployment increases or inflation subsides. The structural deficit measures the impact of fiscal policy.

- "Automatic stabilizers," such as unemployment compensation, *increase* as the economy weakens and decrease when the economy improves.

- When government purchases goods and services, the resources used to produce them are denied to the rest of society. Rates of investment and economic growth may both be reduced when government borrowing pushes interest rates up. This is called "crowding out."

- If you add up all of the Treasury's IOUs that are outstanding, the sum is the national debt. The national debt is a liability of the government, but it represents an asset to those who own it.

- Historically, the United States accrued debt during wars and recessions. Recessions (1980-82 and 1990-92) and massive tax cuts passed in the first Reagan administration pushed the total debt over $5 trillion.

- Most of the debt is owned "internally" by banks and other financial institutions, the Federal Reserve, and individuals. The interest payments redistribute income from taxpayers to bondholders and the opportunity costs are incurred when the debt financed activity occurs.

- Debt that is purchased and held by foreigners is called the external debt. It allows us to avoid opportunity costs presently. When foreign holdings of U.S. debt come due, payment on the debt means that dollars must flow out of the country. As a result, future generations will have less output to consume.

- The Gramm-Rudman-Hollings Act (1985), the Budget Enforcement Act of 1990, and the Republican party's Contract With America were all efforts to stop the continuation of budget deficits and the resulting debt.

Learning Objectives

After reading Chapter 12 and doing the following exercises, you should:

1. Understand the cause of budget deficits and the relationship between deficits and the national debt.
2. Be able to distinguish between discretionary spending and uncontrollables.
3. Be able to describe the operation and importance of automatic stabilizers.
4. Be able to distinguish cyclical deficits from structural deficits.
5. Understand the economic effects of deficits and be able to explain "crowding out."
6. Understand the history of the national debt and how it reached its present size.
7. Know who owns the debt, and understand the implications of internal and external ownership.
8. Understand the real burden of the debt.
9. Understand that the only way to stop the debt from growing is to eliminate budget deficits.
10. Be aware of attempts to address the deficit problem.

Using Key Terms

Fill in the puzzle on the opposite page with the appropriate term from the list of Key Terms at the end of the chapter in the text.

Across

1. Represented by the movement from point a to point b in Figure 12.2 in the text.
6. Tax increases or spending cuts designed to reduce aggregate demand.
10. A spending or revenue item that responds automatically and countercyclically to national income.
12. The twelve-month accounting period used by the federal government.
13. When the government borrows funds to pay for spending that exceeds tax revenues.
14. Promissory notes issued by the U.S. Treasury.
15. The amount by which government spending exceeds revenues.
17. The idea that in order to get more public-sector goods, some private-sector goods must be given up.
18. Equal to the total stock of all outstanding Treasury bonds.
20. Tax cuts or spending increases designed to shift aggregate demand to the right.
21. Equal to $69 billion for 1998 according to Table 12.1 in the text.
22. Equal to 20 percent of the national debt according to Figure 12.4 in the text.
23. The issuance of new bonds to replace the bonds that mature.
24. An explicit limit on the size of the annual budget deficit.
25. An explicit limit on the size of the national debt.

Down

2. Spending decisions not determined by past legislative commitments.
3. The most desirable combination of output given the available resources and technology.
4. U.S. Treasury bonds are an _____ for the people who own them.
5. Payments to individuals for which no current goods or services are exchanged.
7. The U.S. Treasury bonds are a _____ for the federal government.
8. The portion of the budget deficit that widens when unemployment or inflation increases.
9. Use of the government budget to stabilize the economy.
11. The portion of the budget deficit that reflects fiscal-policy decisions.
16. The U.S. government debt owned by U.S. households, institutions, and government agencies.
19. The interest required to be paid each year on outstanding debt.

Puzzle 12.1

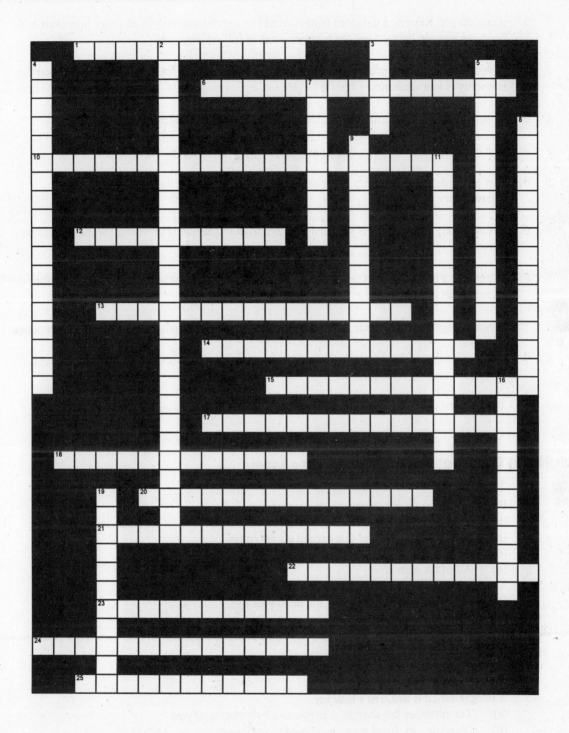

True or False: *Circle your choice and explain why any false statements are incorrect.*

T   F   1.   According to Keynes, a balanced budget would be appropriate only if all other injections and leakages were in balance and the economy was in full employment.

T   F   2.   Automatic stabilizers reduce government expenditures and decrease budget deficits when the economy is in a recession.

T   F   3.   Approximately 20 percent of the expenditures in the federal budget are "uncontrollable."

T   F   4.   The cyclical deficit narrows when unemployment or inflation increase.

T   F   5.   Part of the deficit arises from cyclical changes in the economy; the rest is the result of discretionary fiscal policy.

T   F   6.   Discretionary fiscal policy is stimulative if the structural deficit is shrinking (or the surplus is growing).

T   F   7.   In general, a budget surplus tends to change the mix of output in the direction of more public-sector goods and fewer private-sector goods.

T   F   8.   When foreigners help finance U.S. deficits, U.S. residents can consume more than they produce.

T   F   9.   The true burden of the debt is the reduction in national wealth when the federal government borrows money by selling bonds.

T   F   10.   The national debt is both an asset and a liability to future generations.

Multiple Choice: *Select the correct answer.*

_____   1.   Deficit spending results whenever the government:
(a)   Faces interest expense from government debt amassed from previous deficits.
(b)   Finances expenditures that exceed tax revenues.
(c)   Refinances the debt.
(d)   All of the above.

_____   2.   Deficit spending can be financed in the same year by:
(a)   Borrowing from foreign sources.
(b)   Borrowing from the banking system and the private sector.
(c)   U.S. Treasury bonds.
(d)   All of the above.

_____   3.   A budget deficit is incurred whenever:
(a)   Tax revenues fall short of expenditures over the fiscal year.
(b)   Discretionary fiscal spending is used to achieve macro equilibrium.
(c)   The U.S. Treasury engages in refinancing activities.
(d)   The government uses fiscal policy.

4. According to Keynes, it was acceptable for the budget to be unbalanced if:
   (a) The economy was below full employment.
   (b) Leakages and injections were out of balance.
   (c) The economy was above full employment.
   (d) All of the above.

5. Discretionary fiscal spending includes:
   (a) Income taxes.
   (b) Unemployment benefits.
   (c) A one-time expenditure for a highway.
   (d) Social Security payments.

6. Uncontrollable government spending includes:
   (a) Interest payments on the national debt.
   (b) Medicare benefits.
   (c) Pensions for retired government workers.
   (d) All of the above.

7. Automatic stabilizers tend to stabilize the level of economic activity because:
   (a) They are changed quickly by Congress.
   (b) They increase the size of the multiplier.
   (c) They increase spending during recessions and decrease spending during inflationary periods.
   (d) They control the rate of change in prices.

8. The major reason budget deficits were reduced during the 1990s and surpluses were experienced in 1998-2001 was:
   (a) President Clinton's deficit reduction policies.
   (b) The significant reductions in federal spending implemented by Congress.
   (c) Structural surpluses during the period.
   (d) The growing U.S. economy.

9. In contrast to the structural deficit, the cyclical deficit reflects:
   (a) Fluctuations in economic activity.
   (b) Fiscal-policy decisions.
   (c) Changes in discretionary fiscal policy.
   (d) Changes in the "full-employment" deficit.

10. The structural deficit represents:
    (a) Federal revenues minus federal expenditures at full employment under current fiscal policy.
    (b) Federal revenues minus federal expenditures under current fiscal policy at current output.
    (c) A measure of the size of recessionary or inflationary gaps.
    (d) The difference between expenditures at full employment and expenditures at cyclical unemployment.

11. The magnitude of a fiscal stimulus is measured by the:
    (a) Decrease in the structural deficit (or increase in the structural surplus).
    (b) Increase in the structural deficit (or decrease in the structural surplus).
    (c) Increase in the total budget deficit.
    (d) Increase in the cyclical deficit (or decrease in the cyclical surplus).

12. Crowding out occurs when the government:
    (a) Increases taxes, causing a decrease in consumption.
    (b) Prints money, which displaces currency.
    (c) Borrows, making it more difficult for the private sector to borrow.
    (d) Expenditures displace saving.

13. When the federal government runs a budget surplus, it is:
    (a) Providing a fiscal stimulus to the economy.
    (b) Adding a leakage to the circular flow.
    (c) Adding an injection to the circular flow.
    (d) Reducing leakages to the circular flow.

14. Which of the following uses of a budget surplus has the potential of increasing the private sector's proportion of output?
    (a) Cutting taxes.
    (b) Paying off a portion of the national debt.
    (c) Increasing transfer payments.
    (d) All of the above have the potential.

15. When the U.S. Treasury issues new bonds to replace bonds that have matured, it is engaging in:
    (a) Debt refinancing.
    (b) Debt servicing.
    (c) Income transfers.
    (d) Discretionary fiscal spending.

16. If all of the national debt were owned internally, then:
    (a) We would not have to worry about raising taxes to pay the interest on the debt.
    (b) We would still have to worry about the effect of interest payments on the distribution of income.
    (c) The federal government would have to stop refinancing the debt.
    (d) The Federal Reserve System would have no use for government debt.

17. Externally held U.S. debt results in:
    (a) A burden to the United States when newly issued bonds are sold to foreigners.
    (b) A burden to the United States when foreign-owned bonds are cashed in and proceeds are used to buy goods and services produced in the United States.
    (c) A burden incurred by foreigners when bonds are sold in the United States.
    (d) No burden to the United States.

18. A deficit ceiling limits:
    (a) The amount by which government spending can exceed government revenue.
    (b) The amount of the national debt.
    (c) The trade deficit.
    (d) Inflation.

19. Which of the following statements about the U.S. national debt is *not* correct?
    (a) The national debt represents both a liability and asset.
    (b) The primary burden of the debt is incurred when the deficit-financed activity takes place.
    (c) The primary economic costs of the debt are being passed on to future generations.
    (d) Future generations will bear some of the debt burden when it is externally financed.

20. Which of the following policies can the government use to pay for Social Security in the future?
    (a) An increase in income taxes.
    (b) A decrease in Social Security benefits.
    (c) A decrease in spending for other government programs.
    (d) All of the above.

Problems and Applications

Exercise 1

After doing this exercise you should understand the relationships among deficits, bonds, debt, and interest payments. You should see how continual deficits lead to larger and larger interest payments and larger and larger debt. Keep in mind that it is difficult to eliminate deficits when interest payments are an important factor contributing to the dcficits.

1. Suppose government expenditures for country XYZ in the year 2000 are $1 trillion and taxes are $800 billion. Compute the deficit and place the answer in column 1 of Table 12.1 for the year 2000.

Table 12.1
Deficits, bonds, debts, and interest payments for XYZ
(billions of dollars per year)

Year	(1) Deficit	(2) Newly issued bonds	(3) Total debt	(4) Interest payment
1999	$0	$0	$0	$0
2000				
2001				
2002				
2003				
2004				
2005				
2006				
2007				

2. To finance the deficit, the government must sell bonds of an equivalent amount to cover the revenue shortfall. What is the dollar amount necessary to finance the debt? Place the answer in column 2 of Table 12.1 for the year 2000.

3. Assume that up to 1999 the government had zero debt (as shown in the 1999 row of Table 12.1). What is the total debt after the government has borrowed to cover the deficit in the year 2000? Place the answer in column 3 of Table 12.1 for the year 2000.

4. What will be the interest payment on the total debt in the year 2000 if the interest rate is 10 percent per year? Place the answer in column 4 of Table 12.1 for the year 2000. Assume all bonds are sold January 1 with interest due December 31.

5. For the years 2001 through 2007, the government spends $1 trillion each year plus any interest payment on the previous years' debt and receives tax revenues of only $800 billion each year. The interest rate is still 10 percent per year. Fill in the rest of Table 12.1.

6. Graph and label the deficit (column 1 of Table 12.1) and interest payment (column 4) in Figure 12.1.

Figure 12.1

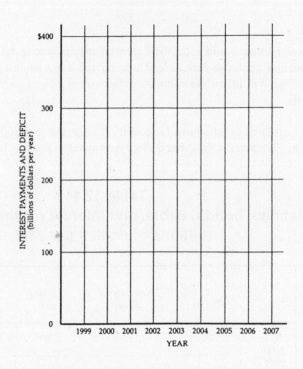

7. T F With continual deficits, interest payments on past deficits will become a bigger part of current deficits, *ceteris paribus*.

8. T F In this example, if both taxes and government expenditures increased at 5 percent per year as a result of bigger government, both the deficit and the debt would become smaller.

Exercise 2

This exercise focuses on the ratio of the national debt to GDP, which is an important measure of the burden of the debt.

Table 12.2 National debt and GDP
(billions of dollars per year)

Year	Country A			Country B		
	Debt	GDP	Debt/GDP	Debt	GDP	Debt/GDP
1999	$200	$1000	_____	$200	$1000	_____
2000	250	1250	_____	250	1150	_____
2001	280	1400	_____	280	1000	_____
2002	320	1600	_____	320	1000	_____
2003	400	2000	_____	400	1200	_____

1. Calculate the debt/GDP ratio for Country A and Country B in Table 12.2.

2. During the period from 1999 to 2003 both countries in Table 12.2 are experiencing (budget deficits, budget surpluses, a balanced budget) each year.

3. Even though the size of the debt is the same for the two countries in Table 12.2 for each year, the debt is likely to be a greater burden for Country _____ because the debt/GDP ratio is _____.

4. Given the information in Table 12.2, what is the most likely cause for the increase in the debt/GDP ratio from 2000 to 2001 for Country B? _____

5. The actual amount of debt increases each year for Country A in Table 12.2. The size of the debt/GDP ratio (increases, decreases, stays the same) because GDP (increases, decreases, stays the same) each year.

Exercise 3

This exercise explores the impact of government spending on private-sector spending.

Use Figure 12.2 to answer questions 1-6.

Figure 12.2

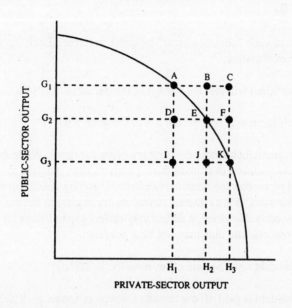

1. If all debt is held internally and the government finances additional spending by borrowing, then an increase in government purchases would move the economy from point K to point _____.

2. If the economy moves from point E to point A because of increased government spending, the amount of private sector spending crowded out is equal to the distance _____.

3. Assume the government has a budget surplus and uses it to reduce the accumulated debt. As a result interest rates (rise, fall) and the economy moves from point E to point _____.

4. The situation described in question 3 is referred to in the text as the _____ effect.

5. External financing of the debt allows the economy to move from point E to point _____.

6. In question 5, external financing allows public-sector goods to (increase, decrease, stay the same) while private-sector goods (increase, decrease, stay the same).

Exercise 4

Reports on fiscal policy typically involve changes in the deficit and the debt.

Reread the article titled "Fiscal Policy in the Great Depression" in the text.

1. President Hoover believed that the federal budget should always be (balanced, in deficit, in surplus).

2. What did President Hoover propose to resolve the problem with the federal budget?
   _____

3. From 1931 to 1933 the structural deficit _____. This fiscal restraint caused the _____ curve to shift to the (left, right).

4. What finally occurred that caused a huge increase in government spending, which ended the Great Depression? _____

Common Errors

The first statement in each "common error" below is incorrect. Each incorrect statement is followed by a corrected version and an explanation.

1. Our grandchildren will feel the burden of the deficit. WRONG!

   Our grandchildren may feel the burden of the debt. RIGHT!

   Deficit and debt are concepts that are often confused. While deficits occur because of the excess of expenditures over taxes during a given year, the debt can be calculated at any given point in time and represents the cumulative effect of running deficits over our entire history. It is the debt on which transfers such as interest payments are made, not the deficit. Such transfers may result in opportunity costs. However, a deficit may reflect expenditures on capital, which will benefit future generations and thus may not be a burden.

2. The national debt must be paid off eventually. WRONG!

   The national debt is paid off continually through refinancing. RIGHT!

   No Treasury bond has a maturity date more than thirty years in the future. Some bonds have maturity dates that come much sooner—in ten or twenty years. Treasury bills are sold at auction and have maturity dates of 360 days or less with 30-day intervals (i.e., 30, 60, 90, and so on). Suppose the federal government has balanced budgets for the next thirty years. The entire debt will have come due at some point. What will happen? It would be refinanced as it comes due and replaced with new debt.

3. There is nothing "behind" the national debt. WRONG!

   The federal government owns many physical assets and has the ability to tax. RIGHT!

   The proceeds of bond sales by the federal government are used to do many things, including the purchase of assets. Every item owned by the federal government—from the White House to

166

Old Faithful—is an asset that could be sold to help pay off the national debt. Stealth bombers, office buildings, computers, and the like, are all assets that were needed over the years and are as much an asset as the debt is a liability. By raising taxes, the government can at least theoretically run a surplus and pay off the debt.

•ANSWERS•

Using Key Terms

Across

1. crowding out
6. fiscal restraint
10. automatic stabilizers
12. fiscal year
13. deficit spending
14. treasury bonds
15. budget deficit
17. opportunity cost
18. national debt
20. fiscal stimulus
21. budget surplus
22. external debt
23. refinancing
24. deficit ceiling
25. debt ceiling

Down

2. discretionary fiscal spending
3. asset
4. optimal mix of output
5. income transfers
7. liability
8. cyclical deficit
9. fiscal policy
11. structural deficit
16. internal debt
19. debt service

True or False

1. T
2. F   As an economy falls into a recession, automatic stabilizers tend to increase government spending (and reduce tax receipts) thus making budget deficits larger.
3. F   Approximately 80 percent of the expenditures in the federal budget are uncontrollable.
4. F   The cyclical deficit widens when unemployment or inflation increases.
5. T
6. F   Such policies are restrictive.
7. F   Unless the government spends the surplus, the proportion of private goods and services produced will tend to increase.
8. T
9. F   The true burden of the national debt is the private goods and services that are forgone (i.e., crowded out) as a result of government borrowing.
10. T

Multiple Choice

1.	b	5.	c	9.	a	13.	b	17.	b
2.	d	6.	d	10.	a	14.	d	18.	a
3.	a	7.	c	11.	b	15.	a	19.	c
4.	d	8.	d	12.	c	16.	b	20.	d

Problems and Applications

Exercise 1

1-5. **Table 12.1 Answer**

Year	(1) Deficit	(2) Newly issued bonds	(3) Total debt	(4) Interest payment
2000	$200	$200	$ 200	$ 20 = (0.10 x 200)
2001	220	220	420 = (200 + 220)	42 = (0.10 x 420)
2002	242	242	662 = (420 + 242)	66 = (0.10 x 662)
2003	266	266	928 = (662 + 266)	93 = (0.10 x 928)
2004	293	293	1,221 = (928 + 293)	122 = (0.10 x 1,221)
2005	322	322	1,543 = (1,221 + 322)	154 = (0.10 x 1,543)
2006	354	354	1,897 = (1,543 + 354)	190 = (0.10 x 1,897)
2007	390	390	2,287 = (1,897 + 390)	229 = (0.10 x 2,287)

6. **Figure 12.1 Answer**

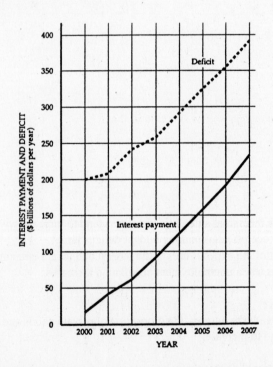

7. T Compare relative sizes of columns 1 and 4 in Table 12.1 Answer.
8. F

Exercise 2

1. **Table 12.2 Answer**

| | Country A | | | | Country B | | |
Year	Debt	GDP	Debt/GDP		Debt	GDP	Debt/GDP
1999	$200	$1000	0.20		$200	$1000	0.20
2000	250	1250	0.20		250	1150	0.22
2001	280	1400	0.20		280	1000	0.28
2002	320	1600	0.20		320	1000	0.32
2003	400	2000	0.20		400	1200	0.33

2. Budget deficits
3. B, greater
4. Recession
5. Stays the same, increases

Exercise 3

1. E
2. H_2-H_1
3. Fall, K
4. Crowding-in
5. B
6. Increase, stay the same

Exercise 4

1. Balanced
2. A decrease in government spending and an increase in taxes
3. Decreased, AD, left
4. World War II

CHAPTER 13

Money and Banks

Quick Review

- Money facilitates market exchanges and allows for specialization. It makes an economy more efficient than one that relies on barter. Anything that serves simultaneously as a medium of exchange, a store of value, and a standard of value can be thought of as money.

- The money supply (M1) is composed of transactions accounts, currency in circulation, and traveler's checks.

- The banking system can create money by making loans. When a bank decides to make a loan, it simply credits the transactions account of the borrower. Because transactions accounts are included in M1, this causes an increase in the money supply.

- In the United States, the Federal Reserve System requires banks to maintain some minimum ratio of bank reserves to total deposits. Any reserves above the required level are considered to be excess reserves. A bank may use its excess reserves to make new loans.

- As the new loans are spent, the dollars flow back into the banking system and additional loans are made. This process continues to occur over and over again and is known as *deposit creation*.

- The banking system as a whole can increase the volume of deposits by the amount of the excess reserves times the money multiplier. The money multiplier is equal to 1/required reserve ratio.

- Banks perform a strategic role in the economy by transferring money from savers to spenders and by creating additional money through lending. An increase in the money supply, because of deposit creation, leads to an increase in aggregate demand. A reduction in the money supply leads to a decrease in aggregate demand.

- Deposit creation is constrained by the willingness of market participants to use and accept checks. It is also constrained by the willingness of businesses and individuals to borrow, and the willingness of banks to make loans. Regulations of the Federal Reserve System also limit deposit creation.

Learning Objectives

After reading Chapter 13 and doing the following exercises, you should:

1. Know the basic history of money and the functions of money.
2. Be familiar with the composition and various measures of the money supply (*M*1, *M*2, etc.).
3. Know how banks create money by making loans.
4. Know the function of the reserve requirement.
5. Be able to calculate required and excess reserves.
6. Be able to work through the steps of deposit creation using balance sheets (T-accounts).
7. Be able to calculate and explain the money multiplier.
8. Know the banking system's role in the circular flow of economic activity.
9. Know the constraints on deposit creation.

Using Key Terms

Fill in the puzzle on the opposite page with the appropriate term from the list of Key Terms at the end of the chapter in the text.

Across

1. Assets held by a bank to fulfill its deposit obligations.
5. Total reserves minus required reserves.
7. An account that allows direct payment to a third party.
9. Represent a leakage from the flow of money because they cannot be used to make loans.
10. The reciprocal of the required reserve ratio.

Down

2. Tends to increase with an increase in the money supply because new loans are used to purchase additional goods and services.
3. The process by which bank lending causes the money supply to increase.
4. The system of exchange in Russia described in the article in the text titled "The Cashless Society."
6. Equal to $1,189 billion according to Figure 13.1 in the text.
8. Equal to 0.20 in Table 13.4 in the text.
10. Throughout history gold coins, tobacco, and bullets have functioned in this role.

Puzzle 13.1

True or False: *Circle your choice and explain why any false statements are incorrect.*

T   F   1.   The terms "transactions-account balances" and "checking accounts" mean the same thing.

T   F   2.   Credit cards are a form of money because they are used to facilitate exchanges.

T   F   3.   When you get a loan at a bank, the bank creates money.

T   F   4.   The withdrawal of money from a checking account causes the money supply to get smaller.

T   F   5.   The minimum-reserve ratio is established by the Federal Reserve System.

T   F   6.   The higher the legal minimum-reserve ratio, the greater the lending power of the banks.

T   F   7.   If the minimum-reserve ratio is 20 percent, then $1 of reserves can support $5 in transactions-account balances.

T   F   8.   The amount any one bank can lend is equal to its total reserves.

T   F   9.   A bank transfers money from savers to spenders by lending a fraction of the deposits it holds.

T   F   10.   If people stop using checks and instead switch to cash, banks will not be able to acquire or maintain reserves and the lending activity will cease.

Multiple Choice: *Select the correct answer.*

_____   1.   Money is anything:
    (a)   That can be used to barter.
    (b)   That a government declares to have value.
    (c)   That has value.
    (d)   Generally accepted as a medium of exchange.

_____   2.   Which of the following is a necessary characteristic of money?
    (a)   It serves as a medium of exchange.
    (b)   Its value must be supported by government reserves of gold and silver.
    (c)   The government declares it to have value.
    (d)   All of the above are necessary characteristics.

_____   3.   Barter:
    (a)   Facilitates specialization in production.
    (b)   Is most efficient for an economy.
    (c)   Is the direct exchange of one good or service for another.
    (d)   All of the above are correct.

_____   4.   The different components of the money supply reflect:
    (a)   Variations in liquidity and accessibility of assets.
    (b)   Whether deposits are domestic or international.
    (c)   How often depositors use their accounts.
    (d)   All of the above.

5. *M*1 refers to:
   (a) One component of the money supply.
   (b) Currency held by the public plus transactions-account balances.
   (c) The smallest of the money-supply aggregates watched by the Fed.
   (d) All of the above.

6. Which of the following appears in *M*2 but not in *M*1?
   (a) Credit-union share drafts.
   (b) Treasury bills.
   (c) Saving account balances.
   (d) U.S. savings bonds.

7. Immediately after cash is deposited into a bank, the composition of the money supply:
   (a) And the size of the money supply both change.
   (b) Changes, but the size of the money supply remains the same.
   (c) Remains the same, but the size of the money changes.
   (d) And the size of the money supply both remain the same.

8. Suppose the total amount of transactions accounts on the books of all of the banks in the system is $1 million and the minimum-reserve ratio is 0.20. The amount of required reserves for the banking system is, then:
   (a) $20,000,000.
   (b) $500,000.
   (c) $200,000.
   (d) $800,000.

9. When the reserve requirement changes, which of the following will change for an individual bank?
   (a) Transactions-account balances, lending capacity.
   (b) Transactions-account balances, total reserves, excess reserves.
   (c) Total reserves, required reserves, excess reserves.
   (d) Required reserves, excess reserves, lending capacity.

10. Banks are required to keep a minimum amount of funds in reserve because:
    (a) Depositors may decide to withdraw funds.
    (b) It provides a constraint on the bank's ability to create money.
    (c) It provides a constraint on the bank's ability to affect aggregate demand.
    (d) All of the above are correct.

11. Suppose a bank has $4 million in deposits, a required reserve ratio of 25 percent, and reserves of $1 million. Then it has excess reserves of:
    (a) $10,000.
    (b) $0.
    (c) $400,000.
    (d) $1,600,000.

12. Suppose a bank has $100,000 in deposits, a required reserve ratio of 5 percent, and bank reserves of $25,000. Then it can make new loans in the amount of:
    (a) $20,000.
    (b) $5,000.
    (c) $2,500.
    (d) $25,000.

13. A higher reserve requirement:
    (a) Further limits deposit creation.
    (b) Increases the ability of banks to make loans.
    (c) Lowers the interest rate.
    (d) Increases the borrowing capability of borrowers.

14. If people never withdrew cash from banks and there was no reserve requirement, how much money could the banking system potentially create for a given amount of new deposits?
    (a) Zero.
    (b) The same amount as the new deposits.
    (c) The amount of new deposits multiplied by the reserve ratio.
    (d) An infinite amount of money.

15. If the minimum-reserve ratio is 10 percent, the money multiplier is:
    (a) 9.
    (b) 10.
    (c) 0.10.
    (d) 1.10.

16. Suppose a banking system has $100,000 in deposits, a required reserve ratio of 15 percent, and total bank reserves for the whole system of $25,000. Then the whole system can potentially make new loans in the amount of:
    (a) $10,000.
    (b) $15,000.
    (c) $66,667.
    (d) $166,667.

17. The main goal of banks is to:
    (a) Earn a profit.
    (b) Create money.
    (c) Lend all of its deposits.
    (d) Minimize its reserve ratio.

18. Which of the following are constraints on the deposit-creation process of the banking system?
    (a) The willingness of consumers and businesses to continue using and accepting checks rather than cash.
    (b) The willingness of consumers, businesses, and government to borrow money.
    (c) The reserve requirement.
    (d) All of the above.

19. Deposit insurance:
    (a) Lowers the bankruptcy rate for banks.
    (b) Lowers the number and magnitude of bank runs.
    (c) Must be subsidized and run by the government in order to have credibility.
    (d) All of the above.

20. Which of the following could cause the money supply to decrease?
    (a) An increase in depositor confidence in the banking system.
    (b) An increase in the amount of borrowing by businesses and individuals.
    (c) A decrease in lending activity by banks.
    (d) Rapid growth on the part of the economy.

Problems and Applications

Exercise 1

Use the information from the Balance Sheet in Table 13.1 to answer questions 1–5.

Table 13.1 Bank of Arlington

Assets		Liabilities	
Required reserves	$200,000	Transactions accounts	$1,000,000
Other assets	800,000		
Total	$1,000,000	Total	$1,000,000

1. Suppose that the Bank of Arlington is just meeting its reserve requirement. The reserve ratio must be _____, and the money multiplier must be _____.

2. To be in a position to make loans, the Bank of Arlington must acquire some _____ (required reserves, excess reserves).

3. If we assume that the reserve ratio is changed to 15 percent, the Bank of Arlington would have required reserves of _____ and excess reserves of _____.

4. With a 15 percent reserve ratio the Bank of Arlington is in a position to make new loans totaling _____.

5. With a 15 percent reserve ratio, the entire banking system can increase the volume of loans by _____.

Exercise 2

This exercise shows how the multiplier process works.

Assume that all banks in the system lend all of their excess reserves, that the reserve ratio for all banks is 0.25, and that all loans are returned to the banking system in the form of transactions deposits. Use the information from the Balance Sheets in Table 13.2, Table 13.3, Table 13.4, and Table 13.5 to answer questions 1–6.

Table 13.2 Bank A - Initial Balance Sheet

Assets		Liabilities	
Required reserves	$25,000	Transactions accounts	$100,000
Excess reserves	0		
Other assets	75,000		
Total	$100,000	Total	$100,000

177

1. Bob takes $10,000 out of his cookie jar and deposits it in a transactions account in Bank A. Fill in the blanks in Bank A's balance sheet in Table 13.3 after the deposit. (Remember that some of the deposit will show up in required reserves and the remainder will become part of excess reserves.)

Table 13.3 Bank A - Balance Sheet After Bill's Deposit

Assets		Liabilities	
Required reserves	$_____	Transactions accounts	$_____
Excess reserves	_____		
Other assets	75,000		
Total	$_____	Total	$_____

Now assume that Bank A lends all of its excess reserves to Maria, who spends the money on a car. The car dealership deposits the money in its transactions account in Bank B. Bank B's initial balance sheet is the same as Bank A's initial balance sheet.

2. Fill in the blanks in Bank B's balance sheet after the car dealership makes its deposit.

Table 13.4 Bank B - Balance Sheet After Car Dealership's Deposit

Assets		Liabilities	
Required reserves	$_____	Transactions accounts	$_____
Excess reserves	_____		
Other assets	75,000		
Total	$_____	Total	$_____

Now assume Bank B lends all of its excess reserves to Mike, who spends the money on college tuition. The university deposits the money in Bank C. Bank C's initial balance sheet is the same as Bank A's initial balance sheet.

3. Fill in the blanks in Bank C's balance sheet after the university makes its deposit.

Table 13.5 Bank C - Balance Sheet After University's Deposit

Assets		Liabilities	
Required reserves	$_____	Transactions accounts	$_____
Excess reserves	_____		
Other assets	75,000		
Total	$_____	Total	$_____

4. Add together the loans made by each bank because of the initial $10,000 deposit made by Bob.

Bank A lent $_____
Bank B lent $_____
Bank C lent $_____

Total loans made so far $_____

5. The money multiplier for this exercise equals _____.

6. The potential deposit creation for the banking system in this exercise is _____.

Exercise 3

Reread the article "The Cashless Society" in the text. Use the article to answer the following questions.

1. Which form of money ($M1$, $M2$,... etc.) is most affected according to the article? _____

2. According to the article, the ruble is no longer accepted as payment for goods and services. In this situation, which of the functions of money is the ruble not performing? _____
_____

3. Because the ruble has lost its value, people are using _____ to acquire goods and services.

4. Which passage indicates the impact on the Russian economy as a result of barter? _____
_____

Exercise 4

This exercise focuses on the reserve requirement and its impact on the money supply.

1. Given the following reserve ratios, calculate the money multiplier for each.

   a. Reserve ratio = 10 percent   Money multiplier = _____
   b. Reserve ratio = 15 percent   Money multiplier = _____
   c. Reserve ratio = 20 percent   Money multiplier = _____

2. As the reserve ratio increases, the money multiplier (increases, decreases).

3. As the money multiplier decreases, potential deposit creation (increases, decreases).

4. T   F   An increase in the reserve ratio functions as a constraint on the deposit creation of the banking system.

Common Errors

The first statement in each "common error" below is incorrect. Each incorrect statement is followed by a corrected version and an explanation.

1. Banks can't create money. WRONG!

   Banks can and do create money. RIGHT!

   It should be obvious by now that banks and other depository institutions are very important participants in the money-supply process. They create money by granting loans to borrowers and accomplish their role by adding to their customers' transactions accounts. The accounts are money just as much as the coins and currency in your wallet are money. The banks create (supply) money, but only in response to borrowers' demands for it. Without customers demanding loans, banks wouldn't be able to create money at all.

2. Banks hold your deposits in their vaults. WRONG!

Banks don't hold your deposits in their vaults. (And neither do other depository institutions.) RIGHT!

You can look at this two ways. First, when you deposit your paycheck, there's nothing for the bank to "hold" in its vault, except the check, and that is returned to the person who wrote it. Second, if you deposited coin or cash, it's all put together and you can't distinguish any one person's deposit from any other person's deposit. Even then, when "cash in vault" becomes too large, much of it is shipped away by armored truck to the Federal Reserve Bank. (This is described in Chapter 14.) Thus, banks don't hold your deposits in their vaults.

3. Gold and silver are intrinsically valuable and are necessary to secure the value of a currency. WRONG!

Money can serve as a store of value, a standard of value, and a medium of exchange without being backed by gold and silver. RIGHT!

While precious metals such as gold and silver have frequently been used to back currencies, they do not back the dollar today. Like other commodities, their value in terms of dollars continually fluctuates in response to supply and demand conditions. International monetary authorities have attempted to "demonetize" the precious metals and have been successful in holding the price of these metals down in terms of the major currencies. Nevertheless, during periods of calamity and fear, these precious metals are hoarded because people believe these items have intrinsic value; they then do take the role of a store of value.

4. Banks are irresponsible if they fail to store all of the money that is deposited with them so that it is available on demand. WRONG!

Banks must lend most of the money that is deposited with them so that they can earn interest and pay interest on those deposits. RIGHT!

If banks allowed money just to sit in the vault, no productive use could be made of the money. Banks are useful as the intermediary between savers, who have the money, and spenders, who wish to borrow the money. Through their lending activity, banks promote efficiency. That means the money is not sitting idle in the bank's vault.

•ANSWERS•

Using Key Terms

Across

1. bank reserves
5. excess reserves
7. transactions account
9. required reserves
10. money multiplier

Down

2. aggregate demand
3. deposit creation
4. barter
6. money supply
8. reserve ratio
10. money

True or False

1. F   Transactions accounts permit direct payment to a third party by check or debit card. In addition to traditional checking accounts, NOW accounts, ATS accounts, credit union share drafts, and demand deposits at mutual savings banks also serve this purpose.
2. F   Credit cards are a payment service, not a final form of payment, i.e., credit card balances must be paid by cash or check.
3. T
4. F   The single action of withdrawal simply changes the composition of the money supply from, for example, a transactions account balance to cash. However, the banking system now has less money to lend out and the potential exists for a reduction in the money supply.
5. T
6. F   The higher the reserve ratio, the lower the lending power of the banks.
7. T
8. F   The amount any one bank can lend is equal to its excess reserves.
9. T
10. T

Multiple Choice

1.	d	5.	d	9.	d	13.	a	17.	a
2.	a	6.	c	10.	d	14.	d	18.	d
3.	c	7.	b	11.	b	15.	b	19.	b
4.	a	8.	c	12.	a	16.	c	20.	c

Problems and Applications

Exercise 1

1. 0.20; 5
2. Excess reserves
3. $150,000; $50,000
4. $50,000
5. $333,333.33

Exercise 2

1. Table 13.3 Answer

Assets		Liabilities	
Required reserves	$27,500	Transactions accounts	$110,000
Excess reserves	7,500		
Other assets	75,000		
Total	$110,000	Total	$110,000

2. Table 13.4 Answer

Assets		Liabilities	
Required reserves	$26,875	Transactions accounts	$107,500
Excess reserves	5,625		
Other assets	75,000		
Total	$107,500	Total	$107,500

3. Table 13.5 Answer

Assets		Liabilities	
Required reserves	$26,406.25	Transactions accounts	$105,625.00
Excess reserves	4,218.75		
Other assets	75,000.00		
Total	$105,625.00	Total	$105,625.00

4. Bank A lent $7,500.00
   Bank B lent $5,625.00
   Bank C lent $4,218.75
   Total loans made so far $17,343.75
5. 1/reserve ratio = 1/0.25 = 4
6. Potential deposit creation = initial excess reserves x money multiplier = $7,500 x 4 = $30,000

Exercise 3

1. $M1$
2. Medium of exchange
3. Barter
4. "Barter is poisoning the development of capitalism . . . because it consumes huge amounts of time that would be better spent producing goods."

Exercise 4

1. a. 10
   b. 6.67
   c. 5
2. Decreases
3. Decreases
4. T

CHAPTER 14

The Federal Reserve System

Quick Review

- The Federal Reserve System (Fed) controls the money supply by limiting the amount of loans that the banking system can provide from any given level of reserves, and it also controls the amount of reserves in the system.

- The Federal Reserve System is composed of twelve regional banks located across the country. The regional banks provide the following services for the private banks in their region: check clearing, holding bank reserves, providing currency, and providing loans to the private banks.

- The Board of Governors of the Federal Reserve System is the key decision-maker in setting monetary policy. Board members are appointed by the president of the United States for fourteen-year terms. The Federal Open Market Committee (FOMC) directs Fed transactions in the bond market.

- There are three primary levers of monetary policy: reserve requirements, discount rates, and open-market operations. Changing the reserve requirement changes both the money multiplier and the level of excess reserves in the banking system. It is the least frequently used tool.

- The process in which the Fed lends money to private banks is known as "discounting." Changing the discount rate makes it more or less attractive for private banks to borrow from the Fed.

- The principal monetary policy tool is open-market operations, which involves the buying or selling of U.S. government bonds in the open market by the Fed. When the Fed buys or sells bonds, this changes the price of bonds and their yields.

- If the Fed buys bonds, there is an increase in bank reserves and the lending capacity for the banking system increases. If the Fed sells bonds, there is a decrease in bank reserves and the lending capacity decreases.

- In order to increase the money supply the Fed can decrease the reserve requirement, decrease the discount rate, or buy bonds. To decrease the money supply the Fed can do just the opposite.

- Congress passed legislation in 1980 to give the Fed greater control of the money supply, but the rise in foreign institutions and nonbank financial entities has made it more difficult for the Fed to control the money supply.

Learning Objectives

After reading Chapter 14 and doing the following exercises, you should:

1. Be familiar with the organization, structure, and functions of the Federal Reserve System.
2. Know that the Fed can use the reserve requirement as one of its tools to change the money supply.
3. Know what the money multiplier is and how it is used.
4. Know that the discount rate can be used by the Fed to change the money supply.
5. Know the significance of the federal funds rate and the Federal Funds Market.
6. Understand how the Open Market Committee can achieve a given policy objective by buying or selling securities.
7. Understand how the Fed can change the price of a bond and its yield.
8. Be able to demonstrate the inverse relationship between interest rates and bond prices.
9. Know the background and provisions of the Monetary Control Act of 1980 and recent changes in the structure of the financial system.

Using Key Terms

Fill in the puzzle on the opposite page with the appropriate term from the list of Key Terms at the end of the chapter in the text.

Across

5. The interest rate one bank charges another bank when lending reserves.
6. Equal to total reserves minus required reserves.
8. The interest rate the Fed charges a bank when lending reserves.
10. Represent a leakage from the flow of money because they cannot be used to make loans.
12. The choice of where to place idle funds.

Down

1. The reciprocal of the required reserve ratio.
2. The use of money and credit controls to influence the macroeconomy.
3. The purchase and sale of government securities by the Fed in order to change bank reserves.
4. The annual interest payment divided by the bond's purchase price.
7. Controlled by the Fed through the use of the reserve requirement, the discount rate, and open market operations.
9. Refers to the Fed lending reserves to private banks.
11. A certificate acknowledging a debt and terms for repayment.

Puzzle 14.1

True or False: *Circle your choice and explain why any false statements are incorrect.*

T   F   1.   The Federal Reserve banks hold deposits of banks and other business firms.

T   F   2.   The Board of Governors is responsible for setting monetary policy.

T   F   3.   The Fed is not one bank but is actually twelve regional banks with central control located in Washington D.C.

T   F   4.   The fourteen-year terms for the Board of Governors give the Fed a measure of political independence.

T   F   5.   Monetary policy is the use of money and government spending to influence macroeconomic activity.

T   F   6.   If the Fed wishes to create the conditions under which the money supply can be increased, it can increase the reserve requirement.

T   F   7.   When the Fed buys bonds from the public, it increases the flow of reserves into the banking system.

T   F   8.   The FOMC implements monetary policy by adjusting reserve requirements and discount rates.

T   F   9.   Open-market operations are the principal mechanism for altering the reserves of the banking system.

T   F   10.   To increase the lending capacity of banks, the Fed sells securities.

Multiple Choice: *Select the correct answer.*

_____   1.   Suppose that Brian receives a check for $100 from a bank in Atlanta. He deposits the check in his account at his Baltimore bank. Brian's Baltimore bank will collect the $100 from the:
   (a)   Atlanta bank.
   (b)   Baltimore bank's regional Federal Reserve Bank.
   (c)   The central Federal Reserve Bank in Washington.
   (d)   Board of Governors.

_____   2.   Which of the following is a service performed by the Federal Reserve banks?
   (a)   Clearing checks between commercial banks.
   (b)   Holding reserves of commercial banks.
   (c)   Providing currency to commercial banks.
   (d)   All of the above.

_____   3.   The formulation of general Federal Reserve policy is the responsibility of the:
   (a)   Federal Open Market Committee.
   (b)   Federal Advisory Council.
   (c)   Board of Governors.
   (d)   Regional Federal Reserve banks.

_____ 4. Members of the Federal Reserve Board of Governors:
  (a) Are appointed to fourteen-year terms by the president of the United States.
  (b) Are relatively immune to short-term political pressures.
  (c) May not be reappointed after serving a full term.
  (d) All of the above are true.

_____ 5. Which of the following is responsible for buying and selling government securities to influence reserves in the banking system?
  (a) The Board of Governors.
  (b) The twelve regional Federal Reserve Banks.
  (c) The Federal Open Market Committee.
  (d) The Executive Branch of the government.

_____ 6. Which of the following is *not* one of the tools of monetary policy used by the Fed?
  (a) Expulsion from Fed membership.
  (b) Changing the reserve requirement.
  (c) Changing the discount rate.
  (d) Performing open-market operations.

_____ 7. When the Fed wishes to increase the excess reserves of the member banks, it:
  (a) Raises the discount rate.
  (b) Buys securities.
  (c) Raises the reserve requirement.
  (d) Sells securities.

_____ 8. The reserve requirement is:
  (a) A powerful tool that can cause abrupt changes in the money supply.
  (b) The most often used tool on the part of the Fed.
  (c) A tool that has little impact on the money supply.
  (d) Effective in changing excess reserves but not the money multiplier.

_____ 9. Which of the following can be used by a bank to increase reserves?
  (a) Selling securities.
  (b) Borrowing from the discount window.
  (c) Borrowing in the Fed funds market.
  (d) All of the above.

_____ 10. The federal funds market is a market in which:
  (a) Banks lend excess reserves to other banks.
  (b) Government securities are bought and sold.
  (c) Reserves are discounted outside the Fed's control.
  (d) The Fed lends to member banks.

_____ 11. Discounting refers to the Fed's practice of:
  (a) Selling securities at the federal funds rate.
  (b) Lending reserves to private banks.
  (c) Lending at the prime rate.
  (d) Purchasing securities at the lowest available federal funds rate.

_____ 12. The most frequently used tool on the part of the Fed is:
  (a) The reserve requirement.
  (b) The discount rate.
  (c) Open-market operations.
  (d) The Fed funds rate.

13. Suppose that the Fed desires to sell more bonds than people are willing to purchase. The most likely result of this situation would be a:
    (a) Decrease in the price of bonds.
    (b) Switch to another type of monetary policy lever by the Fed.
    (c) Switch to fiscal policy.
    (d) Purchase of the unsold bonds by the Fed.

14. When the Fed buys bonds from the public:
    (a) It decreases the flow of reserves to the banking system.
    (b) It increases the flow of reserves to the banking system.
    (c) It decreases the money supply.
    (d) It decreases the discount rate.

15. If the Fed buys bonds from the public, which of the following changes are likely to occur?
    (a) The public's holdings of bonds would decrease.
    (b) M1 would increase.
    (c) Excess reserves would increase.
    (d) All of the above would occur.

16. The Fed can increase the Federal Funds rate by:
    (a) Selling bonds.
    (b) Buying bonds.
    (c) Simply announcing a lower rate since the Fed has direct control of this interest rate.
    (d) Changing the money multiplier.

17. In recent years the Fed has shifted away from:
    (a) Money-supply targets to interest rate targets.
    (b) Interest rate targets to money-supply targets.
    (c) Using fiscal policy.
    (d) Using monetary policy.

18. An increase in the discount rate:
    (a) Reduces the cost of reserves borrowed from the Fed.
    (b) Signals the Fed's desire to restrain money growth.
    (c) Signals the Fed's desire to support credit creation.
    (d) Signals the Fed's eagerness to lend additional reserves.

19. Assuming a reserve requirement of 25 percent, if the Fed sells $10 billion of bonds in the open market, the lending capacity of the banking system will eventually:
    (a) Increase by $2.5 billion.
    (b) Decrease by $2.5 billion.
    (c) Increase by $40 billion.
    (d) Decrease by $40 billion.

20. Which of the following has contributed to the reduction in Fed control of the money supply?
    (a) A network of international money clearinghouses.
    (b) The fact that approximately two-thirds of the U.S. dollars in circulation are held abroad.
    (c) International credit cards.
    (d) All of the above.

Problems and Applications

The first three exercises demonstrate how monetary policy might work in a hypothetical situation.

Exercise 1

This exercise is similar to a problem in the text, which shows how to understand the accounts for the entire banking system. The focus of this exercise is the reserve requirement.

Suppose the Fed wishes to expand $M1$. Carefully read the assumptions below and then work through the exercise step-by-step to achieve the policy objective. Assume:

- The banks in the system have initially $300 million of transactions account liabilities.
- The banking system initially has no excess reserves.
- The initial reserve requirement is 0.20.
- The banks make loans in the full amount of any excess reserves that they acquire.
- All loans flow back into the banking system as transactions accounts.

The combined balance sheet of the banks in the system is as shown in Table 14.1.

Table 14.1
Balance sheet of banking system when reserve requirement is 0.20
(millions of dollars)

Assets		Liabilities	
Total reserves	$ 60	Transactions accounts	$300
Required $60			
Excess $0			
Securities	100		
Loans	140		
Total	$300	Total	$300

1. Suppose the Fed lowers the reserve requirement to 0.10. How many dollars of excess reserves does this create? $ _____.

2. How large are required reserves now? $ _____.

3. How large are total reserves now? $ _____.

4. What is the additional lending capacity of the banking system due to the change in the reserve requirement from 0.20 to 0.10? $ _____.

5. Reconstruct the balance sheet in Table 14.2 to show the new totals for the accounts affected in the banking system because of the loans generated in question 4 above.

Table 14.2
Balance sheet of banking system when reserve requirement is 0.10
(millions of dollars)

Assets		Liabilities	
Total reserves	$_____	Transactions accounts	$_____
Required _____			
Excess _____			
Securities	_____		
Loans	_____		
Total	$_____	Total	$_____

6. The money supply (M1) has expanded by $ _____.

7. Total reserves have increased by $ _____.

8. Loans have increased by $ _____.

Exercise 2

This exercise shows how the money supply can be changed. The focus of this exercise is open-market policy.

Suppose the banking system faces the balance sheet given in Table 14.3 and suppose further that:

- The banking system initially has no excess reserves.
- The reserve requirement is 0.25.
- The banks make loans in the full amount of any excess reserves that they acquire.
- All loans flow back into the banking system as transactions accounts.

Table 14.3
Balance sheet of banking system (millions of dollars)

Assets		Liabilities	
Total reserves	$ 75	Transactions accounts	$300
Required $75			
Excess $0			
Securities	100		
Loans	125		
Total	$300	Total	$300

1. Suppose the Fed Open Market Committee buys $10 million of securities from the commercial banking system. This action causes excess reserves to increase by $ _____.

2. Complete the balance sheet in Table 14.4 after loans have been made. Assume the banking system expands its loans and transactions accounts by the maximum amount. (Remember: The reserve ratio is 0.25.)

Table 14.4
Balance sheet of banking system after expansion of loans and deposits
(millions of dollars)

Assets		Liabilities	
Total reserves	$_____	Transactions accounts	$_____
Required _____			
Excess _____			
Securities	_____		
Loans	_____		
Total	$_____	Total	$_____

3. As a result of the open-market operations, the money supply has expanded by a total of
$ _____.

4. Total reserves have increased by $ _____.

5. Loans have increased by $ _____.

Exercise 3

This exercise demonstrates what might happen when the Fed lowers the discount rate.

Suppose the Fed wants to expand the money supply by changing the discount rate. It is faced with the balance sheet of the banking system as shown in Table 14.5. Carefully read the assumptions below and then work through the exercise step-by-step to achieve the policy objective. Assume that:

- The banking system initially has no excess reserves.
- The initial reserve requirement is 0.20.
- The banks in the system respond to each percentage point drop in the discount rate by borrowing $2 million from the Fed.
- The banks make loans in the full amount of any excess reserves that they acquire.
- All loans flow back into the banking system as transactions deposits.

Table 14.5
Balance sheet of banking system (millions of dollars)

Assets		Liabilities	
Total reserves	$ 70	Transactions accounts	$350
Required $75			
Excess $0			
Securities	70		
Loans	210		
Total	$350	Total	$350

1. Suppose the Fed lowers the discount rate by 1 percentage point and that the banking system responds as indicated in the assumption above. As a result of this policy initiative, the banks in the system will now borrow _____ from the Fed, all of which is (excess/required) reserves. On the basis of this lending potential, the banks together can expand their loans by _____ .

2. In Table 14.6, assume the banks have made the additional loans. Complete the balance sheet to show the final effect of the change in the discount rate.

Table 14.6
Final balance sheet of banking system (millions of dollars)

Assets		Liabilities	
Total reserves	\$_____	Transactions accounts	\$_____
Required _____			
Excess _____			
Securities	_____		
Loans	_____	Borrowed from the Fed	\$_____
Total	\$_____	Total	\$_____

3. The effect of lowering the discount rate is an increase in the money supply of _____ .

Exercise 4

In order to understand how open-market operations work, it is important to understand how the bond market works. The following exercise will demonstrate how the Fed can make bonds more or less attractive for people to buy.

1. Assume you purchase a bond for $1000. The face value of the bond is $1000 and the bond pays 10 percent interest annually. What is the dollar amount of the annual interest payment? _____

2. What is the yield on the bond? (*Hint*: Refer to the formula on page 280 in the text.) _____

3. Now assume that instead of paying $1000 for the bond, you buy the same bond for $850. (The annual interest payment stays the same because it is based on the face value of the bond.) Calculate the yield on the bond now. _____

4. When the price of a bond decreases, the yield (increases, decreases) and the bond becomes (more, less) attractive to people. There is a (direct, inverse) relationship between the bond price and the bond yield.

Exercise 5

This exercise provides information from the media about changes in policy by the Federal Reserve.

Reread the article in the text titled "Fed Cuts Deposit-Reserve Requirements" and answer questions 1-5.

1. What central monetary authority is mentioned in the article?_____

2. What phrase in the article indicates the monetary instrument that is being used by the central monetary authority?_____

3. Which instrument is being used?
   (a) Reserve requirement.
   (b) Open-market operations.
   (c) Discount rate.
   (d) Other (Specify: _____)

4. What passage indicates in which direction the monetary instrument(s) is being changed by the central monetary authority to influence the money supply?_____

_____

5. The policy initiative (lowers, raises) the quantity of money relative to what it would have been without the change.

Common Errors

The first statement in each "common error" below is incorrect. Each incorrect statement is followed by a corrected version and an explanation.

1. Bank reserves are required for the safety of depositors' money. WRONG!

   Bank reserves are for control of the money supply. RIGHT!

   Many people have the idea that bank reserves provide for the safety of depositors' money. They don't. The statistics in this chapter indicate that the amount of demand deposits is several times larger than that of reserves. Reserves are for control of the money supply. The FDIC provides for safety of deposits by insuring them. Reserves are not principally for depositors' safety.

2. Deposits of cash are necessary to start the process of lending and deposit creation. WRONG!

   To start the lending process, the banks must acquire reserves from outside the banking system. RIGHT!

   Many find it difficult to understand that for deposit creation to occur, the banking system needs only to acquire reserves from outside the system or be able to stretch existing reserves further. It may acquire reserves by selling a security to the Fed or by borrowing from the Fed. An individual bank, however, may acquire reserves from another bank. So to the extent that it has increased its reserves, another bank's reserves have shrunk. Thus, the system has no more reserves after the transaction than it had before, and so the system's lending capacity is unchanged.

3. When the Fed sells government bonds in open-market operations, it is increasing the money supply. WRONG!

   When the Fed sells government bonds, the buyers pay with reserves, which means there are fewer reserves and less money. RIGHT!

   The key here is to realize that payment of reserves to the Fed means that there are fewer reserves available to the entire banking system. By selling bonds the Fed is tightening monetary policy.

•ANSWERS•

Using Key Terms

Across

5. federal funds rate
6. excess reserves
8. discount rate
10. required reserves
12. portfolio decision

Down

1. money multiplier
2. monetary policy
3. open market operations
4. yield
7. money supply
9. discounting
11. bond

True or False

1. F   Federal Reserve banks hold *reserves* for banks and other types of financial institutions.
2. T
3. T
4. T
5. F   Monetary policy is the use of changes in the money supply and credit conditions to influence the macroeconomy.
6. F   The Fed has to *reduce* the reserve requirement to increase the money supply.
7. T
8. F   The FOMC implements monetary policy by buying and selling bonds.
9. T
10. F   The Fed *buys* securities to increase the lending capacity.

Multiple Choice

1.	b	5.	c	9.	d	13.	a	17.	a
2.	d	6.	a	10.	a	14.	b	18.	b
3.	c	7.	b	11.	b	15.	d	19.	d
4.	d	8.	a	12.	c	16.	a	20.	d

Problems and Applications

Exercise 1

1. $30 million
2. $30 million
3. $60 million
4. $300 million

5. **Table 14.2 Answer**

Assets		Liabilities	
Total reserves	$ 60	Transactions accounts	$600
Required $60			
Excess $0			
Securities	100		
Loans	440		
Total	$600	Total	$600

6. $300 million
7. Zero
8. $300 million

Exercise 2

1. $10 million

2. **Table 14.4 Answer**

Assets		Liabilities	
Total reserves	$ 85	Transactions accounts	$340
Required $85			
Excess $0			
Securities	90		
Loans	165		
Total	$340	Total	$340

3. $40 million
4. $10 million
5. $40 million

Exercise 3

1. $2 million; excess; $10 million

2. **Table 14.6 Answer**

Assets		Liabilities	
Total reserves	$ 72	Transactions accounts	$360
Required $72			
Excess $0			
Securities	70		
Loans	220	Borrowed from the Fed	$ 2
Total	$362	Total	$362

3. $10 million

Exercise 4

1. $100
2. 10 percent
3. 11.76 percent
4. Increase, more, inverse

Exercise 5

1. The Federal Reserve Board
2. The title, "Deposit-Reserve Requirements"
3. a
4. "The Fed cut to 10% from 12% the percentage of checking-account deposits that banks are required to hold as reserves."
5. Raises

CHAPTER 15
Monetary Policy

Quick Review

- By controlling the banks' ability to make loans ("create money"), the Federal Reserve System controls the money supply. The goal of monetary policy is to provide the appropriate level of aggregate demand in the economy to achieve the output, employment, and price level goals.

- The demand for money includes the transactions demand, the precautionary demand, and the speculative demand. The supply of money and demand for money together determine the equilibrium interest rate, or the price of money.

- From a Keynesian perspective, an increase in the money supply will drive the interest rate down and stimulate greater investment spending, thus shifting the aggregate demand curve to the right. Monetary restraint works in the opposite direction. A decrease in the money supply causes the interest rate to increase, which causes investment to decrease and aggregate demand to decrease.

- There are constraints to be considered, though. Will the banks be willing to lend? Will the increase in the money supply force the interest rate down, or will it fall into the Keynesian liquidity trap? Will low expectations leave the business sector without incentives to increase investment?

- If monetary restraint is being applied and the money supply is reduced, will optimistic firms and households borrow more in spite of higher interest rates? Finally, since the money market is a global one, if domestic interest rates get too high, will borrowers look abroad?

- Monetarists believe that the link between the money supply and aggregate demand is more direct. They use the equation of exchange ($MV = PQ$) to demonstrate the relationship. Assuming V is constant, any increase in M must be translated into greater spending.

- Some monetarists also believe that Q is constant, creating a vertical aggregate supply curve at the natural rate of unemployment. Thus, an increase in M translates into an increase in P. Monetarists, as a result, advocate steady, predictable changes in the money supply.

- Monetarists note that real interest rates are fairly stable. The real interest rate is equal to the nominal interest rate minus the anticipated inflation rate.

- Monetarists and Keynesians argue that monetary policy can affect nominal interest rates. This influences the content of GDP and can influence the distribution of income as well.

- Monetarists and Keynesians are led to radically different views about the effectiveness of monetary *and* fiscal policy. The Fed has adopted an eclectic approach to policy making and uses several measures of the money supply and interest rates to gauge the state of the economy.

Learning Objectives

After reading Chapter 15 and doing the following exercises, you should:

1. Know the determinants of the transactions, precautionary, and speculative demands for money.
2. Know how the equilibrium interest rate is determined and how changes in the money supply affect it.
3. Understand how changes in the money supply are transmitted to aggregate demand.
4. Understand expansionary and restrictive monetary-policy initiatives and know the constraints on both.
5. Know how the equation of exchange is expressed and the assumptions on which it is based.
6. Understand the relationship between the natural rate of unemployment and the aggregate supply curve.
7. Know the mechanism by which changes in *M* affect GDP in the monetarist model.
8. Understand and be able to calculate the real rate of interest.
9. Be able to contrast Keynesian and monetarist views of how monetary policy works.
10. Be able to articulate the effects of monetary policy on the mix of output and the distribution of income.
11. Be able to contrast Keynesian and monetarist views of monetary and fiscal policy.

Using Key Terms

Fill in the puzzle on the opposite page with the appropriate term from the list of Key Terms at the end of the chapter in the text.

Across

2. The Federal Reserve System can use its powers to alter the _____ _____.
4. Money held for future financial opportunities.
8. Equal to the nominal rate of interest minus the inflation rate.
9. Represented by the downward-sloping curve in Figure 15.1 in the text.
11. The choice of how and where to hold idle funds.
12. A decrease in private-sector borrowing and spending because of an increase in government spending.
14. The number of times per year a dollar is used to purchase final goods and services.
15. Determined by the intersection of the money demand curve and the money supply curve in Figure 15.2.
16. The curve that shifts to the right in Figure 15.3 as the result of an increase in the money supply.

Down

1. Money held for everyday purchases.
3. Money held for emergencies.
5. The mathematical formula used by monetarists to explain how monetary policy works.
6. The long-run rate of unemployment determined by structural forces.
7. The use of money and credit controls to influence the macroeconomy.
10. The horizontal portion of the money demand curve in Figure 15.4 in the text.
13. The price paid for the use of money.

Puzzle 15.1

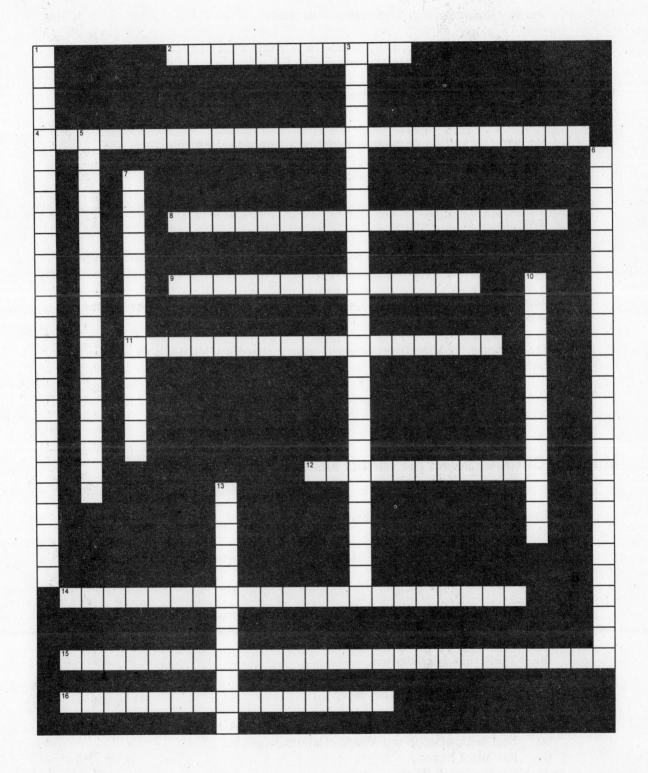

True or False: *Circle your choice and explain why any false statements are incorrect.*

T   F   1.   People who hold idle money balances incur no costs.

T   F   2.   The downward slope of the money-demand curve indicates that the quantity of money people are willing and able to hold increases as interest rates fall.

T   F   3.   When the Fed buys securities and causes interest rates to fall, investment spending increases, thereby increasing AD.

T   F   4.   Monetary policy affects the macro economy by shifting aggregate supply.

T   F   5.   If the interest rate is in the liquidity-trap range, monetary policy is ineffective.

T   F   6.   The liquidity trap occurs because the opportunity cost of holding money is low at low interest rates.

T   F   7.   Monetarists believe that changes in the money supply increase aggregate demand by lowering interest rates.

T   F   8.   According to the equation of exchange, total spending will rise if the money supply grows and velocity is stable.

T   F   9.   The assumption of a natural rate of unemployment implies that M is stable in the equation of exchange.

T   F   10.   Monetarists believe an increase in government spending will lead to the "crowding out" of an equal amount of private spending.

Multiple Choice: *Select the correct answer.*

_____   1.   The opportunity cost of holding money will increase if:
   (a)   Interest rates rise.
   (b)   Bond yields fall.
   (c)   Bond prices rise.
   (d)   All of the above.

_____   2.   By adding together the speculative, transactions, and precautionary demands for money, one can obtain:
   (a)   The market demand curve for money.
   (b)   The Keynesian liquidity trap.
   (c)   The monetarist demand-for-money curve.
   (d)   The market supply curve for money.

_____   3.   The intersection of the market demand for money and the market supply of money establishes the:
   (a)   Equilibrium of supply and demand of investment goods.
   (b)   Real rate of interest.
   (c)   Equilibrium rate of interest.
   (d)   Equilibrium average price level for the economy.

4. If the supply curve of money is vertical, what should happen to the equilibrium interest rate and equilibrium quantity of money as a result of a recession, *ceteris paribus*?
   (a) Equilibrium interest rate should go up.
   (b) Equilibrium interest rate should go down, but equilibrium quantity would remain unchanged.
   (c) Both equilibrium interest rate and equilibrium quantity should go up.
   (d) Equilibrium interest rate should go down, and equilibrium quantity should go up.

5. Given an upward-sloping aggregate supply curve, which of the following is most likely if the Fed pursues restrictive monetary policy?
   (a) The equilibrium price level and output will both increase.
   (b) The equilibrium output will decrease and the price level will stay the same.
   (c) The equilibrium price level will decrease and the output will stay the same.
   (d) The equilibrium price level and output will both decrease.

6. In the Keynesian model, the effectiveness of monetary policy depends on which of the following?
   (a) The Fed's ability to influence the money supply.
   (b) The sensitivity of interest rates to changes in the money supply.
   (c) The sensitivity of investment spending to changes in interest rates.
   (d) All of the above.

7. Which of the following is a series of events used by Keynesians to describe the steps by which expansionary monetary policy works in the short run?
   (a) Increase in M, decrease in interest rate, increase in I.
   (b) Decrease in interest rate, increase in M, increase in I.
   (c) Increase in M, decrease in I, decrease in interest rate.
   (d) Increase in M, increase in interest rate, increase in I.

8. Monetary policy will be most effective if:
   (a) The demand curve for money is horizontal and the investment demand curve is downward sloping.
   (b) The demand curve for money is downward sloping but the investment demand curve is vertical.
   (c) The demand curve for money and the investment demand curve are downward sloping, but neither is vertical nor horizontal.
   (d) The demand curve for money and the investment demand curve are vertical or both curves are horizontal.

9. What should happen to the equilibrium interest rate and the corresponding rate of investment if the Fed lowers the minimum reserve ratio?
   (a) Equilibrium interest rate and the rate of investment should both go up.
   (b) Equilibrium interest rate should go up, and the rate of investment should go down.
   (c) Equilibrium interest rate should go down, and the rate of investment should go up.
   (d) Equilibrium interest rate and the rate of investment should both go down.

10. Which of the following Fed actions is most likely to increase the aggregate demand curve?
   (a) Buying bonds in the open market.
   (b) Raising the discount rate.
   (c) Raising the reserve requirement.
   (d) Raising the federal funds rate.

11. Monetary stimulus will fail if:
   (a) The investment demand curve is perfectly inelastic.
   (b) Expectations of a boom cause the investment demand curve to shift to the right, offsetting interest-rate effects that would stimulate the economy.
   (c) The investment demand curve is elastic.
   (d) All of the above.

203

_____ 12. When the money market is in equilibrium in the liquidity trap:
   (a) The demand for money is perfectly insensitive to interest rates.
   (b) An increase in the money supply does not affect interest rates.
   (c) There is no speculative demand for money.
   (d) Investment spending falls to zero.

_____ 13. Which of the following acts as a constraint on expansionary monetary policy?
   (a) The responsiveness of interest rates to a change in the money supply.
   (b) Low business expectations.
   (c) The reluctance of banks to lend money.
   (d) All of the above.

_____ 14. Which of the following positions can be attributed to the monetarists?
   (a) "Only money matters."
   (b) "Velocity is constant."
   (c) "Government expenditures crowd out private expenditures."
   (d) All of the above are monetarist positions.

_____ 15. Which of the following is a monetarist assumption, which plays a key role in explaining the monetarist view that fiscal policy is ineffective?
   (a) The liquidity trap.
   (b) Crowding out.
   (c) Unstable velocity of money.
   (d) A vertical aggregate demand curve.

_____ 16. Given monetarist assumptions about the shape of the aggregate supply curve, which of the following would most likely result if the Fed pursues expansionary monetary policy?
   (a) The equilibrium price level and output would both increase.
   (b) The equilibrium price level and output would both decrease.
   (c) The equilibrium price level would increase but output would stay the same.
   (d) The equilibrium output would increase but the price level would stay the same.

_____ 17. Monetarists argue that the velocity of money:
   (a) Is constant.
   (b) Is reduced when fiscal policy puts idle money balances to work.
   (c) Increases when there is a recession because people accumulate money balances.
   (d) Increases as much as total spending falls so that MV remains constant.

_____ 18. The existence of a natural rate of unemployment implies that in the long run:
   (a) V in the equation of exchange is actually very unstable.
   (b) Monetary policy affects only the rate of inflation.
   (c) Q in the equation of exchange varies in proportion to M.
   (d) The rate of unemployment can be permanently reduced by more expansionary monetary and fiscal policies.

_____ 19. An increase in the money supply will:
   (a) Always cause inflation.
   (b) Never causes inflation.
   (c) Cause inflation only if aggregate supply is horizontal.
   (d) Cause inflation if aggregate supply is upward sloping or vertical.

204

_____ 20. Which of the following provides the correct policy targets of the three groups mentioned?

    (a)   Keynesians target the money supply, monetarists target interest rates, and the Fed targets a mix of the two.

    (b)   Keynesians target interest rates, monetarists target steady money growth, and the Fed targets a mix of the two.

    (c)   The Fed targets the money supply, monetarists target interest rates, and Keynesians target a mix of the two.

    (d)   The Fed targets interest rates, monetarists target steady money growth, and Keynesians target a mix of the two.

Problems and Applications
Exercise 1

This exercise focuses on the relationship between the money supply, interest rates, and aggregate demand.

Use Figure 15.1 to answer questions 1-7.

Figure 15.1

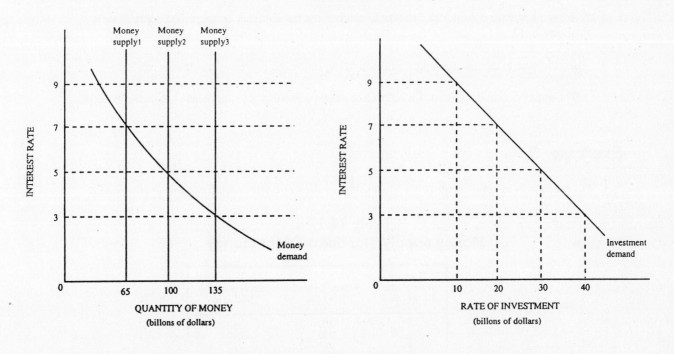

1. Assume the Federal Reserve sets the quantity of money at Money supply 2. The equilibrium interest rate is _____ percent and the equilibrium quantity of money is _____.

2. At the equilibrium interest rate in question 1 the rate of investment is equal to _____.

3. Now, suppose the Federal Reserve increases the money supply by $35 billion. The new equilibrium interest rate is _____ percent.

4. As a result of the (increase, decrease) in the interest rate, the rate of investment will (increase, decrease) to _____.

5: This (increase, decrease) in the rate of investment will cause aggregate _____ to (increase, decrease) or shift to the _____.

6. Now assume the Federal Reserve decides to change the money supply to Money supply 1. As a result of this change the equilibrium interest rate will (rise, fall), which will cause the rate of investment to (rise, fall).

7. Based on question 6, the change in the rate of investment will cause the level of aggregate demand to (rise, fall).

Exercise 2

This exercise examines what might happen if the Federal Reserve decided to change the discount rate.

1. A decrease in the discount rate will cause M1 to (increase, decrease, stay the same).

2. This change in the money supply will cause aggregate (demand, supply) to shift to the (left, right).

3. What other actions could the Fed take to achieve the same impact on aggregate demand as in question 1? _____

4. An increase in the discount rate will cause M1 to (increase, decrease, stay the same).

5. The policy action in question 4 is referred to as (expansionary, contractionary) monetary policy.

Exercise 3

The following exercise examines the relationship between monetary policy and aggregate demand.

Table 15.1
Money supply and demand for money

Nominal interest rate (% per year)	Money demand ($ billions)	Supply of money ($ billions)
2	320	240
4	280	240
6	240	240
8	200	240

On the basis of Table 15.1, answer the indicated questions. Assume for every 1 percentage point decline in the interest rate, aggregate spending shifts upward by $20 billion.

1. In Table 15.1, the equilibrium interest rate is _____ percent per year.

2. If the interest rate in Table 15.1 is 8 percent, then there is a (surplus, shortage) of money, and the interest rate will (rise, fall, remain constant).

3. Assume the anticipated inflation rate is 4 percent. At the equilibrium nominal interest rate in Table 15.1, the real interest rate will be _____ percent per year.

4. If the real rate of interest is negative then, *ceteris paribus*:
   (a) The nominal interest rate is negative.
   (b) Monetary policy is tight.
   (c) The inflation rate is negative.
   (d) It pays to borrow.

5. Suppose the Fed buys $8 billion worth of securities on the open market and that the reserve requirement is 0.2. If the money supply expands to its maximum potential, the new equilibrium rate of interest in Table 15.1 would be, *ceteris paribus*, _____ percent per year.

6. The change in the equilibrium interest rate in Table 15.1 as a result of the Fed's purchase of $8 billion worth of securities would be _____ percentage points.

7. If every 1 percentage point decline in the interest rate causes investment to increase by $20 billion the change in the interest rate in question 6 would cause investment to (increase, decrease) by

   _____ .

Exercise 4

This exercise will help you check your understanding of how monetary and fiscal policy affect the economy.

1. Consider each of the statements in Table 15.2. Decide whether you think each was made by a monetarist or a Keynesian, and place a check in the appropriate column. If you have difficulty, reread Tables 15.2 and 15.3 in the text.

Table 15.2
Comparing Keynesian and Monetarist views on monetary policy

	Monetarist	Keynesian
1. An increase in government spending will raise total spending.	_____	_____
2. A reduction in taxes will leave real output unaffected.	_____	_____
3. Real interest rates are determined by real growth.	_____	_____
4. Prices may be affected by increases in G or reductions in T.	_____	_____
5. Changes in the money supply definitely affect both the price level and aggregate spending.	_____	_____
6. Changes in M definitely affect changes in the normal interest rate.	_____	_____
7. Changes in M may cause changes in V and Q.	_____	_____
8. Changes in M definitely cannot lower the unemployment rate.	_____	_____
9. The liquidity trap may prevent the nominal interest rate from falling.	_____	_____
10. Monetary and fiscal policy must be used together to stabilize aggregate demand.	_____	_____

Exercise 5

The media often feature articles about changes in government policies that affect the money supply or about events that change the demand for money. This exercise will use one of the articles in the text to show the kind of information to look for.

Reread the article titled "Deflation Still Haunts the Bank of Japan." Then answer the following questions.

1. Which passage specifically indicates why the Bank of Japan decided to raise the money supply?
   _____

2. An increase in the money supply should cause the aggregate demand curve to _____
   _____

3. How should the price level respond to this change? _____

4. Prior to targeting the money supply, the Bank of Japan had targeted _____.

Common Errors

The first statement in each "common error" below is incorrect. Each incorrect statement is followed by a corrected version and an explanation.

1. When the interest rate goes down, the demand for money increases. WRONG!

   When the interest rate goes down, the quantity of money demanded increases. RIGHT!

   Don't fail to distinguish between a change in demand and a change in quantity demanded. Remember that each demand schedule (speculative, transactions, precautionary) is drawn on the assumption of *ceteris paribus*. Unless there is a change in one of the things held constant (e.g., expectations), there will be no change in demand when the interest rate falls, only a change in quantity demanded.

2. High nominal rates of interest mean high real rates of interest. WRONG!

   High nominal interest rates and high real interest rates do not necessarily coincide. RIGHT!

   High nominal interest rates and high real interest rates will coincide only if the average level of prices is not changing rapidly enough to offset the differential. For example, if the nominal rate is 10 percent and prices are rising at 10 percent, the real rate of interest is zero.

3. Monetary policy is easy to determine and to administer. WRONG!

   Monetary policy is difficult to determine and to administer. RIGHT!

   One could easily get the idea that monetary policy is easy to administer and that the Fed always knows the rate at which the money supply should grow. This is not true. Many variables intervene to make monetary policy difficult to prescribe and implement. Such variables include timing and the duration of a given policy, unanticipated events on the fiscal side, and problems abroad. The Fed's policy makers analyze the data available and do the best they can to achieve a given objective, which often involves compromises. The process is much more difficult than turning a printing press on and off.

•ANSWERS•

Using Key Terms

Across

2. money supply
4. speculative demand for money
8. real rate of interest
9. demand for money
11. portfolio decision
12. crowding out
14. income velocity of money
15. equilibrium rate of interest
16. aggregate demand

Down

1. transactions demand for money
3. precautionary demand for money
5. equation of exchange
6. natural rate of unemployment
7. monetary policy
10. liquidity trap
13. interest rate

True or False

1. F   Holding money balances incurs an opportunity cost, e.g., giving up interest that could be earned on those balances.
2. T
3. T
4. F   Monetary policy affects the macro economy by shifting aggregate demand.
5. T
6. T
7. F   Monetarists believe that, according to the equation of exchange (MV = PQ), a change in the money supply must alter total spending, regardless of how interest rates change, given the assumption of a constant V.
8. T
9. F   A natural rate of unemployment implies that Q is constant in the equation of exchange.
10. T

Multiple Choice

1. a	5. d	9. c	13. d	17. a
2. a	6. d	10. a	14. d	18. b
3. c	7. a	11. a	15. b	19. d
4. b	8. c	12. b	16. c	20. b

Problems and Applications

Exercise 1

1. $5, $100 billion
2. $30 billion
3. 3
4. Decrease, increase, $40 billion
5. Increase, demand, increase, right
6. Rise, fall
7. Fall

Exercise 2

1. Increase
2. Demand, right
3. An open-market sale of government securities or a decrease in the reserve requirement.
4. Decrease
5. Expansionary

Exercise 3

1. 6
2. Surplus, fall
3. 2
4. d
5. 4
6. -2
7. Increase, $40 billion

Exercise 4

Table 15.1 Answer

	Monetarist	Keynesian
1.		x
2.	x	
3.	x	
4.		x
5.	x	
6.	x	
7.		x
8.	x	
9.		x
10.		x

Exercise 5

1. "... to ease the price declines hammering Japanese companies."
2. Increase or shift to the right
3. Increase
4. Interest rates

CHAPTER 16

Supply-Side Policy: Short-Run Options

Quick Review

- The responses of the economy to demand side policies depend on the slope of the aggregate supply (AS) curve. Monetarists view the aggregate supply as vertical at the natural rate of unemployment, while Keynesians view it as flat until full employment is reached. The consensus view is that aggregate supply is an upward-sloping curve that becomes vertical at full employment.

- If aggregate supply is upward sloping, a shift in aggregate demand (AD) results in tradeoff between output and price level. This relationship between unemployment and inflation is drawn in the Phillips curve.

- If AS shifts to the left, unemployment and inflation both increase and the Phillips curve shifts to the right. This is known as stagflation.

- Supply-side policy attempts to shift the AS curve to the right. This causes a decrease in unemployment and inflation, both positive outcomes for the economy.

- Supply-side tax cuts are incentive-based and work on the assumption that people and firms will produce more if they get to keep a larger fraction of what they earn. Supply-siders favor tax cuts to provide incentives to encourage saving *and* investment

- Just how much supply will respond to a tax cut is measured by the tax elasticity of supply.

- Human capital incentives are important because they emphasize the quality of the labor force and reduce structural employment barriers, thus helping shift the aggregate supply curve to the right. Worker training, spending on education, and affirmative-action programs have a positive impact on the stock of human capital.

- Deregulation of both product and factor markets has provided a powerful stimulus to aggregate supply because it eliminates barriers to the efficient employment of resources, thus reducing costs at every level of output.

- Agreements like the North American Free Trade Agreement (NAFTA), which eliminated trade barriers between Canada, the United States and Mexico, have the potential to shift aggregate supply to the right by reducing the cost of imported inputs and finished goods.

- Infrastructure development enhances aggregate supply by reducing costs in transportation, communication, and so on. This improves market transactions and increases production possibilities.

Learning Objectives

After reading Chapter 16 and doing the following exercises, you should:

1. Understand why the success of demand-side policies depends on the aggregate-supply response.
2. Understand the nature of the inflation–unemployment tradeoff and the Phillips curve.
3. Understand the basic supply-side options for improving the inflation–unemployment tradeoff.
4. Understand why marginal tax rates affect work incentives, investment, and saving.
5. Know the significance of the tax elasticity of supply.
6. Be able to describe human capital and its relationship to structural unemployment.
7. Understand why deregulation of factor and product markets influences aggregate supply.
8. Understand that a reduction in trade barriers increases aggregate supply
9. Know why the development and maintenance of infrastructure is important to aggregate supply.

Using Key Terms

Fill in the puzzle on the opposite page with the appropriate term from the list of Key Terms at the end of the chapter in the text.

Across
4. The amount of output produced by a worker in a given time period.
5. The percentage change in quantity supplied divided by the percentage change in tax rates.
8. The simultaneous occurrence of unemployment and inflation.
10. The vertical curve in Figure 16.1 (b) in the text.
11. Payments such as Social Security, welfare, and unemployment benefits.
12. The transportation, communications, judicial, and other systems that facilitate market exchanges.
13. Business expenditure on new plant and equipment and inventory changes.

Down
1. The skills and knowledge of the workforce.
2. Unemployment because of a mismatch between the skills of the workforce and the requirements of jobs.
3. A lump-sum refund of taxes paid.
6. Disposable income minus consumption.
7. The tax rate imposed on the last dollar of income received.
9. The _____ _____ is drawn in Figure 16.2 in the text.

Puzzle 16.1

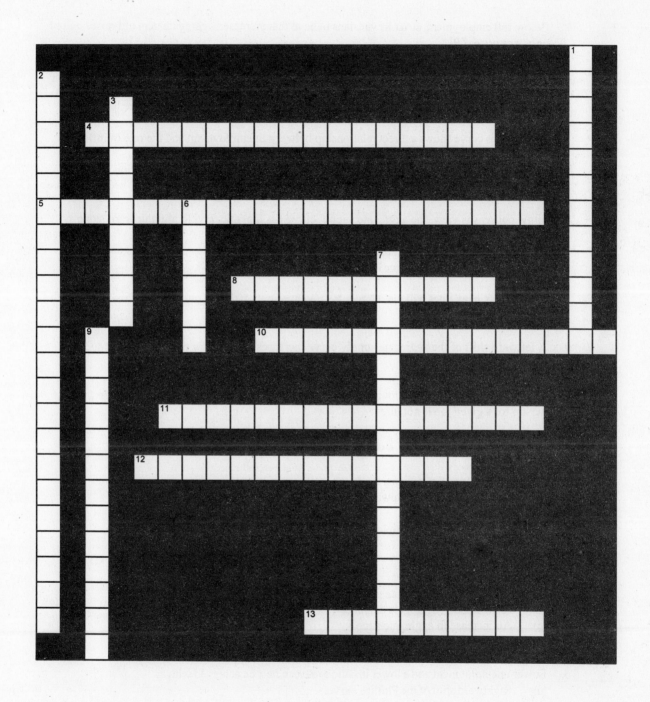

True or False: *Circle your choice and explain why any false statements are incorrect.*

T F 1. Below full employment, strict Keynesians believe that increased aggregate demand raises output only, not prices (*P*).

T F 2. Rightward shifts of the aggregate supply curve decrease both the price level and output.

T F 3. Investment in human capital reduces saving and shifts the aggregate supply curve leftward.

T F 4. The Phillips curve shows a direct relationship between unemployment and the rate of inflation.

T F 5. A basic contention of supply-side economists is that we should decrease regulation of the production process.

T F 6. In the consensus view, the aggregate supply curve has a gentle, accelerating upward slope.

T F 7. As the marginal tax rate increases, there is more incentive to work because workers want to maintain their "after tax" income level.

T F 8. A reduction in tax rates will yield larger tax revenues only if the absolute value of the tax elasticity of supply is greater than 1.0.

T F 9. A leftward shift of the aggregate supply curve increases inflationary pressures and reduces employment.

T F 10. Discrimination against any group can shift the aggregate supply curve to the left when the best person for a given job is not hired.

Multiple Choice: *Select the correct answer.*

_____ 1. According to strict Keynesians, the aggregate supply curve is:
   (a) First horizontal, then upward sloping, and finally vertical.
   (b) Vertical.
   (c) Horizontal until full employment is reached, and then it becomes vertical.
   (d) Upward sloping.

_____ 2. Stagflation is caused by:
   (a) An increase in aggregate demand.
   (b) A decrease in aggregate demand.
   (c) An increase in aggregate supply.
   (d) A decrease in aggregate supply.

_____ 3. Lower unemployment and a lower inflation rate can best be achieved with a:
   (a) Rightward shift of the Phillips curve.
   (b) Rightward shift of the aggregate supply curve.
   (c) Rightward shift of the aggregate demand curve.
   (d) Leftward shift of the aggregate supply curve.

4. The Phillips curve shows:
   (a) An inverse relationship between the unemployment rate and inflation.
   (b) A direct relationship between the unemployment rate and inflation.
   (c) An inverse relationship between output and the unemployment rate.
   (d) A direct relationship between inflation and output.

5. What is the slope of the aggregate supply curve according to monetarists?
   (a) Horizontal until full employment is reached, and then vertical.
   (b) Vertical.
   (c) Horizontal at all production levels.
   (d) Upward sloping.

6. Supply-side policies are designed to achieve:
   (a) A leftward shift in the Phillips curve.
   (b) A rightward shift of the aggregate supply curve.
   (c) Both a lower inflation rate and a lower unemployment rate.
   (d) All of the above.

7. In contrast to monetarists and Keynesians, the supply-side policies are designed to:
   (a) Shift the Phillips curve leftward.
   (b) Raise inflation and lower unemployment.
   (c) Move the economy down the Phillips curve to a lower inflation rate.
   (d) Move the economy down the supply curve.

8. Which of the following shifts, *ceteris paribus*, will cause lower rates of both unemployment and inflation?
   (a) An increase in aggregate demand.
   (b) A decrease in aggregate demand.
   (c) An increase in aggregate supply.
   (d) A decrease in aggregate supply.

9. The impact on the economy of a given shift in aggregate demand depends on the:
   (a) Shape of the aggregate supply curve.
   (b) Response of consumers to a change in spending.
   (c) Position of the aggregate supply curve.
   (d) All of the above.

10. Declining investment in infrastructure:
    (a) Will lead to greater delays and higher opportunity costs.
    (b) Has characterized the United States since 1960.
    (c) Shifts both aggregate demand and aggregate supply.
    (d) All of the above.

11. According to supply-side theory, which of the following would cause a rightward shift in the aggregate supply curve?
    (a) Lifting trade restrictions.
    (b) Increasing transfer payments to the unemployed.
    (c) Eliminating government-funded training programs for the structurally unemployed.
    (d) Eliminating job-search assistance.

12. Which of the following will definitely lead to a larger value on the misery index?
    (a) A movement along the Phillips curve.
    (b) An outward shift of the aggregate demand curve.
    (c) Stagflation.
    (d) A rightward shift of the money supply curve.

13. If the marginal tax rates increase, then:
    (a) The labor supply will increase.
    (b) Entrepreneurship is discouraged.
    (c) Investment increases.
    (d) Savings increases.

14. The tradeoff between unemployment and inflation is the result of an aggregate supply curve that is:
    (a) Horizontal.
    (b) Vertical.
    (c) Upward sloping.
    (d) Downward sloping.

15. Which of the following groups would use a decrease in government regulation to increase the incentive to work and produce?
    (a) Supply-siders.
    (b) Monetarists.
    (c) Keynesians.
    (d) All of the above.

16. If the absolute value of the tax elasticity of supply is 0.5, a tax *cut* of 5 percent would:
    (a) Increase output by 2.5 percent and decrease tax revenues.
    (b) Increase output by 10 percent and decrease tax revenues.
    (c) Increase output by 2.5 percent and increase tax revenues.
    (d) Decrease output by 2.5 percent and decrease tax revenues.

17. Which of the following changes in trade policy will increase aggregate supply?
    (a) Increased tariffs on imported factors of production.
    (b) The implementation of a quota on finished goods.
    (c) The relaxation of immigration laws to allow more immigration.
    (d) All of the above.

18. The marginal tax rate indicates the:
    (a) Change in taxes resulting from a change in fiscal policy.
    (b) Tax rate imposed on total income.
    (c) Tax rate imposed on taxable income.
    (d) Tax rate imposed on the last dollar of income.

19. If a new tax policy raises the tax rate 2% but causes the quantity supplied to fall by 10%, the absolute value of the tax elasticity of supply is:
    (a) 0.5.
    (b) 2.
    (c) 5.
    (d) 10.

_____ 20. If the government reduces the regulations that impact businesses, supply-side economists believe unemployment will:
   (a)   Increase and the price level will decrease.
   (b)   Decrease and the price level will decrease.
   (c)   Increase and the price level will increase.
   (d)   Decrease and the price level will increase.

Problems and Applications

Exercise 1

This exercise will focus on how aggregate supply and demand changes affect the equilibrium output and price index.

The aggregate demand curve and aggregate supply curve for all of the goods in an economy are presented in Figure 16.2. The economy is assumed to be on aggregate demand curve B in the current fiscal year.

Figure 16.1
Aggregate supply and demand curves

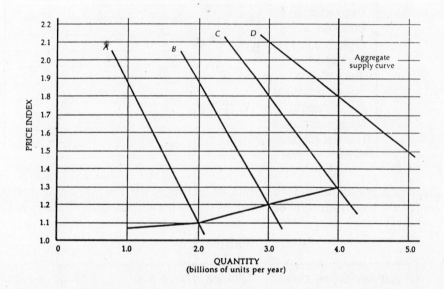

1. Four aggregate demand curves (A, B, C, and D) are shown in Figure 16.1, corresponding to four alternative government policies for the upcoming fiscal year.

   For the following government policy initiatives, choose the aggregate demand curve in Figure 16.1 that best portrays the expected impact of each policy. Place the letter of your choice in the blank provided. Each letter can be used more than once, and some blanks can have more than one letter.

   a. _____   Money supply is expanded, taxes are cut, government increases its expenditures.
   b. _____   Government does nothing.
   c. _____   Government decides to balance the budget by reducing government spending and raising taxes.
   d. _____   Government increases expenditures and cuts taxes.

2. Indicate the equilibrium price index and output for each policy in Table 16.1.

Table 16.1
Equilibrium prices for four government policies

Aggregate demand curve	A	B	C	D
Equilibrium price index	_____	_____	_____	_____
Equilibrium output	_____	_____	_____	_____

3. Place an "X" in the appropriate column in Table 16.2 to indicate the aggregate demand curve that is most likely to result in each of the outcomes listed. More than one answer per outcome is possible.

Table 16.2
Macroeconomic outcomes

(Place an "X")	Aggregate demand curve			
	A	B	C	D
Depression	___	___	___	___
Deflation	___	___	___	___
Highest unemployment	___	___	___	___
Recession	___	___	___	___
Zero inflation	___	___	___	___
Full employment	___	___	___	___
Price stability	___	___	___	___
Maximum output	___	___	___	___
Highest inflation	___	___	___	___

4. Suppose aggregate demand shifts to the left. Determine the change to the equilibrium price level and output level (increase or decrease) for each of the aggregate supply curves in Table 16.3.

Table 16.3

Aggregate supply curve	Change in price level	Change in output level
upward sloping	_____	_____
horizontal	_____	_____
vertical	_____	_____

Exercise 2

1. Suppose the price index is currently 1.2 as shown by demand curve *B* in Figure 16.1. Compute the inflation rate under each of the four policies, assuming the supply curve remains the same. The formula is:

$$\frac{\text{equilibrium price index} - 1.2}{1.2} \times 100\%$$

Enter your answers for each policy in the appropriate blank of column 1 in Table 16.4.

Table 16.4 Inflation rates, equilibrium output, and unemployment rates under four government policies

Aggregate demand curve	(1) Equilibrium price change	(2) Equilibrium output (billions of units per year)	(3) Unemployment rate
A	_____%	_____	_____%
B	_____	_____	_____
C	_____	_____	_____
D	_____	_____	_____

2. In column 2 of Table 16.4, indicate the equilibrium output associated with each of the policies. Use Figure 16.1 to find this information.

3. Which of the following best represents the U.S. unemployment rate?
   (a) The number of people divided by the U.S. labor force.
   (b) The number of people employed divided by the U.S. population.
   (c) The number of people counted as unemployed divided by the U.S. labor force.
   (d) The number of people unemployed divided by the U.S. population.

4. Table 16.5 shows hypothetical data for the U.S. population, the labor force, the number of people who are employed, and the number of people who are unemployed at each production rate for the economy. Compute the unemployment rate at each production rate in the table.

Table 16.5 Computation of the unemployment rate

Production rate (billions of units per year)	2	3	4
U.S. population (millions)	200	200	200
Labor force (millions)	100	100	100
Number of people unemployed (millions)	15	8	5
Number of people employed (millions)	85	92	95
Unemployment rate (percent)	_____	_____	_____

5. Using the information in Table 16.5, complete column 3 in Table 16.4, which shows the unemployment rate corresponding to each government policy.

6. The government's dilemma is:
   (a) That it cannot reach an unemployment level of 5 percent without experiencing inflation of at least 8 percent.
   (b) That it cannot reach stable prices (0 percent increase) without experiencing an unemployment rate of 8 percent or more.
   (c) That when it makes gains in holding inflation below 8 percent, unemployment increases.
   (d) Expressed by all of the above statements.

219

7. Which of the four aggregate demand curves from Figure 16.1 places the economy closest to full-employment output and moderate inflation?
   (a) Aggregate demand curve A.
   (b) Aggregate demand curve B.
   (c) Aggregate demand curve C.
   (d) Aggregate demand curve D.

Exercise 3

Suppose corporate taxes are reduced to encourage productivity and as a result firms in the economy supply $1 trillion more in output at every price level. As a result, the average price level decreases by $50 at every level of real GDP.

Figure 16.2

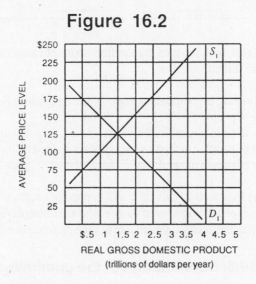

REAL GROSS DOMESTIC PRODUCT
(trillions of dollars per year)

1. Draw the new aggregate demand curve (label it D₂) or aggregate supply curve (label it S₂) in Figure 16.2.

2. What is the new equilibrium price level? _____

3. What is the new equilibrium output level? _____

4. Which type of economic policy is this tax change most consistent with? _____

5. The shift that occurred in Figure 16.2 (above) should result in:
   (a) Stagflation (inflation and a higher unemployment rate).
   (b) Inflation and a lower unemployment rate.
   (c) Deflation and a higher unemployment rate.
   (d) A lower price level and lower unemployment rate.

220

Exercise 4

Suppose taxpayers are required to pay a base tax of $400 plus 20 percent on any income over $1,000.

1. Compute the amount of taxes to be paid at the income levels in Table 16.6 by filling in columns 2, 3, and 4.

Table 16.6
Tax calculations

(1) Income ($ per year)	(2) Base tax + ($ per year)	(3) Tax on income over $1,000 ($ per year)	(4) = Total tax ($/year)	(5) Total tax after change In base tax	(6) In marginal tax rate
$ 5,000	_____	_____	_____	_____	_____
$10,000	_____	_____	_____	_____	_____
$15,000	_____	_____	_____	_____	_____

2. Suppose further that the taxing authority wishes to raise taxes by $500 for people with incomes of $10,000. If the marginal tax rates remain unchanged, what will the new base tax have to be? _____

3. In column 5 of Table 16.6, compute the resulting taxes at each income level with the new base tax.

4. If the base tax of $400 is to remain unchanged, what will the *marginal tax rate* have to be if $500 is to be added to the tax paid by people with incomes of $10,000? _____

5. Use the new marginal tax rate to complete column 6.

6. If taxes are to be increased (columns 5 and 6), a change in the base is:
    (a) More progressive and helpful to work incentives than raising taxes by changing the marginal tax rate.
    (b) More progressive and harmful to work incentives than raising taxes by changing the marginal tax rate.
    (c) More regressive and helpful to work incentives than raising taxes by changing the marginal tax rate.
    (d) More regressive and harmful to work incentives than raising taxes by changing the marginal tax rate.

Common Errors

The first statement in each "common error" below is incorrect. Each incorrect statement is followed by a corrected version and an explanation.

1. Labor productivity increases when more is produced per dollar of wages. WRONG!

    Labor productivity increases when more units of product are produced per unit of labor. RIGHT!

    Productivity changes are not directly related to wage levels. Wage levels reflect a large number of influences embodied in the demand and supply curves for labor. Productivity, however, is a physical measure of the relation between units of product and the amount of labor needed to produce them.

2. The Phillips curve is simply a demand curve. WRONG!

Although the Phillips curve is related to supply and demand curves, it is not the same as either a demand or a supply curve. RIGHT!

Table 16.7 shows some of the major differences separating Phillips curves, market demand curves, and aggregate demand curves. The axes of the three curves are very different.

Table 16.7
Characteristics of three types of demand curve

| | Sources of differences | | |
Type of curve	x-axis	y-axis	Market
Phillips curve	Unemployment	Inflation	Aggregate labor market
Market demand curve	Quantity per time period	Price	Single market
Aggregate demand curve	Quantity per time period	Price index	Aggregate product market

3. We can't have full employment with price stability. WRONG!

Full employment with price stability is possible, although it may be difficult to achieve. RIGHT!

Look at the definition of full employment again. It is the lowest rate of unemployment with price stability. Although we may be able to increase production above full employment, it will cause inflation.

4. Minimum-wage legislation provides more income to workers. WRONG!

Minimum-wage legislation eliminates low-paying jobs, which may decrease total income received by workers. RIGHT!

A higher wage may mean that businesses cannot afford to hire as many people. The lost wages of those people who are unemployed because of the minimum wages must be weighed against the higher wages received by those who are able to hold onto their jobs.

•ANSWERS•

Using Key Terms
Across
4. labor productivity
5. tax elasticity of supply
8. stagflation
10. aggregate supply
11. transfer payments
12. infrastructure
13. investment

Down

1. human capital
2. structural unemployment
3. tax rebate
6. saving
7. marginal tax rate
9. Phillips curve

True or False

1.	T	
2.	F	Increases in AS decrease the price level but increase output.
3.	F	Investment in human capital can shift AS rightward.
4.	F	The Phillips curve indicates an inverse relationship between unemployment and inflation.
5.	T	
6.	T	
7.	F	There is less incentive to work when the additional income earned is taxed at a higher rate.
8.	T	
9.	T	
10.	T	

Multiple Choice

1.	c	5.	b	9.	d	13.	b	17.	c
2.	d	6.	d	10.	d	14.	c	18.	d
3.	b	7.	a	11.	a	15.	a	19.	c
4.	a	8.	c	12.	c	16.	a	20.	b

Problems and Applications

Exercise 1

1. a. C or D   b. B   c. A   d. C or D

2. **Table 16.1 Answer**

Aggregate demand curve	A	B	C	D
Equilibrium price index	1.1	1.2	1.3	1.8
Equilibrium output	2.0	3.0	4.0	4.0

3. **Table 16.2 Answer**

(Place an "x")	Aggregate demand curve			
	A	B	C	D
Depression	X	—	—	—
Deflation	X	—	—	—
Highest unemployment	X	—	—	—
Recession	—	X	—	—
Zero inflation	—	X	—	—
Full employment	—	—	X	—
Price stability	—	X	—	—
Maximum output	—	—	X	X
Highest inflation	—	—	—	X

4. **Table 16.3 Answer (millions of dollars)**

Aggregate supply curve	Change in price level	Change in output level
upward sloping	decrease	decrease
horizontal	no change	decrease
vertical	decrease	no change

Exercise 2

1. See Table 16.4 answer, column 1.

Table 16.4 Answer

Aggregate demand curve	(1) Equilibrium price change	(2) Equilibrium output (billions of units per year)	(3) Unemployment rate
A	– 8.3%	2.0	15%
B	0.0	3.0	8
C	8.3	4.0	5
D	50.0	4.0	5

2. See Table 16.4 answer, column 2.
3. c

4. **Table 16.5 Answer**

Production rate (billions of units per year)	2	3	4
Unemployment rate (percent)	15	8	5

5. See Table 16.4 answer, column 3.

6. d
7. c

Exercise 3

1. See Figure 16.2 answer, S_2.

Figure 16.2 Answer

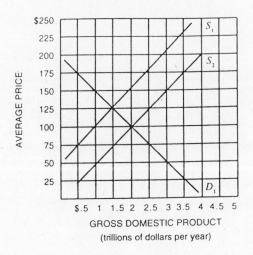

GROSS DOMESTIC PRODUCT
(trillions of dollars per year)

2. $100
3. $2 trillion
4. Supply-side policy
5. d

Exercise 4

1. See Table 16.6 Answer, columns 2-4.

Table 16.6 Answer

(1)	(2)	(3)		(4)	(5)	(6)
		Tax on income		Total	Total tax after change	
Income	Base tax +	over $1,000	=	tax		In marginal
($ per year)	($ per year)	($ per year)		($/year)	In base tax	tax rate
$ 5,000	$400	$ 800 (= $ 4,000x0.2)		$1,200	$1,700	$1,424
$10,000	$400	1,800 (= 9,000x0.2)		2,200	2,700	2,704
$15,000	$400	2,800 (= 14,000x0.2)		3,200	3,700	3,984

2. $900 (= \$400 + \$500)$
3. See Table 16.6 Answer column 5.
4. 25.6 percent. This is found by solving the following equation, which indicates people with \$10,000 in income have a tax of \$2,700 $(= \$2,200 + \$500)$:

$$\$2,700 = \$400 + (\$10,000 - \$1,000)X$$
$$\$2,300 = \$9,000X$$
$$X = 25.6 \text{ percent}$$

5. See Table 16.6 Answer column 6.
6. c

CHAPTER 17

Growth and Productivity: Long-Run Possibilities

Quick Review

- Economic growth refers to increases in real GDP. Growth is desired by virtually every society because it provides for possible improvements in the standard of living.

- In the short run, economic growth can be achieved by increased capacity utilization, represented by a movement toward the production-possibilities curve.

- In the long run, growth requires an increase in capacity itself, represented by a rightward shift of the production-possibilities curve. This results in a rightward shift in the long-run aggregate supply curve as well.

- GDP per capita is a basic measure of living standards. GDP per worker is a measure of productivity. Increases in productivity, rather than increases in the quantity of resources available, have been the primary source of U.S. economic growth in the past.

- The sources of productivity gains include improved labor skills, increased investment and the resulting increase in the nation's capital stock, technological advances, and improved management skills and techniques.

- Government policies play a role in fostering economic growth. Policies that encourage growth include education and training, immigration, and programs that promote investment and saving. All of these can lead to increases in both the quality and quantity of resources available.

- Macroeconomic policies impact the long-run aggregate supply curve. Budget deficits may reduce the level of economic growth through "crowding out." This occurs when increased government spending, financed by borrowing, causes a reduction in the level of private investment. Budget surpluses can increase economic growth and cause "crowding in."

- Political and economic stability and economic freedom also contribute to economic growth.

- Continued economic growth is desirable as long as it brings a higher standard of living for a country and an increased ability to produce and consume goods and services that society desires.

Learning Objectives

After reading Chapter 17 and doing the following exercises, you should:

1. Know the difference between economic growth in the short run versus the long run.
2. Know the difference between GDP per capita and GDP per worker.
3. Understand the sources of productivity growth.
4. Understand how government policy can promote economic growth.
5. Know that economic freedom and stability can foster growth.
6. Understand the nature of environmental constraints that can limit growth.
7. Recognize what society can do to reduce the external costs imposed by economic growth.
8. Understand how the market mechanism automatically generates solutions to resource exhaustion and constraints on growth.

Using Key Terms

Fill in the puzzle on the opposite page with the appropriate term from the list of Key Terms at the end of the chapter in the text.

Across

2.   The proportion of the adult population that is employed.
5.   According to the text, Malthus believed food supplies would increase in this manner.
9.   According to Figure 17.5 in the text, _____ grew at an average pace of 1.4 percent from 1973 to 1995 for the U.S.
12.   An increase in private-sector borrowing and spending because of a decrease in government borrowing.
13.   All persons over the age of sixteen who are working for pay or are looking for work.
14.   An increase in quantity by a constant proportion each year.
15.   Gross investment minus depreciation.

Down

1.   The percentage change in real output from one period to another.
3.   This curve is used in Figure 17.1 in the text to demonstrate long-run growth.
4.   The time period used for comparative analysis.
6.   A decrease in private-sector borrowing and investment because of increased government borrowing.
7.   The knowledge and skills possessed by the labor force.
8.   Used to measure average GDP and equal to $35,714 for the U.S. in 2000 according to the text.
10.   Shown in Figure 17.1(b) in the text as a rightward shift in the production-possibilities curve.
11.   The actual quantity of goods and services produced, valued in constant prices.

Puzzle 17.1

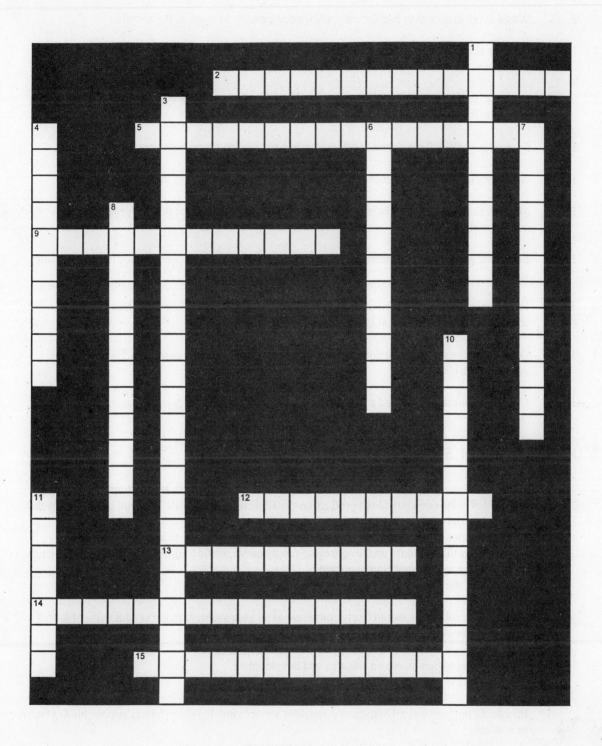

True or False: *Circle your choice and explain why any false statements are incorrect.*

T F 1. World economic growth has virtually eliminated poverty in most of the world.

T F 2. Once an economy is on its production-possibilities curve, further increases in output require an expansion of productive capacity.

T F 3. An increase in nominal GDP always means there has been an outward shift in the production-possibilities curve.

T F 4. Growth in real GDP per capita is achieved when population grows more rapidly than output.

T F 5. A primary determinant of labor productivity is the rate of capital investment.

T F 6. Malthus believed that population grew arithmetically and that the means of subsistence grew geometrically.

T F 7. Economic growth is an exponential process because gains made in one year accumulate in future years.

T F 8. Increases in the size of the labor force and capital stock have been less important than productivity advances in causing U.S. real GDP to grow.

T F 9. Over time, research and development are credited with the greatest contributions to economic growth in the U.S.

T F 10. Overall, immigration has had a negative impact on the U.S. economy over time.

Multiple Choice: *Select the correct answer.*

_____ 1. A major difference between short-run and long-run economic growth is that short-run growth:
    (a) Moves the economy to the production-possibilities curve, while long-run growth shifts the curve outward.
    (b) Increases capacity utilization, while long-run economic growth increases capacity.
    (c) Moves the economy up the aggregate supply curve, while long-run economic growth shifts the aggregate supply curve outward.
    (d) All of the above.

_____ 2. Which of the following would likely contribute to an improvement in the productivity of labor?
    (a) Greater expenditures on training and education.
    (b) Policies to stimulate the saving and investment process.
    (c) Greater expenditures on research and development.
    (d) All of the above.

_____ 3. In order to produce a combination of goods and services outside the production-possibilities curve, an economy:
    (a) Would have to use more of its existing resources.
    (b) Would have to raise the prices of goods and services so that firms would produce more.
    (c) Would have to find more resources or develop new technology.
    (d) Will never be able to produce a combination of goods and services outside its current production-possibilities curve.

4. A sustained net growth in real output of 4 percent per year will cause real output to double in about:
   (a) 4 years.
   (b) 18 years.
   (c) 10 years.
   (d) 25 years.

5. The best measure of productivity could be calculated with data on:
   (a) Real GDP and hours worked by the labor force.
   (b) Real GDP and the population of the United States.
   (c) Nominal GDP and the number of people in the U.S. labor force.
   (d) Nominal GDP and the population of the United States.

6. A major goal of short-run macroeconomic policy is to:
   (a) Shift the production-possibilities curve outward.
   (b) Move toward the production-possibilities curve.
   (c) Shift the aggregate supply curve leftward.
   (d) Shift the aggregate supply curve rightward.

7. Which of the following is the best measure of the standard of living?
   (a) The ratio of current GDP to GDP in the base period.
   (b) Investment as a percentage of GDP.
   (c) GDP per capita.
   (d) GDP per worker.

8. Assume U.S. real GDP in 1929 was $942 billion with a population of 122 million people and U.S. real GDP in 1930 was $858 billion with 123 million people, then the real GDP per capita for this time period:
   (a) Increased.
   (b) Increased and then decreased.
   (c) Remained unchanged.
   (d) Decreased.

9. Which of the following measures the growth rate of an economy?
   (a) The ratio of current real GDP to real GDP in the base period.
   (b) Investment as a percentage of GDP.
   (c) Real GDP divided by nominal GDP.
   (d) GDP per worker.

10. Which of the following measures productivity?
    (a) The ratio of current GDP to GDP in the base period.
    (b) Percentage increase in GDP.
    (c) GDP per capita.
    (d) GDP per worker.

11. When the production-possibilities curve shifts outward, we can also be sure that:
    (a) Aggregate supply has increased.
    (b) Output has increased.
    (c) GDP per capita has increased.
    (d) All of the above occur when the production possibilities curve shifts outward.

12. The exponential process:
    (a) Explains why increases in GDP in one year accumulate in future years.
    (b) Is a measure of productivity.
    (c) Is included in an arithmetic progression.
    (d) All of the above.

_____ 13. Which of the following policy levers definitely enhances productivity?
   (a) Higher taxes.
   (b) More government regulation.
   (c) Development of human capital.
   (d) A higher labor to capital ratio.

_____ 14. In recent decades, a primary source of growth in U.S. output has been:
   (a) Rapid growth of the money supply.
   (b) Increased capacity utilization.
   (c) Increased number of workers.
   (d) Increased productivity per worker.

_____ 15. Sources of productivity growth include:
   (a) Higher skills.
   (b) More capital.
   (c) Improved management.
   (d) All of the above.

_____ 16. Which of the following could impede productivity improvements?
   (a) Crowding out.
   (b) Technological advances.
   (c) Higher ratios of capital to labor.
   (d) All of the above.

_____ 17. Which of the following situations will cause the greatest increase in labor productivity?
   (a) An increase in the labor force and capital remains constant.
   (b) An increase in both the labor force and capital, but the labor force increases more rapidly.
   (c) An increase in both the labor force and capital, but the capital increases more rapidly.
   (d) A decrease in capital and the labor force remains constant.

_____ 18. Current U.S. problems with congested highways, air quality and global warming are primarily the result of:
   (a) Too many goods and services.
   (b) The mix of output produced.
   (c) Too much government regulation.
   (d) Excessively high levels of GDP per capita.

_____ 19. Growth in GDP per capita is attained only when:
   (a) There is growth in population.
   (b) There is growth in output.
   (c) The growth of output exceeds population growth.
   (d) Population is held constant.

_____ 20. From the long run perspective of economic growth, household saving:
   (a) Threatens growth because of the paradox of thrift.
   (b) Is the basic source of investment financing in the U.S.
   (c) Is a leakage that constrains economic growth.
   (d) Shifts the institutional production-possibilities curve inward.

Problems and Applications

Exercise 1

This exercise focuses on the difference in short-run growth versus long-run growth.

Refer to Figure 17.1 to answer questions 1-4.

Figure 17.1

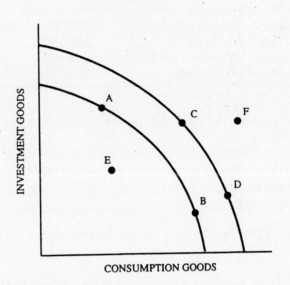

1. Assume the economy is producing at point E. A movement to point B represents an increase in (short-run, long-run) growth.

2. The movement from point E to point B results in increased output because of (increased use of existing capacity, increased capacity).

3. Assume the economy is now producing at point B. A movement to point D represents an increase in (short-run, long-run) growth.

4. The movement from point B to point D results in increased output because of (increased use of existing capacity, increased capacity). This type of growth implies a (leftward, rightward) shift in the _____ _____ curve.

Exercise 2

The following exercise shows how gross domestic product can be used to indicate the standard of living and the rate of economic growth in an economy.

1. Using the data provided complete Table 17.1.

Table 17.1

	1990	1998	Percentage change
(1) U.S. real GDP (billions of dollars)	$6707.9	$8515.7	_____
(2) U.S. population (thousands)	249,973	270,509	_____
(3) U.S. per capita GDP (dollars per person)	$26,834	$31,480	_____
(4) World population (thousands)	5,329,000	5,927,000	_____

2. Using the information in Table 17.1, the U.S. standard of living (increased, decreased) from 1990 to 1998.

3. Why must the world economic growth be greater than the U.S. economic growth to maintain the same standard of living? _____
_____

4. From 1990 to 1998, what was the average annual growth rate for real GDP in the U.S? _____

5. If the growth rate calculated in question 4 was the actual growth rate each year (not the average), how long should it take for real GDP to double according to Table 17.1 in the text? _____

Exercise 3

The focus of this exercise is on the value of investment in spurring economic growth. This exercise will help you with a problem at the end of the chapter.

Reread the *World View* article titled "Comparative Investment and Growth." Suppose two hypothetical economies are currently characterized by the following data:

	Country A	Country B
GDP	$10 trillion	$5 trillion
Consumption	4 trillion	3 trillion
Investment	4 trillion	1 trillion
Government spending	2 trillion	1 trillion

1. What is the investment rate (I/GDP) for Country A? _____

2. What is the investment rate (I/GDP) for Country B? _____

3. Based on the information above, which country is likely to have the higher growth rate of GDP? _____ Why? _____

4. According to the article in the text, which two countries had the highest investment rate?

    _____

5. Which two countries had the highest growth rate for GDP? _____

Common Errors

The first statement in each "common error" below is incorrect. Each incorrect statement is followed by a corrected version and an explanation.

1. Zero economic growth treats everyone equally. WRONG!

    Zero economic growth treats groups unequally. RIGHT!

    Zero economic growth in its simplest dimensions means that GDP would not grow from year to year. Income per capita therefore could not grow unless population declined. Yet we know that U.S. population is growing, although slowly, as a result of new births and increased longevity, and more recently as a result of immigration. If GDP were not to grow, the only way for those at the bottom of the income distribution to have more would be for someone at the top to take less.

2. As long as output increases as rapidly as the population, the standard of living will improve. WRONG!

    As long as output increases more rapidly than the population, the standard of living will improve. RIGHT!

    Standard of living is typically measured using real GDP per capita. In order for the standard of living to increase, real GDP must grow faster than the population. If they both grow at the same rate, the standard of living will remain constant.

3. There is no way to hold off the doomsday prophecy. WRONG!

    Much has been done in the last decade to avoid the cataclysmic predictions of the doomsday prophets. RIGHT!

    Much has been done by federal, state, and local governments to overcome some of the problems that seemed most acute. The air is cleaner in many areas and so is the water. Actions on the part of OPEC over the last three decades have helped in this regard. Higher oil prices spur research into new sources of power and new ways to conserve energy. All of this activity helps us meet the doomsday challenge each time it arises.

4. Zero economic growth will alleviate the pollution problem. WRONG!

    Zero economic growth will maintain the rate of pollution. RIGHT!

    Some people mistakenly think that stifling economic growth is a way to cut down on pollution. It isn't. The best that a zero economic growth policy could do is cut down on the *growth* in pollution. With the same output level and output mix, the rate of pollution would be the same from year to year. To cut pollution would require cutting GDP—that is, a *negative* economic growth policy! The economy has the capability of cleaning up pollution as well as generating pollution as it grows.

Using Key Terms

Across

2. employment rate
5. arithmetic growth
9. productivity
12. crowding in
13. labor force
14. geometric growth
15. net investment

Down

1. growth rate
3. production possibilities
4. base period
6. crowding out
7. human capital
8. GDP per capita
10. economic growth
11. real GDP

True or False

1. F Over half of the world's population lives in poverty.
2. T
3. F An increase in *nominal* GDP does not necessarily mean that production has increased.
4. F Growth in real GDP per capita is achieved when output grows more rapidly than population.
5. T
6. F Malthus believed that population grew geometrically but the means of subsistence grew only arithmetically.
7. T
8. T
9. T
10. F Immigration has significantly increased the labor force and contributed to the outward shift of the U.S. production possibilities curve over time.

Multiple Choice

1.	d	5.	a	9.	a	13.	c	17.	c
2.	d	6.	b	10.	d	14.	d	18.	b
3.	c	7.	c	11.	a	15.	d	19.	c
4.	b	8.	d	12.	a	16.	a	20.	b

Problems and Applications

Exercise 1

1. Short-run
2. Increased use of existing capacity
3. Long-run
4. Increased capacity, rightward, long-run AS

236

Exercise 2

Table 17.1 Answer

	1990	1998	Percentage change
(1) U.S. real GDP (billions of dollars)	$6707.9	$8515.7	27.0%
(2) U.S. population (thousands)	249,973	270,509	8.2%
(3) U.S. per capita GDP (dollars per person)	$26,834	$31,480	17.3%
(4) World population (thousands)	5,329,000	5,927,000	11.2%

2. Increased
3. Since the world population growth rate is faster than that of the U.S., it takes higher economic growth to maintain the same standard of living.
4. 3.375%
5. 21.33 years

Exercise 3

1. I/GDP is $4trillion/$10trillion = 0.40 or 40 percent
2. I/GDP is $1trillion/$5trillion = 0.20 or 20 percent
3. Country A, because it has a higher investment rate.
4. China and Thailand
5. China and Thailand

CHAPTER 18
Global Macro

Quick Review

- Trade impacts domestic economic performance. Exports (X) are an injection into the circular flow and imports (IM) are a leakage from it.

- The multiplier in an open economy reflects consumers' desire to spend some of every extra dollar on imports, which is called the marginal propensity to import (MPM). The multiplier for the open economy becomes 1/(MPS + MPM).

- The marginal propensity to import may interfere with fiscal policy in achieving domestic goals. Because the multiplier is smaller in an open economy than in a closed economy, any tax or spending change will have to be larger to achieve a given income or employment goal.

- Our exports (determined abroad) are seldom equal to our imports (determined at home). We expect either a trade surplus, $(X - IM) > 0$, or a trade deficit, $(X - IM) < 0$. Although the trade deficit permits us to consume more goods than we produce, it may complicate fiscal policy. A fiscal expansion will worsen any trade deficit, *ceteris paribus*.

- If the U.S. has a trade deficit, our trading partners must have an overall trade surplus.

- Capital flows involve the movement of money across international borders. Capital inflows occur when foreigners lend to us (e.g., by purchasing Treasury bonds or other U.S. assets) and outflows occur when we purchase assets from other countries.

- Capital flows are seldom in balance. When the outflow of dollars exceeds the inflow of dollars, the U.S. experiences a capital deficit; when the inflow exceeds the outflow, there is a capital surplus.

- Capital imbalances can alter macro outcomes. If the Fed decreases the growth of the money supply, domestic interest rates increase. This action attracts foreigners to U.S. bonds and other assets, which causes a capital inflow and an increase in the money supply.

- The critical link between economies in both trade and finance is the exchange rate.

- Specialization and trade increase world efficiency and output, and stimulate improvements in productivity, as producers anywhere must compete with producers everywhere. As a result, consumption possibilities increase.

- The gains from trade and cooperation among nations are enormous and have been pursued with great resolve by blocks of countries. The International Monetary Fund, the Group of Seven, and the European Union are all attempts at global coordination.

Learning Objectives

After reading Chapter 18 and doing the following exercises, you should:

1. Understand how international transactions affect U.S. economic performance and the ability to use macroeconomic policy.
2. Be able to explain why the open-economy multiplier is smaller than the closed-economy multiplier.
3. Understand why the marginal propensity to import *changes the slope* of the aggregate expenditure curve.
4. Be able to demonstrate how a change in exports *shifts* the aggregate expenditure curve.
5. Be able to show how trade and capital flows can counteract normal macro policy initiatives.
6. Be aware of the foreign repercussions of U.S. policy initiatives.
7. Know the principal vocabulary of the trade and capital accounts.
8. Be able to relate exchange rate changes to the question of competitiveness in international trade.
9. Understand the various attempts at global coordination.

Using Key Terms

Fill in the puzzle on the opposite page with the appropriate term from the list of Key Terms at the end of the chapter in the text.

Across
2. The ability of a country to produce a specific good at a lower opportunity cost than its trading partners.
3. Income diverted from the circular flow, such as imports.
9. Equal to 1-MPC.
12. Equal to exports minus imports.
13. The amount by which exports exceed imports.
14. Equal to 1/1-MPC.
15. The amount by which the capital outflow exceeds the capital inflow.

Down
1. The fraction of each additional dollar of income that is spent on imports.
4. Goods and services purchased from foreign sources.
5. A situation in which capital inflows are greater than capital outflows.
6. A decrease in private-sector borrowing and spending because of an increase in government borrowing.
7. A situation in which imports exceed exports.
8. Output per unit of input.
10. Goods and services sold to foreign sources.
11. The price of one country's currency in terms of another country's currency.

Puzzle 18.1

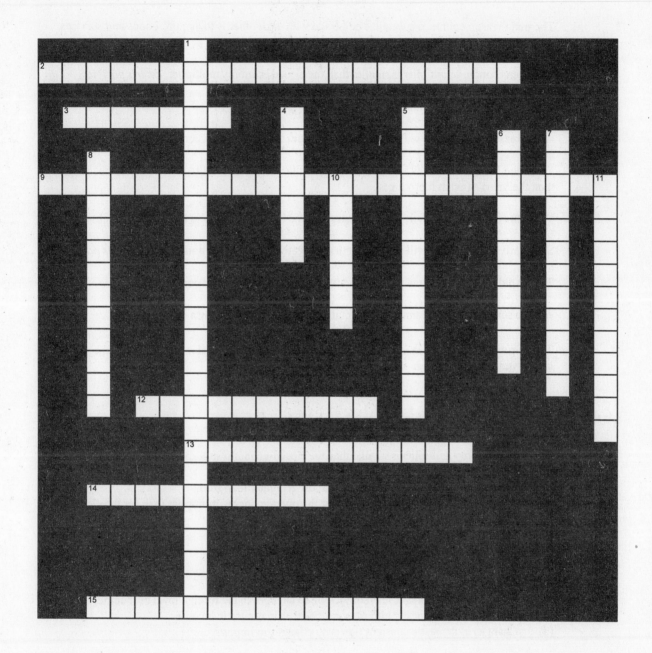

True or False: *Circle your choice and explain why any false statements are incorrect.*

T F 1. The main reason countries specialize and trade with each other is to acquire goods and services they cannot produce themselves.

T F 2. The open economy multiplier is smaller than the closed economy multiplier, *ceteris paribus*.

T F 3. Imports act like an automatic stabilizer for the economy.

T F 4. An increase in net exports will lower the equilibrium level of income, *ceteris paribus*.

T F 5. When the United States has a trade deficit, the value of what the United States consumes is more than the value of what it produces.

T F 6. When the dollar gets weaker, U.S. products become less competitive in the world market.

T F 7. Stimulative fiscal policy will increase both aggregate demand and a trade deficit, *ceteris paribus*.

T F 8. Trade stimulates improvements in productivity because of increased competition.

T F 9. A trade surplus is accompanied by a capital inflow; a trade deficit, by a capital outflow.

T F 10. The "Group of Seven" is an informal attempt to coordinate the global macro policy of the seven largest industrial countries.

Multiple Choice: *Select the correct answer.*

_____ 1. The open-economy multiplier is smaller than the closed-economy multiplier:
  (a) Because imports are a leakage from the circular flow.
  (b) Because the marginal propensity to import is greater than zero.
  (c) Because the denominator is greater for the open-economy multiplier than for the closed-economy multiplier.
  (d) For all of the above reasons.

_____ 2. The marginal propensity to import relates:
  (a) Domestic consumption to the foreign level of income.
  (b) Changes in the domestic level of income to changes in the foreign level of income.
  (c) Changes in the domestic imports with changes in domestic income.
  (d) Changes in domestic consumption with changes in imports.

_____ 3. An increase in U.S. exports:
  (a) Must increase unemployment in the rest of the world.
  (b) Means the rest of the world must be importing more.
  (c) Means the rest of the world must have a trade deficit.
  (d) Means the rest of the world must have a trade surplus.

4. If the marginal propensity to import is 0.2 and the marginal propensity to consume is 0.8, the open-economy multiplier is:
   (a) 0.4.
   (b) 2.5.
   (c) 4.0.
   (d) 2.0.

5. A decrease in the marginal propensity to import will:
   (a) Reduce the size of the open-economy multiplier.
   (b) Shift the aggregate supply curve rightward.
   (c) Increase the size of the open-economy multiplier.
   (d) Shift the aggregate demand curve leftward.

6. With respect to the circular flow of economic activity:
   (a) Exports are a leakage.
   (b) Imports are a leakage.
   (c) Imports and exports are both leakages.
   (d) Exports and imports are both injections.

7. World output of goods and services increases with specialization because:
   (a) The world's resources are being used more efficiently.
   (b) Each country's production possibilities curve is shifted outward.
   (c) Each country's workers are able to produce more than they could before specialization.
   (d) All of the above are correct.

8. When a trade deficit rises:
   (a) Exports rise, imports fall, or both.
   (b) Net exports fall.
   (c) The aggregate demand curve increases.
   (d) The level of income will rise, *ceteris paribus*.

9. An increase in U.S. imports:
   (a) Means the rest of the world must be exporting more.
   (b) Must increase unemployment in the rest of the world.
   (c) Means the rest of the world must have a trade deficit.
   (d) Means the rest of the world must have a trade surplus.

10. There is a tradeoff between the objective of reducing a trade deficit and the objective of reaching full employment because:
    (a) Net exports rise as income increases.
    (b) As income increases, the trade deficit rises.
    (c) Imports fall as income increases.
    (d) Fiscal policy and monetary policy must be used to achieve the objective.

11. Comparative advantage refers to the ability of a country to:
    (a) Produce a specific good with fewer resources than other countries.
    (b) Sell a good at a higher price than other countries.
    (c) Produce a specific good at a lower opportunity cost than other countries.
    (d) Maximize its economic welfare by producing all the goods and services it needs domestically.

12. French wine producers would gain an advantage over U.S. wine producers in world markets if:
    (a) The French franc weakened relative to the U.S. dollar.
    (b) The American dollar weakened against other currencies.
    (c) The French inflation rate rose relative to the American inflation rate.
    (d) French interest rates rose relative to American interest rates.

_____ 13. A net capital inflow into the U. S. means that the U. S. is:
   (a)   Consuming more than it produces, and net exports are positive.
   (b)   Consuming more than it produces, and net exports are negative.
   (c)   Consuming less than it produces, and net exports are positive.
   (d)   Consuming less than it produces, and net exports are negative.

_____ 14. The International Monetary Fund (IMF):
   (a)   Receives its funds from contributions from all the countries of the world.
   (b)   Lends funds to nations whose currency is in trouble.
   (c)   Often insists on changes in a nation's monetary, fiscal and/or trade policies as a condition for an IMF loan.
   (d)   All of the above are correct.

_____ 15. A capital outflow occurs for the U.S. when, _ceteris paribus_:
   (a)   Citizens of the United States buy foreign stock.
   (b)   U.S. corporations abroad repatriate their profits.
   (c)   Foreigners purchase real estate in the United States.
   (d)   All of the above occur.

_____ 16. If the Fed cuts interest rates to stimulate aggregate demand, this could cause:
   (a)   A capital outflow.
   (b)   A capital inflow.
   (c)   The value of the dollar to increase.
   (d)   The value of the Euro to decrease.

_____ 17. When the U.S. dollar is strong, _ceteris paribus_:
   (a)   Imports become more expensive.
   (b)   U.S. producers become more competitive in foreign markets.
   (c)   U.S. goods become more expensive for foreigners to buy.
   (d)   U.S. exports should increase.

_____ 18. A common currency, like the Euro, facilitates trade by:
   (a)   Eliminating the uncertainties associated with fluctuating exchange rates.
   (b)   Eliminating currency conversion costs.
   (c)   Easing the flow of financial capital across national boundaries.
   (d)   All of the above facilitate trade.

_____ 19. For a given amount of fiscal stimulus, an open economy will experience, _ceteris paribus_, a shift in aggregate demand that is:
   (a)   Greater than in a closed economy resulting in a larger increase in GDP.
   (b)   Less than in a closed economy resulting in a larger increase in GDP.
   (c)   Less than in a closed economy resulting in a smaller increase in GDP.
   (d)   Greater than in a closed economy resulting in a smaller increase in GDP.

_____ 20. Which of the following is true about the Group of Seven?
   (a)   It is composed of the seven largest industrialized nations.
   (b)   It assesses the global economic outlook.
   (c)   It coordinates global macroeconomic policy.
   (d)   All of the above.

Problems and Applications

Exercise 1

Using the consumption function and the marginal propensity to import, it is possible to compare the multiplier effect for an open economy versus the multiplier effect for a closed economy.

Assume that an economy is characterized by the consumption function

$$C = 100 + 0.75Y_D$$

where all figures are in billions of dollars.

1. What is the marginal propensity to consume for this closed economy? _____

2. Compute the marginal propensity to save for the closed economy. _____

3. Compute the multiplier for this closed economy. _____

4. If government expenditures were to increase $100 billion, how much would income increase in this closed economy? _____

5. Now suppose the economy has been opened up to imports and has a marginal propensity to import equal to 0.25.

    Assuming that the consumption function is the same as in the beginning of this exercise, compute the multiplier for this open economy. _____

6. Now, if government expenditures increase $100 billion, how much does income increase in this open economy? _____

7. T   F   Imports reduce the effectiveness of fiscal policy. (Compare your answers in questions 4 and 6 above.)

Figure 18.1

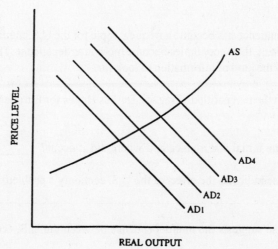

8. Refer to Figure 18.1. Assume the economy is originally on AD$_1$. For a closed economy, a fiscal policy stimulus shifts aggregate demand to AD$_3$. In an open economy, the same fiscal policy stimulus would shift aggregate demand to _____, *ceteris paribus*.

Exercise 2

This exercise shows the impact of fiscal policy on the trade balance.

Assume the following information for a hypothetical economy.

Table 18.1 Data in billions of dollars

	Year 1	Year 2
GDP	$800	$_____
Exports	50	50
Imports	60	_____
Net exports	_____	_____
Import/GDP ratio	_____	_____

1. Calculate the level of net exports in Year 1 in Table 18.1.

2. Assume the government increases spending form Year 1 to Year 2, which causes GDP to increase by $200 billion. Calculate GDP for Year 2 in Table 18.1.

3. As a result of the increase in government spending, the demand for imports increases. Assume imports increase by $10 for every $100 increase in GDP. Calculate the level of imports for Year 2 in Table 18.1.

4. Assume exports do not change. Calculate the level of net exports for Year 2 in Table 18.1.

5. Calculate the import/GDP ratio for Year 1 and for Year 2 in Table 18.1.

6. In an open economy, fiscal stimulus tends to (increase, decrease) a trade deficit by (increasing, decreasing) imports.

Exercise 3

Economic interdependence has become a frequent topic for the U.S. media. As countries forge greater links through trade and investment, their economies become more interdependent. This exercise will use one of the articles in the text to show the kind of information to look for.

Reread the article in the text entitled "Tragedy Dashes Hopes for Europe's Economy." Then answer the following questions.

1. What was the initial disturbance and where did it occur? _____

2. Which phrase indicates the effect of the U.S. economy's problems on the level of European exports? _____

3. Which phrase suggests the interdependence between the U.S. economy and Europe? _____
_____

246

Common Errors

The first statement in each "common error" below is incorrect. Each incorrect statement is followed by a corrected version and an explanation.

1. A stronger dollar means American firms are stronger and more competitive. WRONG!

   A stronger dollar puts U.S. firms at a competitive disadvantage, *ceteris paribus.* RIGHT!

   When the dollar becomes stronger, this means the dollar can now purchase more of a foreign currency. It also means it takes more of a foreign currency to purchase one U.S. dollar. U.S. manufactured items now cost more. The stronger dollar effectively causes the price of U.S. manufactured items to increase for foreign countries, and this puts U. S. firms at a competitive disadvantage.

2. Foreign trade does not impact the effectiveness of domestic fiscal and monetary policy. WRONG!

   Foreign trade can significantly impact the effectiveness of domestic fiscal and monetary policy. RIGHT!

   Imports and exports result in financial flows into and out of the economy. The movement of goods across borders not only affects the exchange rates, but also the spending multipliers. In a closed economy the spending multiplier is equal to 1/MPS, while in an open economy the spending multiplier is equal to 1/(MPS + MPM). Thus, in an open economy, the spending multiplier is smaller and fiscal and monetary policies have less impact than in a closed economy.

3. American firms have trouble competing with foreign firms because wages are so low. WRONG!

   American firms may have trouble competing with foreign firms because of changes in exchange rates. RIGHT!

   Wage rates are typically a reflection of labor productivity. American workers are paid more because they are more productive than foreign workers are, in general. For many products, the labor cost per unit is actually less in the United States. But the wage rate is not the only factor that determines the international price of a product. Exchange rates are also a determinant. When Americans buy foreign goods and send American dollars abroad, they provide the money with which foreigners can buy American goods. If American goods are being bought in large quantities by foreigners and Americans are buying few foreign goods, a trade imbalance will develop. The value of the dollar will rise as foreign exchange markets move to eliminate such an imbalance. This rise in the value of the dollar will increase the international price of American made items and make all American goods less competitive internationally.

4. Trade surpluses are good for the economy, and trade deficits are bad for the economy. WRONG!

   Trade surpluses and deficits are neither *inherently* bad nor *inherently* good. RIGHT!

   When we run a trade deficit, we get the benefits of foreign resources *net*. That's good. But persistent deficits can be bad for the economy if they lead to restrictive policies designed to cut down on imports and to a continual depreciation of the exchange rate. Our persistent trade deficits (foreigners' trade surpluses) mean foreigners will eventually accumulate more of our currency than they want to hold. Capital inflows will not be able to stem the glut of the currency. As a result, our currency will depreciate and foreign goods will become more expensive.

247

5. The U.S. trade deficit means U.S. producers are inefficient. WRONG!

   The U.S. trade deficit means U.S. producers are having difficulty competing. RIGHT!

   The trade deficit reflects more than our (in)efficiency. As an example, U.S. agricultural producers are extremely efficient, but they have had difficulty exporting because the dollar was so strong for so long. A weaker dollar helps our producers compete. Before we believe the rhetoric concerning competitiveness, we need to know what is happening to exchange rates.

•ANSWERS•

Using Key Terms

Across
2. comparative advantage
3. leakage
9. marginal propensity to save
12. net exports
13. trade surplus
14. multiplier
15. capital deficit

Down
1. marginal propensity to import
4. imports
5. capital surplus
6. crowding out
7. trade deficit
8. productivity
10. exports
11. exchange rate

True or False

1. F   Getting goods and services they can't produce themselves is one reason to trade, but the main reason countries specialize and trade is to increase total output, incomes, and living standards.
2. T
3. T
4. F   Net exports are a part of GDP, so an increase will cause equilibrium income to increase.
5. T
6. F   U.S. products become more competitive (i.e. relatively lower priced) when the U.S. dollar becomes weaker.
7. T
8. T
9. F   A trade deficit is associated with a capital inflow and a trade surplus is associated with a capital outflow.
10. T

Multiple Choice

1. d	5. c	9. a	13. b	17. c
2. c	6. b	10. b	14. d	18. d
3. b	7. a	11. c	15. a	19. c
4. b	8. b	12. a	16. a	20. d

Problems and Applications

Exercise 1

1. 0.75. See the consumption function.
2. $0.25 (= 1 - 0.75)$
3. $4 (= 1/MPS)$
4. $400 billion (= \$100 billion \times 4)$
5. $2 [= 1/(MPS + MPM) = 1/(0.25 + 0.25)]$
6. $200 billion (= \$100 billion \times 2)$
7. T
8. AD_2

Exercise 2

1. **Table 18.1 Answer**

	Year 1	Year 2
GDP	$800	$1,000
Exports	50	50
Imports	60	80
Net exports	-10	-30
Import/GDP ratio	0.075	0.080

2. See Table 18.1 Answer.
3. See Table 18.1 Answer.
4. See Table 18.1 Answer.
5. See Table 18.1 Answer.
6. Increase, increasing

Exercise 3

1. Terrorist attacks on the United States.
2. "The U.S. buys 22 percent of Europe's exports."
3. "Economists estimate a percentage-point drop in U.S. economic growth translates into a half-percentage point decline in European growth."

CHAPTER 19
Theory and Reality

Quick Review

- Government policy-makers have many tools with which to design and implement the ideal "package" of macro policies.

- The basic tools of fiscal policy are taxes and government spending. Automatic stabilizers, such as income taxes and unemployment benefits, help to stabilize any disruptions in the economy by responding automatically to changes in national income.

- Monetary policy, controlled by the Federal Reserve, uses open market operations, changes in the discount rate, and occasional changes in the reserve requirement to impact the macroeconomy. Both monetary and fiscal policy shift the aggregate demand curve.

- Supply-side policy focuses on shifting the aggregate supply curve, which allows for economic growth. Tax cuts, government deregulation, education, training, and research are supply-side tools.

- To end a recession, we can cut taxes, increase government spending, or expand the money supply. To curb inflation, we can reverse each of these policy levers. To overcome stagflation, fiscal and monetary policies can be combined with supply-side incentives.

- Recurring economic slowdowns with accompanying increases in unemployment and nagging inflation suggest that obstacles may stand in the way of successful policy-making. In addition, there are opportunity costs for all policy decisions, and economic goals may even conflict with one another.

- Measurement problems exist because data is always dated and incomplete, and we must rely on forecasts of future economic activity that have inherent accuracy problems. Design problems exist as well because we are frequently unsure of just how the economy will respond to specific policy initiatives. Implementation problems reflect the time it takes Congress and the president to agree on an appropriate plan of action. And there is always the chance that policy approaches will reflect political needs rather than economic needs.

- Those who favor discretionary policies believe that active intervention is necessary. Others (monetarists and new classical economists) believe fine-tuning is not possible and favor fixed policy rules.

Learning Objectives

After reading Chapter 19 and doing the following exercises, you should:

1. Know the three basic types of policies and each of the policy levers.
2. Know how the concept of "opportunity cost" defines the basic policy tradeoffs faced in the economy.
3. Be able to prescribe policies to eliminate an AD shortfall.
4. Be able to design policies to deal with excess AD.
5. Be able to suggest policies to control stagflation.
6. Know the general theories of several groups of economists.
7. Evaluate how effective policy makers have been in battling inflation and unemployment.
8. Be able to explain how measurement problems impede the development of effective policies.
9. Understand the concept of a leading indicator.
10. Understand the design problems encountered in administering policy and the problems that are inherent in economic forecasting.
11. Know the "rational-expectations" argument about the effectiveness of policy.
12. Recognize the lags involved in policy implementation.
13. Know the advantages and problems of both rules and discretion in making policy.

Using Key Terms

Fill in the puzzle on the opposite page with the appropriate term from the list of Key Terms at the end of the chapter in the text.

Across

4. Spending or revenue item that responds automatically and countercyclically to changes in national income.
5. Alternating periods of economic expansion and contraction.
8. The idea that people make decisions on the basis of all available information, including the anticipated effects of government intervention.
9. A period during which real GDP grows, but at a rate below the long-term trend.
10. A situation of inflation and substantial unemployment.
11. Equal to 1/1-MPC.
12. Spending increases or tax cuts intended to increase aggregate demand.
13. Focuses on providing incentives to work, invest, and produce.
14. The use of money and credit controls to change macroeconomic outcomes.
16. The difference between equilibrium GDP and full-employment GDP when there is demand-pull inflation.
17. The use of spending and revenue items to change macroeconomic outcomes.

Down

1. The lowest rate of unemployment compatible with price stability.
2. Continuous responses to changing economic conditions.
3. The number of times money turns over in a given time period.
6. Federal revenues at full employment minus federal expenditures at full employment.
7. Spending decreases or tax hikes intended to decrease aggregate demand.
15. The difference between full-employment GDP and equilibrium GDP.

Puzzle 19.1

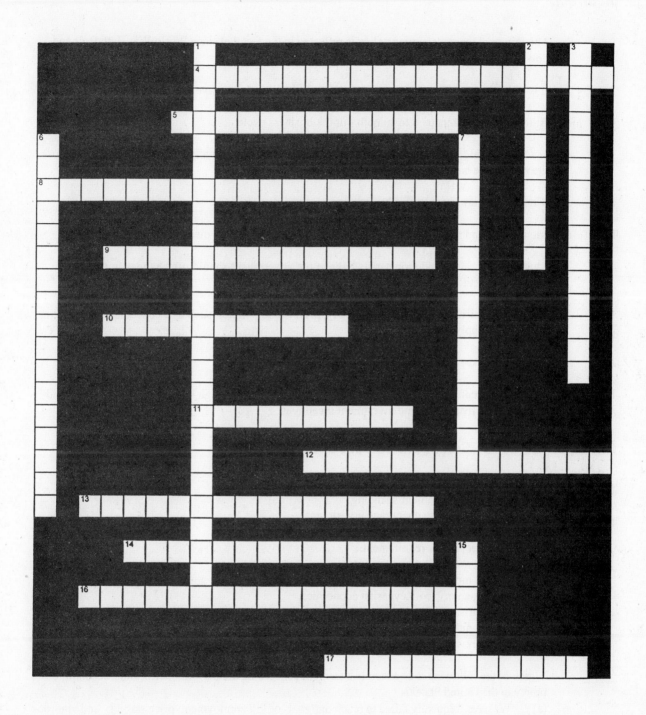

True or False: *Circle your choice and explain why any false statements are incorrect.*

T F 1. The failure of macroeconomic policy is reflected in the fact that since World War II, the ups and downs of the business cycle have become more severe.

T F 2. It is often the case that good economic policy and political objectives are in conflict.

T F 3. Automatic stabilizers tend to smooth out the business cycle.

T F 4. Macroeconomic forecasts from different computer models are usually surprisingly similar because the models are based on the same macroeconomic theories.

T F 5. Monetary policy is controlled by Congress.

T F 6. Monetarists and new classical economists favor rules rather than discretionary macro policies.

T F 7. Modern Keynesians and monetarists believe the government should use changes in the money supply as a method to eliminate a GDP gap.

T F 8. The new classical economists favor steady, predictable policies, such as a constant growth rate in the money supply.

T F 9. External shocks can make economic forecasts invalid.

T F 10. Supply-side economists focus on the expansion of capacity through lower marginal tax rates and policies to increase work and investment incentives.

Multiple Choice: *Select the correct answer.*

_____ 1. A supply-side policy cure to stagflation would include:
    (a) Reduced government spending.
    (b) Tax incentives to encourage investment.
    (c) Open-market operations when the Fed buys securities.
    (d) A higher reserve requirement.

_____ 2. Fine-tuning is most consistent with:
    (a) Keynesian or Neo-Keynesian economics.
    (b) Monetarist or new classical economics.
    (c) Supply-side economics or new classical economics.
    (d) A laissez -faire policy.

_____ 3. Which of the following is an accurate statement concerning the performance of macroeconomic policy in the United States?
    (a) We have frequently failed to reach our goals of full employment, price stability and vigorous economic growth.
    (b) The business cycle continues to exist.
    (c) The ups and downs of the business cycle have been less severe since World War II.
    (d) All of the above are accurate.

_____ 4. Monetary policy to eliminate a recession might include:
    (a)   Infrastructure development.
    (b)   The sale of securities in the open market by the Fed.
    (c)   A decrease in the marginal tax rate.
    (d)   A decrease in the discount rate.

_____ 5. When Federal Reserve Board chairman Alan Greenspan announced a goal of "zero inflation," which of the following was most consistent with his new goal?
    (a)   A lower discount rate.
    (b)   A lower minimum reserve ratio.
    (c)   Sales of securities in the open market.
    (d)   Increased government spending.

_____ 6. Which of the following groups feels that output and employment gravitate to a long-term rate determined by structural forces in the labor and product markets?
    (a)   Monetarists.
    (b)   Keynesians.
    (c)   New classical economists.
    (d)   Supply-side economists.

_____ 7. An increase in the discount rate during an inflationary period would be a policy consistent with the views of:
    (a)   Monetarists.
    (b)   Modern Keynesians.
    (c)   Monetarists and supply-siders.
    (d)   New classicals and "Old" Keynesians

_____ 8. A supply-side policy to reduce AD excess would include:
    (a)   Tax incentives to encourage saving.
    (b)   Reduced government spending.
    (c)   The purchase of securities by the Fed.
    (d)   A higher reserve requirement.

_____ 9. Which of the following is the Monetarist policy for fighting a recession?
    (a)   Increase government spending.
    (b)   Expand the money supply at a faster rate.
    (c)   Provide tax incentives to increase investment.
    (d)   Patience (i.e., laissez faire).

_____ 10. Which of the following supply-side efforts has the George W. Bush administration embraced?
    (a)   Deficit reduction.
    (b)   Reduced marginal tax rates.
    (c)   A zero-inflation target.
    (d)   All of the above.

_____ 11. Expansionary fiscal and monetary policy are _not_ effective when the aggregate:
    (a)   Supply curve is horizontal.
    (b)   Supply curve is vertical.
    (c)   Supply is upward sloping but not vertical.
    (d)   Demand curve is vertical.

12. The opportunity costs of different policies must be weighted to solve which of the following obstacles?
    (a) Design problems.
    (b) Measurement problems.
    (c) Goal conflicts.
    (d) Implementation problems.

13. Which of the following is a reason that many economic policies fail, even if they are properly designed to achieve economic goals?
    (a) Measurement difficulties prevent policy makers from correctly identifying what is actually happening in the economy.
    (b) People often react in ways that may undercut new government policies.
    (c) There are significant lags in response to policy.
    (d) All of the above are reasons for the failure of economic policy.

14. Advocates of "fixed policy rules" believe:
    (a) That "fixed policy rules" can improve macro outcomes.
    (b) Appropriate macro policy would include constant increases in the money supply and balanced federal budgets.
    (c) That in view of the many practical problems associated with implementing fiscal and monetary policy, the economy would be better off if discretionary policy were abandoned.
    (d) All of the above.

15. During a severe recession, appropriate economic policy might include:
    (a) An open market sale by the Fed, a decrease in the discount rate, or an increase in the budget deficit.
    (b) A decrease in government spending, a decrease in the discount rate, or a decrease in government regulations.
    (c) An open market purchase by the Fed, a decrease in the discount rate, or a decrease in government regulations.
    (d) An open market purchase by the Fed, a decrease in tax rates, or a decrease in the budget deficit.

16. Which of the following groups feels that output and employment gravitate to their natural levels?
    (a) Keynesians.
    (b) Monetarists.
    (c) New Classical economists.
    (d) Marxists.

17. Leading economic indicators are used to address:
    (a) Goal conflicts.
    (b) Design problems.
    (c) Measurement problems.
    (d) Implementation problems.

18. Congress is responsible for:
    (a) Monetary policy.
    (b) Fiscal policy and supply-side policy.
    (c) Monetary and fiscal policy.
    (d) Monetary, fiscal, and supply-side policy.

19. The order of policy lags can best be stated as follows:
    (a) Formulation, recognition, and implementation lags.
    (b) Implementation, formulation, and recognition lags.
    (c) Recognition, formulation, and implementation lags.
    (d) Formulation, implementation, and recognition lags.

_____ 20. Which of the following groups believes that people will realize what the government is attempting to do and will take action to offset government policy?
- (a) Modern Keynesians.
- (b) Keynesians.
- (c) Monetarists.
- (d) Marxists.

Problems and Applications

Exercise 1

This exercise will help you recognize the inherent tradeoffs in the economy.

Table 19.1 presents data on interest rates, government expenditures, taxes, exports, imports, investment, consumption, a price index, and unemployment for four levels of equilibrium income (GDP). These items appear frequently in newspaper articles about the economy.

Table 19.1 Level of key economic indicators, by GDP level
(billions of dollars per year)

Interest rate	30%	20%	10%	0%
Government expenditures	$ 100	$ 100	$ 100	100
Taxes	25	75	125	175
Budget balance	___	___	___	___
Exports	300	300	300	300
Imports	260	280	300	320
Investment	10	90	170	250
Consumption	750	790	830	870
Nominal GDP				
Price index	1.00	1.00	1.02	1.10
Real GDP (constant dollars)	___	___	___	___
Unemployment rate	15%	7%	4%	3.5%

1. Compute the federal budget balance, nominal GDP, and real GDP in Table 19.1, for each level of interest rate. (*Hint:* Remember the formula $C + I + G + [X - M] = $ GDP.)

2. Which policy is the government most likely using to reach each of the situations in Table 19.1?
- (a) Fiscal policy.
- (b) Monetary policy.
- (c) Wage and price controls.
- (d) Labor policy.

3. Which of the following statements best explains why the amount paid in taxes might change as the level of GDP changes, as shown in Table 19.1?
- (a) Taxpayers experience stagflation as income increases.
- (b) As taxpayers' incomes rise, their marginal tax rates rise.
- (c) The income tax is regressive.
- (d) Automatic stabilizers link taxes with income.

4. The most likely explanation for why the price index changes as the level of GDP changes, as shown in Table 19.1, is that as:
   (a) People receive greater income, they can be more discriminating buyers and find the lowest prices.
   (b) Firms receive more orders, productivity rises allowing inflation to ease.
   (c) People receive greater income, they spend it, and if the economy is near full employment, prices begin to rise.
   (d) Businesses receive greater income, they have an incentive to expand capacity and must pass the cost of the increased capacity on to consumers in the form of higher prices.

5. The most logical reason for why unemployment changes as the level of GDP changes, as shown in Table 19.1, is that as GDP rises:
   (a) People do not need jobs and leave the labor force.
   (b) Automatic stabilizers provide increased benefits to the unemployed, keeping them out of the labor force.
   (c) Inflation causes real income to fall and employment to decrease.
   (d) Aggregate demand rises, stimulating the derived demand for labor.

Exercise 2

This exercise shows the difficulties faced by policy makers because of the inevitable tradeoffs in the economy.

Table 19.2 presents data on government expenditure, taxes, the price index, unemployment, and pollution for four levels of equilibrium income (GDP). These items appear frequently in newspaper articles about the economy.

Table 19.2 Level of key economic indicators, by GDP level (billions of dollars per year)

Indicator	Nominal GDP $120	$160	$200	$240
Government expenditure	$ 0	$ 20	$ 35	$ 50
Taxes	$ 18	$ 24	$ 30	$ 36
Budget balance	$____	$____	$____	$____
Price index	1.00	1.00	1.02	1.20
Real GDP (constant dollars)	$____	$____	$____	$____
Unemployment rate	15%	7%	4%	3.5%
Pollution index	1.00	1.10	1.80	1.90

1. Compute the federal budget balance and real GDP in Table 19.2 for each level of nominal GDP.

2. Choose the government expenditure level that is best at accomplishing all of the following goals, according to Table 19.2. $_____
   • Lowest level of taxes.
   • Lowest pollution index.
   • Lowest inflation rate.

258

3. Which of the following might induce a policy maker to choose a higher government expenditure level than the one that answers question 2?
   (a) High unemployment.
   (b) An inability by government to provide public goods and services.
   (c) Low real income.
   (d) All of the above.

4. Choose the government expenditure level that is best at accomplishing all of the following goals, according to Table 19.2. $_____
   • Lowest unemployment rate.
   • Largest amount of government spending.
   • Highest level of real income.

5. The policy that best satisfies the goals in question 4, is most likely to result in:
   (a) A recession.
   (b) Rapid economic growth accompanied by inflation.
   (c) Stagflation.
   (d) Deflation.

6. Choose the government expenditure level that is best at accomplishing all of the following goals, according to Table 19.2. $_____
   • Balancing the federal budget.
   • Maintaining pollution at reasonably low levels.
   • Maintaining price stability.

7. At which government expenditure level does full employment occur? (Use 4 percent unemployment as full employment.) $_____

8. If you are a policy maker faced with the alternatives in Table 19.2, can you say that one of the alternative government expenditure levels is clearly better than all the others? _____

Exercise 3

This exercise tests your ability to choose the appropriate policy initiative to overcome various undesirable economic conditions.

Choose a policy from the list below that would be appropriate to correct the economic conditions at the top of Table 19.3. Place the letter of each item in Table 19.3 only once.

a. Deregulation.
b. Discount rate lowered.
c. Discount rate raised.
d. Government spending decreases.
e. Government spending increases.
f. Open-market operations (Fed buys government securities).
g. Open-market operations (Fed sells government securities).

h. Reserve requirement higher.
i. Reserve requirement lower.
j. Job and skill training.
k. Tax cuts.
l. Tax incentives to alter the structure of supply and demand.
m. Tax incentives to encourage saving.
n. Tax increases.

Table 19.3 Economic policies

	Recession	Inflation	Stagflation
Fiscal policy	1._____	6._____	
	2._____	7._____	
Monetary policy	3._____	8._____	
	4._____	9._____	
	5._____	10._____	
Supply-side policy		11._____	12._____
			13._____
			14._____

Exercise 4

The media often provide information about the government's slow response to the economy's needs. This exercise will use one of the articles in the text to show the kind of information to look for.

Reread the article in the text titled "Deficit-Cutting Wilts in Heat from Voters." Then answer the following questions.

1. Which *one* of the following obstacles to success is best illustrated by the article?
   (a) Goal conflicts.
   (b) Measurement problems.
   (c) Design problems.
   (d) Implementation problems.

2. Which passage specifically mentions the obstacle you have chosen? _____
   _____

3. Which passage indicates the decision-maker who is responsible for determining the policy?
   _____

4. Which passage indicates the situation that requires a policy response? _____
   _____

Common Errors

The first statement in each "common error" below is incorrect. Each incorrect statement is followed by a corrected version and an explanation.

1. Fiscal and monetary policy should be consistently applied to stimulate the economy. WRONG!

   Fiscal and monetary policies must be tailored to the specific economic problems faced by the government. RIGHT!

The government sometimes needs to apply apparently contradictory monetary and fiscal policies in order to attain quite different goals. For example, an expansionary fiscal policy may be needed to stimulate the economy, but a contractionary monetary policy may be needed to raise interest rates so that foreign capital will be enticed into the United States. A policy maker must weigh the various goals and decide on the appropriate mix of tools to achieve them.

2. Fiscal, monetary, and stagflation policies are effective regardless of the income level of the economy. WRONG!

The state of the economy in relation to full employment is important in determining the effectiveness of the various policies. RIGHT!

If the economy is experiencing an excess aggregate demand, wage–price controls will prove ineffective in curbing inflation. At relatively low levels of GDP, however, wage–price controls can be effective in holding down inflation. Work-force policies are often more effective in matching people with jobs when many people are looking for work than when unemployment is low. It is easier for the government to increase expenditures to stimulate the economy when there is a recession than to cut them back when there is excess aggregate demand.

3. The government has the power to prevent unemployment and inflation, but it just doesn't want to use it. WRONG!

While the government has the power to move the economy closer to any one goal, it faces a tradeoff between different goals that prevents it from achieving all of them. RIGHT!

Remember that the Phillips curve shows that a tradeoff exists between unemployment and inflation. Government policies to lower unemployment may lead to a worsening of inflation. The government must choose between the different goals.

•ANSWERS•

Using Key Terms

Across

4. automatic stabilizer
5. business cycle
8. rational expectations
9. growth recession
10. stagflation
11. multiplier
12. fiscal stimulus
13. supply-side policy
14. monetary policy
16. inflationary GDP gap
17. fiscal policy

Down

1. natural rate of unemployment
2. fine tuning
3. velocity of money
6. structural deficit
7. fiscal restraint
15. GDP gap

True or False

1. F The ups and downs of the business cycle have become less severe since World War II, possibly indicating partial success.
2. T
3. T
4. F Macroeconomic forecasts often differ because the models are based on different macroeconomic theories (e.g., Keynesian, supply-side).
5. F Monetary policy is controlled by the Federal Reserve.
6. T
7. F Modern Keynesians would agree to the use of changes in the money supply, but monetarists would take a "hands off" approach, believing that as sales and output decline, interest rates will decline (because of lower demand) and the lower rates will stimulate investment without government intervention.
8. F New classicals believe that the only policies that work are those that are unexpected because rational people will anticipate the impact of announced policies and take protective actions that will render the announced policies ineffective.
9. T
10. T

Multiple Choice

1.	b	5.	c	9.	d	13.	d	17.	c
2.	a	6.	a	10.	b	14.	d	18.	b
3.	d	7.	b	11.	b	15.	c	19.	c
4.	d	8.	a	12.	c	16.	b	20.	a

Problems and Applications

Exercise 1

1. **Table 19.1 Answer (billions of dollars per year)**

Interest rate	30%	20%	10%	0%
Budget balance	$ –75	$ –25	$ 25	$ 75
Nominal GDP	900	1,000	1,100	1,200
Real GDP (constant dollars)	900	1,000	1,078	1,091

At the 30 percent interest rate, the following calculations should have been made, in billions of dollars per year:

Budget balance = $25 - $100 = - $75

Nominal GDP = $750 + $10 + $100 + $40 = $900

2. b   3. b   4. c   5. d

Exercise 2

1. **Table 19.2 Answer (billions of dollars per year)**

Indicator	Nominal GDP			
	$120	$160	$200	$240
Budget balance	$ 18	$ 4	$ -5	$ -14
Real GDP (constant dollars)	120	160	196	200

2. $0
3. d

4. $50 billion
5. b

6. $20 billion
7. $35 billion

8. No

Exercise 3

1. **Table 19.3 Answer**

	Recession	Inflation	Stagflation
Fiscal	1. k Tax cuts 2. e Government spending increases	6. n Tax increases 7. d Government spending decreases	
Monetary policy	3. b Discount rate lowered 4. f Open-market operations (Fed buys government securities) 5. i Reserve requirement lower	8. c Discount rate raised 9. g Open-market operations (Fed sells government securities) 10. h Reserve requirement higher	
Supply-side policy		11. m Tax incentives to encourage saving	12. a Deregulation 13. l Tax incentives to alter the structure of supply and demand 14. j Job and skill training

263

Exercise 4

1. a However, there is implicit evidence of design problems concerning the best way to cut the deficit.

2. "Even before his proposal [to cut the deficit] took shape, more than 3,000 New Mexico constituents sent him identical postcards opposing any effort to cap entitlement programs." The passage shows the conflict between deficit cutting and the need for inflation-indexed entitlement programs to protect different groups.

3. "Senate, which voted 69 to 28 to reject the proposal"

4. "digging out of the massive federal deficit"

CHAPTER 20

International Trade

Quick Review

- The trade balance for any country is the difference between its exports and imports. Since the mid-1970s, the United States has experienced a trade deficit.

- Without trade, each country's consumption possibilities are limited to its production possibilities. With trade, a country may concentrate its resources on the goods it produces relatively efficiently. Trade allows for specialization and increases total world output. For each country, consumption possibilities will exceed production possibilities.

- For trade to be mutually beneficial, each country must exploit its comparative advantage. Comparative advantage is based on relative efficiency in production. If Country A produces a specific good, and in doing so gives up less in terms of other goods than Country B gives up to produce the same good, then Country A has a comparative advantage. Comparative advantage relies on a comparison of relative opportunity costs.

- For trade to be mutually beneficial, the terms of trade—the rate at which one good is exchanged for another—must lie between the opportunity costs for each of the individual countries. The closer the terms of trade are to the slope of a country's production-possibilities curve, the fewer benefits it receives, and vice versa.

- Not everyone benefits from trade. Those involved in import competing industries will object to trade because they may lose jobs to foreign producers. Other arguments against free trade include concerns about national security, dumping, and protection of infant industries. Those engaged in export industries will favor trade because jobs and profits are likely to increase.

- There are several different types of trade barriers. An embargo prohibits the trade of certain goods. Tariffs discourage imports by making the goods more expensive. Quotas set a limit on the quantity of a particular good that may be imported. Nontariff barriers can also restrict trade.

- The World Trade Organization (WTO) polices world trade and looks for trade agreement violations. Regional pacts, such as NAFTA and the EU, are designed to reduce trade barriers.

Learning Objectives

After reading Chapter 20 and doing the following exercises, you should:

1. Know some basic facts about U.S. trade patterns.
2. Understand the macroeconomic impact of international trade.
3. Understand why specialization and trade increase both production possibilities and consumption possibilities.
4. Be able to explain comparative advantage using opportunity costs.
5. Know how to determine the limits to the terms of trade.
6. Be able to calculate the gains from specialization and trade at given terms of trade.
7. Be able to show how trade allows a country to consume beyond its production-possibilities curve.
8. Recognize the sources of pressure that result in restricted trade.
9. Know some of the arguments used by those wishing to restrict trade.
10. Be able to discuss tariff and nontariff barriers to trade.
11. Be able to discuss the reasons for the rise of regional trading arrangements.

Using Key Terms

Fill in the puzzle on the opposite page with the appropriate term from the list of Key Terms at the end of the chapter in the text.

Across

2. Alternative combinations of goods and services that can be produced with available resources and technology.
3. Alternative combinations of goods and services that a country can consume.
5. The ability to produce a good at a lower opportunity cost than another country.
9. A negative trade balance.
11. The sale of goods in export markets at prices below domestic prices.
13. A limit on the quantity of a good that may be imported.
14. The most desired goods and services that are foregone in order to obtain something else.
15. A tax imposed on imported goods.
16. The amount of good A given up for good B in trade.

Down

1. An agreement to reduce the volume of trade in a specific good.
4. Determined by the intersection of market demand and market supply.
6. The ability of a country to produce a good with fewer resources than other countries.
7. A prohibition on exports or imports.
8. The amount by which exports exceed imports.
10. Goods and services sold to foreign buyers.
12. Goods and services purchased from foreign sources.

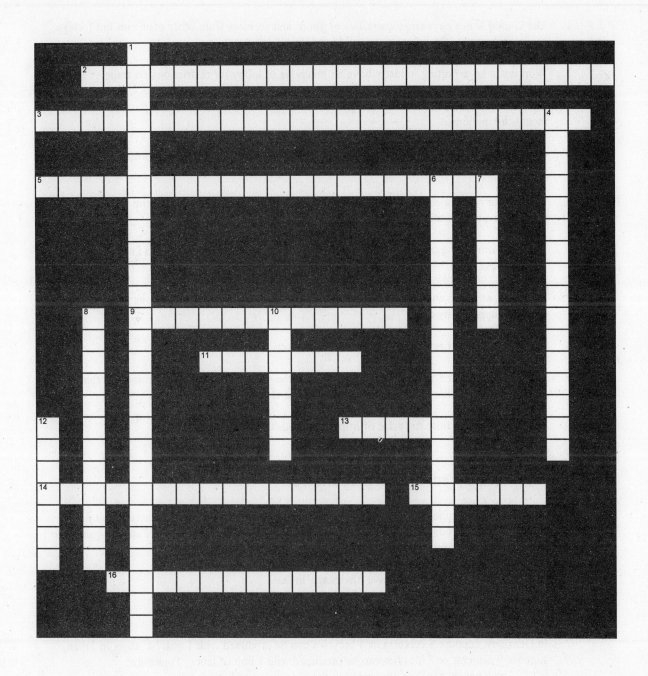

True or False: *Circle your choice and explain why any false statements are incorrect.*

T   F   1.   The United States buys large quantities of goods and services from other countries but foreign countries buy very few of our goods and services.

T   F   2.   Workers in an exporting industry have an incentive to lobby for restrictions on trade.

T   F   3.   The United States relies less on foreign trade, as measured by the ratio of exports to GDP, than most other nations.

T   F   4.   Comparative advantage refers to the ability to produce output with fewer resources than any other country.

T   F   5.   If one country has a comparative advantage in producing one of two goods, the other country must have a comparative advantage in the other good.

T   F   6.   It is impossible for a country to consume a mix of goods and services beyond its production-possibilities curve.

T   F   7.   The terms at which countries will trade one good for another will occur between their respective domestic opportunity costs.

T   F   8.   Everybody wins when countries specialize and trade.

T   F   9.   From the consumer's point of view, quotas have the potential to inflict more damage than do tariffs because additional imports are not available at any price.

T   F   10.   Tariffs and quotas raise the price of imported goods to consumers.

Multiple Choice: *Select the correct answer.*

_____   1.   Suppose the production of 1 ton of steel in the United States requires the same amount of resources as the production of 100 metric tons of wheat. In Canada, 2 tons of steel requires the same amount of resources as 200 metric tons of wheat. This means that:
   (a)   Neither country has a comparative advantage.
   (b)   Canada has the comparative advantage in steel.
   (c)   The United States has an absolute advantage in steel.
   (d)   The United States has the comparative advantage in steel.

_____   2.   In Germany, suppose 6 cameras or 4 bicycles can be produced with 1 unit of labor. In Japan, suppose 9 cameras or 5 bicycles can be produced with 1 unit of labor. Therefore:
   (a)   Japan has an absolute advantage in the production of both goods.
   (b)   Japan has a comparative advantage in the production of both goods.
   (c)   Germany has a comparative advantage in the production of cameras.
   (d)   Japan has a comparative advantage in the production of bicycles.

_____   3.   If a country is completely self-reliant in producing goods for its own consumption needs, then:
   (a)   It is consuming more than it could with trade.
   (b)   Its consumption possibilities will equal its production possibilities.
   (c)   It is promoting specialization.
   (d)   It will achieve a higher standard of living by exporting.

_____ 4. The expansion of world output as a result of trade is mainly due to the effects of:
   (a) Higher trade barriers.
   (b) Improved terms of trade.
   (c) Specialization according to comparative advantage.
   (d) Specialization according to absolute advantage.

_____ 5. When one country can produce a given amount of a good using fewer inputs than any other country:
   (a) It has an absolute advantage in producing the good.
   (b) It has a comparative advantage in producing the good.
   (c) Specialization will definitely increase worldwide consumption possibilities.
   (d) All of the above.

_____ 6. "Terms of trade" refers to:
   (a) The opportunity costs incurred in trade.
   (b) The rate at which goods are exchanged.
   (c) The degree to which one country has an absolute advantage.
   (d) Which country pays the transportation costs when trade occurs.

_____ 7. To say that a country has a comparative advantage in the production of wine is to say that:
   (a) It can produce wine with fewer resources than any other country can.
   (b) Its opportunity cost of producing wine is greater than any other country's.
   (c) Its opportunity cost of producing wine is lower than any other country's.
   (d) The relative price of wine is higher in that country than in any other.

_____ 8. America's tariffs on foreign goods result in:
   (a) Lower domestic prices than those that would prevail in their absence.
   (b) A stimulus to efficient American firms that are not protected.
   (c) Higher employment and output in protected industries than would otherwise be the case.
   (d) A more efficient allocation of resources than would occur in their absence.

_____ 9. A principal objective of GATT is to:
   (a) Reduce barriers to trade.
   (b) Settle domestic tax disputes internationally.
   (c) Equalize income tax structures in various countries.
   (d) Protect domestic producers from foreign competition.

_____ 10. World output of goods and services increases with specialization because:
   (a) The world's resources are being used more efficiently.
   (b) Each country's production possibilities curve is shifted outward.
   (c) Each country's workers are able to produce more than they could before specialization.
   (d) All of the above are correct.

_____ 11. Suppose the production of 12 tons of copper in the United States requires the same amount of resources as the production of 1 ton of aluminum. In Mexico, 12 tons of copper requires the same amount of resources as 2 tons of aluminum. This means that:
   (a) Mexico has an absolute advantage in producing copper.
   (b) The United States has a comparative advantage in producing copper.
   (c) The United States has an absolute advantage in producing aluminum.
   (d) All of the above.

Suppose the production possibilities of Japan and the U.S. are given in Table 20.1. Use Table 20.1 to answer questions 12 and 13.

Table 20.1
Output per worker day in the United States and Japan

Country	TV sets (per day)	Bicycles (per day)
Japan	2	10
United States	1	8

_____ 12. Which of the following statements is true?
(a) The United States has an absolute advantage in the production of bicycles.
(b) Japan has an absolute advantage in the production of bicycles only.
(c) Japan has an absolute advantage in the production of TV sets only.
(d) Japan has an absolute advantage in the production of both bicycles and TV sets.

_____ 13. Suppose the terms of trade are established in such a way that 1 TV set equals 5 bicycles. Which of the following statements would be true?
(a) These terms of trade provide gains for the United States, but Japan is worse off.
(b) These terms of trade provide gains for Japan, but the United States is worse off.
(c) These terms of trade provide gains for the United States, and Japan is no worse off.
(d) These terms of trade provide gains for Japan, and the United States is no worse off.

_____ 14. As a result of specialization and trade, total world output of goods and services:
(a) Decreases along with consumption levels.
(b) Increases along with consumption levels.
(c) Decreases, but consumption levels increase.
(d) Increases, but consumption levels decrease.

_____ 15. "Dumping" is said to occur when:
(a) Foreign producers sell more of a particular good in the United States than domestic producers sell.
(b) Foreign producers sell their goods in the United States at prices lower than the U.S. average cost of production.
(c) Foreign producers sell their goods in the United States at prices lower than those prevailing in their own countries.
(d) The foreign countries have trade surpluses and the United States has a trade deficit.

_____ 16. What should happen to the equilibrium price and quantity in a market as a result of a tariff on imports?
(a) Equilibrium price and quantity should both go up.
(b) Equilibrium price should go up, and equilibrium quantity should go down.
(c) Equilibrium price should go down, and equilibrium quantity should go up.
(d) Equilibrium price and quantity should both go down.

_____ 17. With regard to international trade, the market mechanism:
(a) Provides a profit incentive to producers who specialize in the goods and services for which a comparative advantage exists.
(b) Provides a profit incentive to producers who trade in the goods and services for which a comparative advantage exists.
(c) Determines the terms of trade.
(d) Does all of the above.

_____ 18. International trade:
   (a) Lowers prices to consumers.
   (b) Alters the mix of domestic production.
   (c) Redistributes income toward export industries.
   (d) All of the above.

_____ 19. Suppose that Brazil has a comparative advantage in coffee and Mexico has a comparative advantage in tomatoes. Which of the following groups would be worse off if these two countries specialize and trade?
   (a) Brazilian tomato producers.
   (b) Brazilian coffee producers.
   (c) Mexican tomato producers.
   (d) Everyone is better off when specialization and trade take place.

_____ 20. If we add together all the gains from specialization and trade and then subtract all the losses, the net result would be:
   (a) Zero; the gains and losses would cancel out.
   (b) Positive; a net gain for the world and each country.
   (c) Negative; a net loss for the world and each country.
   (d) Impossible to tell; the net result could be zero, positive, or negative.

Problems and Applications

Exercise 1

This exercise shows how trade leads to gains by all trading partners through specialization and comparative advantage.

Suppose that Japan has 20 laborers in total and that the United States has 40 laborers. Suppose their production possibilities are given in Table 20.2. (*Be careful:* The table tells you that a worker in Japan can produce 2 TV sets per day *or* 10 bicycles per day, *not* two TV sets *and* 10 bicycles!)

Table 20.2
Output per worker day in the United States and Japan

Country	TV sets (per day)	Bicycles (per day)
Japan	2	10
United States	1	8

1. Draw the production-possibilities curves for each country in Figure 20.1. Assume constant costs of production.

Figure 20.1

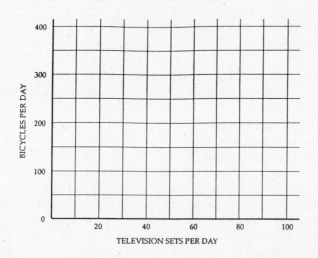

2. Suppose that before trade, Japan uses 12 laborers to produce bicycles and 8 laborers to produce television sets; suppose also that in the United States 20 workers produce bicycles and 20 produce television sets. Complete Table 20.3.

Table 20.3
Output produced and consumed without trade

Country	TV sets (per day)	Bicycles (per day)
Japan	_____	_____
United States	_____	_____
Total	_____	_____

3. Before trade, the total output of television sets is _____ ; of bicycles, _____ .

4. What is the opportunity cost of 1 television set in Japan? _____ In the United States? _____

5. What is the opportunity cost of 1 bicycle in Japan? _____ In the United States? _____

6. If Japan and the United States specialize according to their respective comparative advantages, Japan will produce _____ and the United States will produce _____ . They will do so because the opportunity cost of bicycles in terms of television sets is (lower, higher) in the United States than in Japan, and the opportunity cost of television sets in terms of bicycles is (lower, higher) in Japan than in the United States.

7. After specialization, the total output of television sets is _____ and the total output of bicycles is _____ . (*Hint:* Assume 20 Japanese produce only TV sets, and 40 Americans produce only bicycles.)

8. This output represents an increase of _____ bicycles and _____ television sets over the pre-specialization output. (*Hint:* Compare answers to questions 3 and 7.)

Exercise 2

This exercise will help you understand how the terms of trade are determined. Refer to Exercise 1 for the data.

If Japan and the United States are to benefit from the increased production, trade must take place. The Japanese will be willing to trade television sets for bicycles as long as they get back more bicycles than they could get in their own country.

1. The terms of trade will be between 1 television set equals _____ bicycles and 1 television set equals _____ bicycles.

2. If the terms of trade were 4 bicycles equals one television set:
   (a)   Neither country would buy bicycles, but both would buy TV sets.
   (b)   Neither country would buy TV sets, but both would buy bicycles.
   (c)   Both countries would buy bicycles and TV sets.

3. Suppose that the two countries agree that the terms of trade will be 6 bicycles equals 1 television set. Let Japan export 20 television sets per day to the United States. Complete Table 20.4. Assume that Japan produces 40 television sets per day and the United States produces 320 bicycles.

Table 20.4
Consumption combination after trade

Country	TV sets (per day)	Bicycles (per day)
Japan	_____	_____
United States	_____	_____
Total	40	320

4. As a result of specialization and trade, the United States has the same quantity of television sets and _____ more bicycles per day. (Compare Tables 20.3 and 20.4.)

5. As a result of specialization and trade, Japan has the same number of bicycles and _____ more television sets per day.

Now suppose that at the exchange rate of 6 bicycles to 1 TV set, Japan would like to export 10 TV sets and import 60 bicycles per day. Suppose also that the United States desires to export 90 bicycles and import 15 television sets per day.

6. At these terms of trade there is a (shortage, surplus) of television sets.

7. At these terms of trade there is a (shortage, surplus) of bicycles.

8. Which of the following terms of trade would be more likely to result from this situation?
   (a)   5 bicycles equal 1 television set.
   (b)   6 bicycles equal 1 television set.
   (c)   7 bicycles equal 1 television set.

Exercise 3

When protection is provided to producers of a particular product, consumers of that product are harmed because they must pay higher prices than in the absence of protection. In addition, the effects of the protection in one market spill over into related factor and product markets, thus distorting both production and consumption patterns. This exercise will help you to discover how this occurs.

Reread the World View article entitled "Sugar Quota a Sour Deal," and then answer the following questions.

1. What was the estimated overall cost to U.S. consumers in 2001 due to the quota on sugar?

   _____

2. If the U.S. sugar quota was abolished, which of the following would be the most likely equilibrium world price for sugar, *ceteris paribus*?
   (a) 7 cents per pound.
   (b) 15 cents per pound.
   (c) 22 cents per pound.
   (d) 24 cents per pound.

3. If the sugar quota was abolished, what would you predict to happen to the number of sugar producers in the United States?_____

4. Suppose the next best use of land used to produce sugar beets in the U.S. was to produce wheat. What would you predict to happen to the price of wheat in the U.S. market, *ceteris paribus*, if the sugar quota was abolished?_____

5. If the sugar quota was abolished, what would you predict to happen to the marginal revenue product of labor and the level of employment of labor in the Caribbean sugar industry, *ceteris paribus*?_____

Common Errors

The first statement in each "common error" below is incorrect. Each incorrect statement is followed by a corrected version and an explanation.

1. A country must have an *absolute advantage* in order to gain from trade with another country. WRONG!

   A country must have a *comparative advantage* in order to gain from trade with another country. RIGHT!

   Mutually advantageous trade requires only that the opportunity costs of producing goods differ between the two countries, *ceteris paribus*. Another way of stating this is that the production-possibilities curves of the two countries must have different slopes. The two circumstances noted above are indicated in Figure 20.2 below.

Figure 20.2

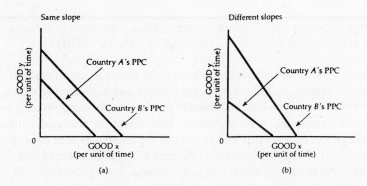

In diagram (a), in which country B has an absolute advantage over country A, the production-possibilities curves have the same slope; thus mutually advantageous trade *is not* possible. In diagram (b), each country has a comparative advantage because the production-possibilities curves of the two countries have different slopes; thus mutually advantageous trade *is* possible.

2. Foreign trade costs a country jobs. WRONG!

Although jobs may be lost, new ones will be created by the opportunities opened up with trade. RIGHT!

When countries specialize and trade according to the law of comparative advantage, some particular workers and firms may be hurt by imports, but the economy as a whole gains by trade. More output per resource input will be attainable. Because the economy is able to reach full employment with trade as well as without trade, there is no reason to assume there will be fewer jobs.

3. A country is well off only as long as it exports more than it imports. WRONG!

Countries may, at times, be well off when they experience a trade surplus; they may also be well off when they have a trade deficit. RIGHT!

Both trade deficits and trade surpluses can be problems if either situation persists for a long period of time. Trade surpluses mean that a country is giving more of its limited, precious resources in trade than it is acquiring from other countries. The currencies of deficit countries tend to depreciate, which means they will be unable to buy as many foreign goods with a unit of currency.

4. Countries tend to enter into trade to get things they cannot produce themselves. WRONG!

Countries very often trade for things they could produce themselves. RIGHT!

Be careful! Countries often trade for things they could produce themselves because the relative costs of domestic production would be prohibitive. Take baskets as an example. Producers in the U.S. could certainly produce baskets if they really wanted to. The technique is not difficult to learn and the materials are abundant. But baskets do not lend themselves to machine production, and hand labor is expensive here. The cost in terms of goods forgone would be tremendous. (So would the price of the baskets.) We're better off specializing in something like computers, where we have a comparative advantage, and trading for baskets, where we clearly do not have a comparative advantage.

5. The effects of protection affect only workers in the protected industry and the domestic consumers of the protected commodity. WRONG!

    The effects of protection spread to many other markets both here and abroad as producers and consumers adjust their production and consumption patterns. RIGHT!

    Protection and output changes in any market are bound to set off additional changes in related markets. Higher prices for a protected product lead consumers to seek out substitutes with lower prices. This should increase the demand for the substitute and set off a host of other changes in related input and product markets. Similarly, if the protected commodity is used as an input, an increase in its price will lead to a search for substitutes with lower prices and have consequent impacts on related markets. In the case of sugar, corn based high-fructose corn syrup has replaced sugar to such an extent that corn growers, fearing a reduction in the demand for their output, now lobby their congressional delegations to maintain the sugar quota! Similar impacts can be expected in the markets of foreign producers.

•ANSWERS•

Using Key Terms

Across

2. production possibilities
3. consumption possibilities
5. comparative advantage
9. trade deficit
11. dumping
13. quota
14. opportunity cost
15. tariff
16. terms of trade

Down

1. voluntary restraint agreement
4. equilibrium price
6. absolute advantage
7. embargo
8. trade surplus
10. exports
12. imports

True or False

1. F   Approximately 11 percent of U.S. GDP is exported. In dollar terms, the U.S. is the world's largest exporter of goods and services.
2. F   Workers in an exporting industry typically benefit from trade so they would not lobby for trade restrictions.
3. T
4. F   Comparative advantage refers to the ability to produce output at a smaller opportunity cost than another country, i.e., giving up fewer alternative goods and services.
5. T

6. F   With specialization and free trade it is possible for a country to consume a mix of goods and services beyond its production-possibilities curve although it is never possible for a country to produce beyond its production-possibilities curve.

7. T

8. F   Although countries as a whole benefit from specialization and free trade, there are always individuals and groups that may lose, e.g. import-competing firms.

9. T

10. T

Multiple Choice

1. a	5. a	9. a	13. c	17. d
2. a	6. b	10. a	14. b	18. d
3. b	7. c	11. b	15. c	19. a
4. c	8. c	12. d	16. b	20. b

Problems and Applications

Exercise 1

1. **Figure 20.1 Answer**

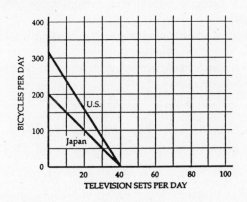

2. **Table 20.3 Answer**

Country	TV sets	Bicycles
Japan	16	120
United States	20	160
Total	36	280

3. 36; 280
4. 5 bicycles; 8 bicycles
5. 1/5 television set; 1/8 television set
6. Television sets; bicycles; lower; lower
7. 40; 320
8. 40; 4

Exercise 2

1. 5; 8
2. a
3. **Table 20.4 Answer**

Country	TV sets	Bicycles
Japan	20	120
United States	20	200
Total	40	320

4. 40
5. 4
6. Shortage, The Japanese wish to export fewer (10) TV sets than Americans want to import (15).
7. Surplus, The Americans wish to export more (90) bicycles than the Japanese want to import (60).
8. c   The shortage of TV sets will cause their price to increase.

Exercise 3

1. The estimated cost to U.S. consumers due to the price difference between the U.S. market and the world market was $2 billion.
2. b   The market should reach equilibrium between the previous world price and the protected U.S. price.
3. The absence of protection should cause economic losses in the U.S. sugar industry and the number of producers should decrease.
4. As sugar producers reallocate their land to wheat production, the market price of wheat should fall.
5. Their marginal product should increase as the world price of sugar rises; the level of employment should increase.

CHAPTER 21

International Finance

Quick Review

- All of the trade between nations must somehow be financed. Since each country has its own money and in order to facilitate trade, markets for foreign exchange have developed.

- When goods are traded between countries, there is an exchange of currency. The exchange rate is the price of one currency in terms of another currency.

- A currency will appreciate or depreciate in value based on the supply and demand for the currency. Factors that shift the foreign exchange supply or demand include changes in relative incomes, relative prices, and interest rates.

- If a nation's currency appreciates, its goods become more expensive for foreigners and it exports less, *ceteris paribus*. The opposite is true if the currency depreciates.

- The balance of payments is an accounting statement of a country's international economic transactions. It is composed of the trade balance, the capital-account balance, and the current-account balance.

- Countries resist exchange rate movements because any change in the exchange rate automatically alters the price of all exports and imports. These changes complicate the conduct of domestic monetary and fiscal policy.

- Under a fixed exchange rate system, the value of a currency does not change because of shifts in the supply or demand for the foreign exchange. In this case balance of payments deficits or surpluses occur because of the excess demand or excess supply of foreign exchange.

- To maintain fixed rates, governments must intervene. Intervention requires a country to accumulate reserves (foreign currencies, gold, etc.) sometimes and to release reserves at other times.

- A flexible exchange rate system does not require government intervention because the exchange rate automatically adjusts to the equilibrium rate. But a totally flexible system can result in many changes. To avoid this problem a system of "managed rates" has evolved in which governments still intervene, but now with the idea of reducing, rather than eliminating, fluctuations.

Learning Objectives

After reading Chapter 21 and doing the following exercises, you should:

1. Understand that an exchange rate is the price of a currency.
2. Know the forces that operate on the demand side of the foreign exchange market.
3. Know the forces that operate on the supply side of the foreign exchange market.
4. Understand how supply and demand interact to determine the equilibrium exchange rate.
5. Understand the essentials of balance-of-payments accounting.
6. Be able to demonstrate graphically the forces that cause a currency to appreciate or depreciate.
7. Understand why there is resistance to exchange-rate changes.
8. Be able to describe several exchange-rate systems and their consequences.
9. Understand the macroeconomic and microeconomic consequences of exchange-rate movements.
10. Be able to describe a balance-of-payments problem.
11. Be aware of the recent history of currency bailouts.

Using Key Terms

Fill in the puzzle on the opposite page with the appropriate term from the list of Key Terms at the end of the chapter in the text.

Across

2. Places where foreign currencies are bought and sold.
4. The amount by which the quantity demanded exceeds the quantity supplied.
6. A system in which governments intervene in foreign-exchange markets to limit exchange-rate fluctuations.
8. Stocks of gold held by a government to purchase foreign exchange.
9. A rise in the price of a currency relative to another.
10. The price of one currency in terms of another currency.
11. A fall in the price of one currency relative to another.
13. A mechanism for fixing the exchange rate.
14. The price at which the quantity demanded equals the quantity supplied.
15. An excess demand for domestic currency at current exchange rates.

Down

1. An excess demand for foreign currency at current exchange rates.
2. Holdings of foreign exchange by official government agencies.
3. Floating exchange rates.
5. A summary record of a country's international economic transactions.
7. An abrupt depreciation of a currency whose value was fixed or managed by the government.
12. A situation in which the value of imports exceeds the value of exports.

Puzzle 21.1

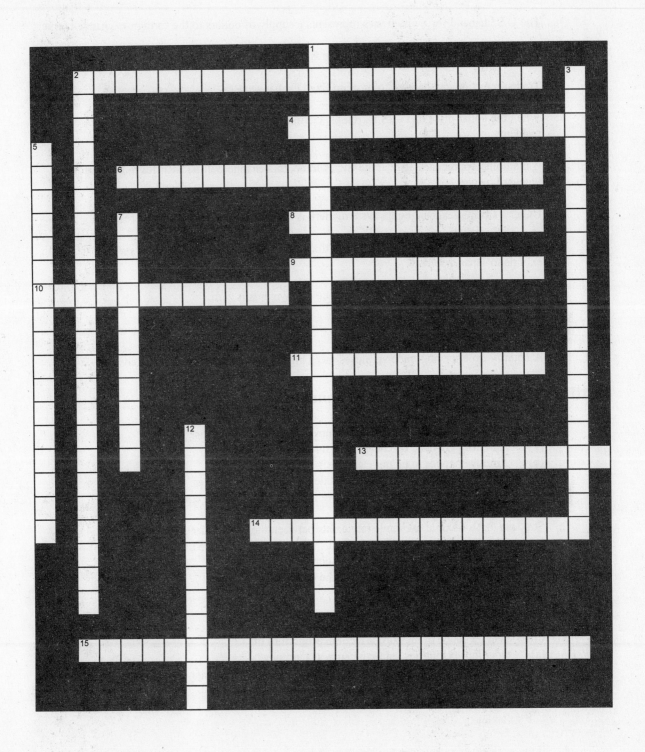

True or False: *Circle your choice and explain why any false statements are incorrect.*

T F 1. The U.S. demand for Swiss francs represents a supply of dollars to the foreign-exchange market.

T F 2. Increased foreign travel by Americans tends to cause the dollar to appreciate, *ceteris paribus*.

T F 3. Trade protection can be used to prop up fixed exchange rates.

T F 4. When the dollar price of Euros increases, German machinery becomes more expensive to U.S. residents.

T F 5. If the dollar appreciates against the Swiss franc, this change will be harmful to California vineyard owners.

T F 6. Under a flexible-exchange-rate system, there is no need for foreign-exchange reserves.

T F 7. If the U.S. price level rises more rapidly than the Japanese price level, *ceteris paribus*, U.S. exports to Japan will rise.

T F 8. When exchange rates are fixed, the balance of payments is zero.

T F 9. If there is a deficit in the capital account, it must be offset by a surplus in the current account.

T F 10. A country experiencing trade surpluses faces higher foreign debt and interest costs.

Multiple Choice: *Select the correct answer.*

_____ 1. An increase in the dollar price of other currencies will tend to cause:
  (a) American goods to be cheaper for foreigners.
  (b) American goods to be more expensive for foreigners.
  (c) Foreign goods to be cheaper to residents of the United States.
  (d) Foreign goods to be more expensive to residents of foreign countries.

_____ 2. Suppose that a flexible exchange rate exists between the U.S. dollar and the Japanese yen. An increase in the supply of yen (a rightward shift in the supply curve of yen) will tend to:
  (a) Increase U.S. imports of Japanese goods.
  (b) Push the U.S. balance of trade in the direction of a surplus.
  (c) Lower the yen price of the dollar.
  (d) Raise the dollar price of the yen.

_____ 3. Changes in the value of the euro affect the economies of:
  (a) Only those countries using the euro as currency.
  (b) All European countries but there would no significant impact on countries outside Europe.
  (c) Potentially the entire world.
  (d) There would be no significant impact on any economies as long as exchange rates are flexible.

_____ 4. If the exchange rate between U.S. dollars and Japanese yen changes from $1 = 100 yen to $1 = 90 yen:
  (a) All Japanese producers and consumers will lose.
  (b) U.S. auto producers and autoworkers will lose.
  (c) U.S. consumers of Japanese TV sets will gain.
  (d) Japanese tourists to the U.S. will gain.

_____ 5. A country will experience a reduction in its balance-of-payments deficit, *ceteris paribus,* if:
  (a) Its level of GDP rises relative to foreign levels of GDP.
  (b) Its prices fall relative to foreign price levels, *ceteris paribus.*
  (c) The domestic price of the foreign currency falls.
  (d) It lowers its tariffs.

_____ 6. A result of the Asian Crisis of 1997-98 was:
  (a) A general increase in the value of the U.S. dollar in relation to Southeast Asian currencies.
  (b) A major decrease in the level of U.S. exports to Southeast Asia.
  (c) Political unrest in many Southeast Asian countries.
  (d) All of the above.

_____ 7. Greater volatility of floating exchange rates results in:
  (a) Greater costs because of uncertainty.
  (b) Balance-of-payments instability.
  (c) Smaller market shortages and surpluses of currencies.
  (d) Depletion of foreign reserves.

_____ 8. Which of the following changes will tend to cause a shift in the domestic demand curve for foreign currencies?
  (a) Changes in domestic incomes, *ceteris paribus.*
  (b) Changes in domestic prices of goods, *ceteris paribus.*
  (c) Changes in consumer taste for foreign goods, *ceteris paribus.*
  (d) All of the above.

_____ 9. An increase in the U.S. trade deficit could be caused by:
  (a) A depreciation of the dollar in terms of other currencies.
  (b) An appreciation of the dollar in terms of other currencies.
  (c) The imposition of a tariff on imported goods.
  (d) An increase in the capital-account deficit.

_____ 10. In a floating-exchange-rate system, the capital-account balance equals:
  (a) The negative of the current-account balance.
  (b) Foreign purchases of U.S. assets minus U.S. purchases of foreign assets.
  (c) The balance of payments minus the sum of the trade balance, the services balance, and unilateral transfers.
  (d) All of the above.

_____ 11. American citizens planning a vacation abroad would welcome:
  (a) Appreciation of the dollar.
  (b) Depreciation of the dollar.
  (c) Devaluation of the dollar.
  (d) Evaluation of the dollar.

_____ 12. A change in the exchange rate for a country's currency alters the prices of:
  (a) Exports only.
  (b) Imports only.
  (c) Both exports and imports.
  (d) Only domestic goods and services.

_____ 13. In a floating exchange-rate regime, the overall "balance" of the balance of payments must be:
  (a) Equal to zero.
  (b) Positive if exports of goods and services exceed imports of goods and services.
  (c) Positive if the capital account is in surplus.
  (d) Negative if the current account is in deficit.

_____ 14. When exchange rates are flexible, they are:
- (a) Determined by proclamation of the monetary authorities of a country.
- (b) Determined by the relative levels of gold reserves.
- (c) Permitted to vary with changes in supply and demand in the foreign exchange market.
- (d) Determined by the provisions of the Bretton Woods agreement.

_____ 15. If the U.S. dollar depreciates, the United States should experience in the long run, a:
- (a) Lower inflation rate.
- (b) Smaller deficit on the U.S. trade balance.
- (c) Larger deficit on the U.S. current account.
- (d) Larger deficit on the U.S. capital account.

_____ 16. The major drawback to a system of managed exchange rates is that:
- (a) A country's efforts to manage exchange-rate movements may arouse suspicion and retaliation.
- (b) A country's efforts to affect changes in exchange rates are almost totally ineffective.
- (c) Government efforts to alter exchange rates usually result in violent disruptions of the domestic economy.
- (d) It requires enormous gold reserves.

_____ 17. If French speculators believed the yen was going to appreciate against the dollar, they would:
- (a) Purchase francs.
- (b) Purchase dollars.
- (c) Purchase yen.
- (d) Sell yen.

_____ 18. Suppose that at the prevailing yen-dollar exchange rate, there is an excess demand for yen. To prevent the dollar from depreciating, the United States might:
- (a) Raise taxes.
- (b) Reduce government spending.
- (c) Raise interest rates.
- (d) Do all of the above.

_____ 19. A currency bailout:
- (a) Occurs when an economy is lent money in order to increase or maintain the value of its currency.
- (b) Can help avoid a "domino effect" of depreciating currencies in other economies.
- (c) Can be ultimately self-defeating because it saves the country receiving the bailout from implementing politically unpopular domestic policies which could have prevented the problem in the first place.
- (d) All of the above are correct.

_____ 20. The capital account includes:
- (a) Trade in goods.
- (b) Foreign purchases of U.S. assets.
- (c) Unilateral transfers.
- (d) Trade in services.

Problems and Applications

Exercise 1

This exercise provides practice in determining exchange rates.

1. Table 21.1 depicts the hypothetical demand for and supply of British pounds in terms of U.S. dollars. Use the information in Table 21.1 to plot the demand and supply of British pounds at the exchange rates indicated in Figure 21.1. Then answer questions 2-4.

Table 21.1
Monthly demand for and supply of British pounds in the United States

Dollars per British pound	Quantity demanded	Quantity supplied
4.50	100	700
4.00	200	600
3.50	300	500
3.00	400	400
2.50	500	300
2.00	600	200
1.50	700	100

Figure 21.1
Demand and supply curves for pounds

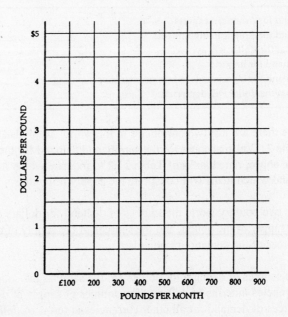

2. What is the equilibrium rate of exchange? _____

3. At a price of $2 per pound there would be excess:
   (a)   Demand, and the exchange rate for pounds would rise.
   (b)   Demand, and the exchange rate for pounds would fall.
   (c)   Supply, and the exchange rate would rise.
   (d)   Supply, and the exchange rate would fall.

285

4. Suppose that Americans suddenly increased their demand for British exports. The dollar price of pounds would (rise, fall).

5. T   F   Whenever one currency depreciates, another currency must appreciate.

6. As a result of the increased demand for British exports, the pound price of the dollar would (rise, fall).

Exercise 2

This exercise shows why one currency appreciates when another currency depreciates. It also shows why the demand for dollars represents the supply of other currencies, while the supply of dollars represents the demand for other currencies in the foreign-exchange markets. In learning these things, you will get practice in making calculations with exchange rates.

1. Table 21.2 includes the sources of demand and supply of dollars. In the first column, check off the items that are the source of the demand for dollars. In the second column, check off the items that are the source of the supply of dollars. (*Hint*: There are two kinds of speculators—those who think the dollar will rise and those who think it will fall. You must sort the two types of speculators to determine which type will supply dollars and which will demand dollars.)

Table 21.2
Sources of supply and demand for dollars and pounds

	(1) Demand for $	(2) Supply of $	(3) Demand for £	(4) Supply of £
Foreign demand for American exports	___	___	___	___
Foreign demand for American investments	___	___	___	___
Speculation that the dollar will appreciate	___	___	___	___
American demand for imports	___	___	___	___
American demand for investments in foreign countries	___	___	___	___
Speculation that the dollar will depreciate	___	___	___	___

2. If we assume there are just two currencies in the world, the dollar ($) and the pound (£), then the items in Table 21.2 also account for the supply and demand for the pound. Once again place checks in the appropriate blanks of Table 21.2 to indicate which items will constitute the demand for pounds and which items will constitute the supply of pounds.

3. T   F   In a two country world the sources of demand for dollars are the same as the sources of the supply of the pound, and the sources of the supply of dollars are the same as the sources of the demand for pounds.

4. T   F   The sources of demand for dollars are the same as the sources of supply for all other currencies in terms of dollars. The sources of supply of dollars are the same as the sources of demand for all other currencies in terms of dollars.

5. Let's return to our assumption that there are only two countries. Use your observations in the previous two questions and your knowledge of converting one currency into another to find the quantities of dollars supplied (column 3) and quantities of dollars demanded (column 6) in Table 21.3. Use the information in Table 21.3, which is the same as the data we used in Exercise 1 above, to compute the supply and demand for pounds.

Table 21.3
Supply and demand for dollars ($) and pounds (£)

(1) Price of a £ ($/£)	(2) Quantity of £ demanded	(3) Quantity of $ supplied	(4) Price of a $ (£/$)	(5) Quantity of £ supplied	(6) Quantity of $ demanded
4.50	100	_____	_____	700	_____
4.00	200	_____	_____	600	_____
3.50	300	_____	_____	500	_____
3.00	400	_____	_____	400	_____
2.50	500	_____	_____	300	_____
2.00	600	_____	_____	200	_____
1.50	700	_____	_____	100	_____

6. Complete column 4 of Table 21.3 by converting the price of pounds (£) in terms of dollars ($) in column 1 to the price of dollars in terms of pounds. (*Hint*: They are reciprocals of each other. Remember that to find the price of any good or currency, that good or currency appears in the denominator!)

7. From the data on the demand for the dollar (columns 4 and 6 of Table 21.3), draw the demand curve for the dollar in Figure 21.2. From the data on the supply of the dollar (columns 3 and 4 of Table 21.3), draw the supply curve for the dollar in Figure 21.2.

Figure 21.2
Demand and supply of dollars

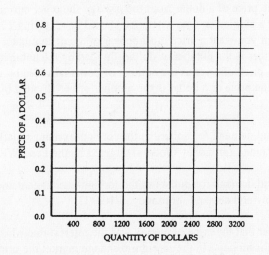

8. The equilibrium value of the dollar is _____ , and the equilibrium quantity of dollars is _____ .

9. When you multiply the equilibrium quantity of dollars by the equilibrium exchange rate for the dollar in terms of pounds (£), you find the quantity of pounds is _____ . When you find the reciprocal of the equilibrium exchange rate for the dollar, you find the exchange rate for pounds is _____ .

10. T   F   When you multiply the equilibrium quantity of dollars by the equilibrium exchange rate for the dollar in terms of pounds (£), you have calculated the equilibrium quantity of pounds. (Compare your answer to question 9 in this exercise with your answer to question 2, Exercise 1 above.)

11. T   F   The equilibrium exchange rate for the dollar equals the equilibrium exchange rate for the pound.

Exercise 3

The media often feature articles about international financial issues.

Read the article entitled "Nobel Prize Was Nobler in October." Then answer the following questions.

1. According to the article, what was the dollar value of the Nobel Prize at the time it was announced?_____

2. How much was it worth two months later?_____

3. Why did the value change so much? _____

Common Errors

The first statement in each "common error" below is incorrect. Each incorrect statement is followed by a corrected version and an explanation.

1. The price of a dollar in terms of yen is the number of dollars per yen. WRONG!

    The price of a dollar in terms of yen is the number of yen per dollar. RIGHT!

    This mistake can cost a bundle if you are in a foreign country and don't know how to distinguish the price of a dollar from the price of the other currency. In Japan you don't want to give $100 for a single yen note when you should be receiving 100 yen for $1! Remember that the item for which you want a price must appear in the denominator of the price. For example, the price of tomatoes is the number of dollars divided by the number of tomatoes that are purchased. Similarly, the price of a yen is the number of dollars divided by the number of yen that are purchased. The price of a dollar is the number of yen divided by the number of dollars that are purchased.

2. The supply and demand for dollars in the foreign-exchange market is the same thing as the supply and demand for money (dollars) targeted by the Fed. WRONG!

    The supply and demand for dollars in the foreign-exchange market is a totally different concept from the supply and demand for money. RIGHT!

    Remember that the price of money was the interest rate when we were focusing on the supply and demand for money. In the foreign-exchange market the price is the exchange rate, not the interest rate. Furthermore, the supply and demand for money (dollars), which is the focus of the Fed, occurs geographically within the United States. The foreign-exchange market occurs between countries—literally on the phone lines between banks of different countries. We can visualize the foreign-exchange market as an area totally outside of borders in which money temporarily enters for the purpose of being exchanged. While domestic monetary policies may influence the amount of money going into the foreign-exchange market, the link is often indirect. In fact, when the Fed tightens monetary policy to reduce the supply of dollars, the foreign-exchange market may see an *increase* in the supply of dollars as foreigners seek the higher interest rates from a tighter U.S. monetary policy.

3. A country is well off if its currency appreciates steadily over a long period of time. WRONG!

   Both appreciating currencies and depreciating currencies create problems. RIGHT!

   Be careful! There are problems associated with steadily appreciating currencies *and* with steadily depreciating currencies. People sometimes view a depreciating currency as a source of national shame and dislike the higher cost (and inflation) associated with higher prices of foreign goods. However, depreciation may make a country's exports more competitive, may lead to more jobs, and may help correct a trade deficit. By contrast, a country with an appreciating currency develops employment problems and a loss of competitiveness against other countries, even if it has more buying power as a result of its stronger currency.

4. When countries have trade deficits, money really flows out. When they have surpluses, money really flows in. WRONG!

   Money is not physically sent in most transactions, but the claim to ownership is. RIGHT!

   Most foreign trade is transacted by check and is just a "flow" of bookkeeping entries. Even when gold is sold, it seldom *physically* flows anywhere. In the case of the United States, under a fixed-exchange-rate system, it stays in Fort Knox even though someone else owns it. Thus, it is the claim to ownership that flows, not the money. When countries run trade deficits, their trading partners add to their claims against them. For countries with a trade surplus, the reverse is true.

5. There are balance-of-payments surpluses and deficits under floating exchange rates. WRONG!

   The balance of payments is always zero under floating exchange rates. RIGHT!

   Under fixed exchange rates, the government must balance surpluses and deficits on the balance of payments with changes in reserves. With floating exchange rates, there is no reserve currency and any transfers abroad by the government are simply classified as unilateral transfers and are included in the current account. By definition, the current account and the capital account balance each other under a floating exchange-rate system.

•ANSWERS•

Using Key Terms

Across

2. foreign-exchange markets
4. market shortage
6. managed exchange rates
8. gold reserves
9. appreciation
10. exchange rate
11. depreciation
13. gold standard
14. equilibrium price
15. balance-of-payments surplus

Down

1. balance-of-payments deficit
2. foreign exchange reserves
3. flexible exchange rate
5. balance of payments
7. devaluation
12. trade deficit

True or False

1. T
2. F   Increased foreign travel by Americans tends to increase the demand for foreign currency, thus increasing the supply of U.S. dollars and reducing the value of the dollar.
3. T
4. T
5. T
6. T
7. F   U.S. goods will be relatively more expensive to Japan thus reducing exports.
8. F   Fixed exchange rates tend to cause balance-of-payments deficits and surpluses because they cause shortages and surpluses of currencies.
9. T
10. F   A country experiencing trade deficits will have higher foreign debt and interest rates because that country will have to borrow to finance the additional goods and services it is consuming over what it is producing.

Multiple Choice

1.	a	5.	b	9.	b	13.	a	17.	c
2.	a	6.	d	10.	d	14.	c	18.	d
3.	c	7.	a	11.	a	15.	b	19.	d
4.	d	8.	d	12.	c	16.	a	20.	b

Problems and Applications

Exercise 1

1. **Figure 21.1 Answer**

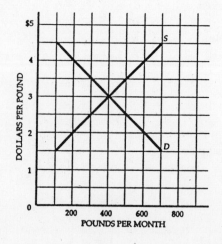

2. $3 per British pound   3. a   4. rise   5. T   6. fall

Exercise 2

1. and 2.   **Table 21.2 Answer**

	(1) Demand for $	(2) Supply of $	(3) Demand for £	(4) Supply of £
Foreign demand for American exports	X	__	__	X
Foreign demand for American investments	X	__	__	X
Speculation that the dollar will appreciate	X	__	__	X
American demand for imports	__	X	X	__
American demand for investments in foreign countries	__	X	X	__
Speculation that the dollar will depreciate	__	X	X	__

3. T
4. T

5. and 6.   **Table 21.3 Answer**

Price of a £ ($ / £) (1)		Quantity of £ demanded (2)		Quantity of $ supplied (3)	Price of a $ (£ / $) (4)	Quantity of £ supplied (5)	Quantity of $ demanded (6)
4.50	x	100	=	450	0.222 = 1/4.50	700	3,150
4.00	x	200	=	800	0.25 = 1/4	600	2,400
3.50	x	300	=	1,050	0.29 = 1/3.50	500	1,750
3.00	x	400	=	1,200	0.33 = 1/3	400	1,200
2.50	x	500	=	1,250	0.40 = 1/2.50	300	750
2.00	x	600	=	1,200	0.50 = 1/2	200	400
1.50	x	700	=	1,050	0.67 = 1/1.50	100	150

7.   **Figure 21.2 Answer**

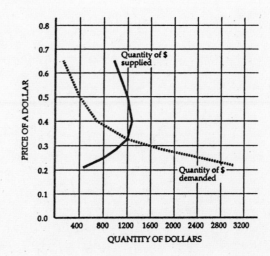

291

8. 1/3 £ per dollar; $1,200
9. 400 (= 1,200 x 1/3); $3 per pound [= 1/(1/3)]
10. T
11. F   The equilibrium exchange rate for the dollar equals the *reciprocal* of the equilibrium exchange rate for the pound.

Exercise 3

1. $1.2 million
2. $958,000
3. The Swedish krona depreciated, which caused the value of the prize to decrease.